WHICH MONEY PERSONALITY BEST DESCRIBES YOU

THE NESTER... wants nothing so much as security. She views risk with a guarded eye. Her goal is to keep what she has.

THE REACHER... enjoys spending. She sees money as a token of love and lavishes it on herself. An optimist, she believes something—or someone—will turn up to make things better for her.

THE DRIVER... is imbued with a sense of power. She is willing to take risks to make money. Yet she is determined to control those risks by controlling her environment.

Once your know your money style (take the quiz inside to be sure!), you're ready for *The Working Woman Financial Advisor's* S-T-A-I-R Program to success. You'll learn how to use your personal money strengths and compensate for your weaknesses, how to make your funds grow in the chapter that covers *your* rung on the career ladder, and how to adapt your plans and your goals as the world around you changes. Written by a woman financial expert who deeply understands—and solves—the most common money problems women face, *The Working Woman Financial Advisor* is every woman's guide to financial security—having the money you need for the life you want to live.

ABOUT THE AUTHOR:

Bonnie Siverd is money columnist and contributing editor for *Working Woman* magazine. A former *Business Week* editor and author of *Count Your Change,* she appears weekly on Cable News Network's "Business Morning," and has also covered business and financial topics for *Time* and the *Congressional Quarterly*.

OTHER BOOKS BY BONNIE SIVERD

Count Your Change:
A Woman's Guide to Sudden Financial Change

THE WORKING WOMAN FINANCIAL ADVISOR

WHAT TO DO WITH THE MONEY YOU MAKE

Bonnie Siverd

A Warner Communications Company

Warner Books, Inc., 666 Fifth Avenue, New York, NY 10103

Printed in the United States of America
First Printing: January 1987
10 9 8 7 6 5 4 3 2 1

Library of Congress Cataloging-in-Publication Data

Siverd, Bonnie.
The working woman financial advisor.

Includes index.
1. Women—Finance, Personal. 2. Women—Employment.
3. Investments. I. Title.
HG179.S522 1987 332.024'042 86-13225
ISBN 0-446-38169-1 (U.S.) (pbk.)
ISBN 0-446-38170-5 (Canada) (pbk.)

Cover design by Bob Silverman
Book design by Giorgetta Bell McRee

To my parents

ACKNOWLEDGMENTS

The fact that this book exists at all is a testament to the help and support of a great many people.

My appreciation goes first of all to my colleagues at *Working Woman,* present and past, who saw the need for this book and gave their wholehearted support over the course of the project. Thank you, Anne Mollegen Smith, for championing the importance of money in a working woman's life. My gratitude also goes to Gay Bryant, who brought me onto the *Working Woman* team and was the first supporter of this book, as well as to Jacqueline Giambanco, whose insightful reading of the manuscript made it immeasurably stronger. Thanks also to Jeanne Rhode and Leslie Erickson for their tireless research help.

Countless professionals helped me frame the personalities and the advice offered here. My deepest appreciation to Robin Oegerle, president of Financial Strategies Inc., in Washington, D.C., who brainstormed with me to develop many of the ideas and kindly read the manuscript and offered suggestions. I also value all of the thoughts generously shared by George Barbee, president, the Consumer Financial Institute; the financial planning team at New England Life, especially Linda Sheldon and Charlotte Neagle; Sandra Goodstein, C.F.P., the Philadelphia district manager for IDS/American Express; David Rhine, CPA, Seidman & Seidman; Paul Silby, CPA, Mann Judd Landau in New York City.

For their unending support I also thank Fredda Isaacson, my editor at Warner, who always had words of encouragement, even in the face of one of the biggest tax reform moves in history, and my agent, Denise Marcil, who believed in this project from the beginning.

My most special thanks go to good friends, Nora Tulchin, Paula Saunders and Carol Ott, who truly helped make this book happen, and to all the readers of *Working Woman* whose stories inspired and enriched it.

CONTENTS

INTRODUCTION

We've done it.

The real money story of the '80s is us. Working women. From first job to career peak, we are succeeding—superlatively—in our work. Pulling down real money. And enjoying the rewards that come with a job well done. As we move toward the '90s our mandate is clear: to *manage* our money with every bit of the guts and verve that we used to earn it. As hardworking women we deserve no less.

The problem is most of us have spent so much time making money that we've scarcely had time to manage it. My talks with scores of money managers, financial planners, and fellow women have made one thing clear: that will never do. We women stand to lose too much if we fail to take charge now.

It's not that we don't care. Or that we don't try. Our stumbling block is far more subtle, and all too easy for successful professional women to hit. Most women who fail financially do so because they work against, not with, themselves. It's that simple. We make investments but do not consider why we want them. We spend money, but never quite seem to get what we want. We make plans, in fact, for our whole lives without truly taking our deepest needs and values into account.

Women who *achieve* financial success, by contrast, take a markedly different tack. They know themselves and act on that knowledge. How *you* can get to know yourself, what you should look for, and how to profit from your insight is the driving force behind this book.

Whatever your approach to money, wherever you work, and however you live, you will find part of yourself in the pages ahead. For this book is based on a truly personal premise: you. What is important to you, what you want to accomplish, and the steps you feel comfortable taking are yours alone to decide. By helping you see yourself clearly, this book will show you how to make a financial plan that will get you where you want to go, in one piece, on schedule. In the process, you'll see how to play to your strengths and keep your weaknesses from doing you in.

Money smarts are required to win this game, sure. But learning them is easy, and most of what you need you'll find in the chapters that follow. The hard part—the part that takes time, thought, and honesty but in the end is more important than whether you buy stock index options or can even define them—is knowing yourself.

Don't we know ourselves already? Not really. Or at least not enough. Most successful career women are too busy barrelling through life to have much time to get to know themselves. In the few hours left over each week after we take care of our jobs, partners, children, parents, and friends, we are more likely to curl up with a novel than with our bankbooks.

This book will help you change that. It starts out personal. Financially speaking, there is nothing more important than your money personality. You'll see what money personalities consist of, find out which one *you* fit, and learn how you are likely to think, feel, and behave as a result. With that in mind, you will learn how to make your own financial plan. Then, in the most important lesson this book will teach you, you'll put the two together. Only by creating a plan that flows from your money style can you be sure your plan will meet your needs.

In Part Two, we will look more closely at the lives we lead. Whatever our money personalities and whatever our goals, they are played out in individual situations. Each of us is, in fact, several selves at any point in time. We straddle roles of manager, subordinate, mother, daughter, best friend, entertainer, wife, lover. Different roles bring out different sides of our money personalities. And at different times in our lives we see our personalities change.

A longed-for promotion or the sudden loss of a job can shatter comfortable patterns. Less abruptly but no less surely, our money styles shift as we pile up assets, choose to stay single or marry, go on to have children, divorce, retire. In each of the six chapters that form the core of this book, we'll see how our money personalities influence our financial decisions—for better and for worse—and how to control them to come out ahead.

In Part Three, you will see when and how to change your plans to suit the ever-changing times around us. You'll learn when borrowed money can backstop your own funds. And how to build a team of money advisors to help you win the profits you seek.

For every working woman, managing money well is as important as making money in the first place. Just as we have taken charge of our professional lives, and succeeded, we must take charge of our money and find success there, too.

And we can. We would not have come so far so fast if we weren't achievers. We wouldn't be earning the money now at our disposal if we couldn't manage it.

For now, taking charge of your financial life may seem a daunting task. After reading this book, you will see that it really is an opportunity. It's the chance to gain some of the most valuable lessons you ever will learn about yourself and what makes you happy. And in the process, you will give yourself the best reward of all, one that only you can give: lifelong financial security.

—Bonnie Siverd
Contributing Editor, *WORKING WOMAN*

I

HOW TO BUILD A FINANCIAL PLAN

ONE

WHAT'S YOUR MONEY STYLE?

Most working women have already devoted a lot of time to money. We've opened bank accounts, filed tax returns, bought insurance, perhaps picked up a few investments. We've spent hours poring over decimal points and dollars. And hours feeling frustrated.

In many ways, we'd all be better off if we simply abolished percentages, dollar signs, and other money measures. Unlike many things in life, money can be quantified, right down to the penny. But that very precision can be deceptive—if not downright dangerous.

All this exactness clouds the real issue where money is concerned. In focusing too intently on objective measures—how much we have and how fast it is growing—we stand to overlook the most important financial yardstick of all—our hearts.

Feelings count. In our relationships, women know this well. As wives and daughters, mothers and friends, we listen for clues to the feelings of others. In the workplace, too, our successes spring as often from our insights into bosses, staffs, and competitors as from our ability to draw up a budget or meet a deadline.

When we turn to the paychecks we earn with these skills, however, it is as though we become other women entirely. We strive to wring any traces of sentiment from our thinking. Prudence is the prize. How we *feel* about the money we make seems entirely beside the point.

How wrong. For that approach is destined to fail; it overlooks reality. As much as any other topic in life, we feel deeply, strongly, at times passionately about money. Money lies at the heart of some of the most intimate questions any of us face—how to take care of our loved ones and how to take care of ourselves. When money is there for us, it can make our dreams come true. When it's not, our most cherished plans will be stymied. It can leave us feeling elated and powerful—or uncertain, anxious, and, face it, like fools. No matter the question, if it involves money, we *react*.

More important, **each of us reacts to money in distinctly different ways, ways that over years become a pattern. Your pattern, your peculiar set of beliefs and behavior, is what this book will call your money personality.**

Your money personality is a powerful force. It spans every feeling you hold about money: how important it is to you, what you want it to do for you, and most vital, what you need it to do for you. As the summing up of who you are and where you've been, it becomes the force that determines where you are going.

Think about it. Two women working side by side can strike out after vastly different money goals. One may squirrel away funds for an early retirement. Another cannot imagine quitting and instead lavishes her pay on life's pleasures now. Even when they share similar aims, women with different money personalities will follow markedly different paths to reach them.

Every decision you make about money—to buy a fur or buy insurance, to invest in staid bank CDs or in junk bonds, to keep careful records or to dawdle over a stash of unpaid bills—springs directly from your money style. Yet **most of us are only dimly aware of our money personalities, if we think of them at all. As a result, our feelings can sabotage even the most carefully crafted attempts to plan for the future.**

Take Cathy. When interest rates started to skid last year, she was determined to trade her money market account for a higher-yielding plan. She spent two months carefully researching her options. In the meantime, interest rates sank another point and a half and the stock market soared.

Leslie has a different approach. Part of her money style is not to plan at all. She saves whatever's left at the end of the month, which—despite her salary in the mid-30's—does not usually come to much. Instead, she boasts the most beautiful collection of antique pins and bracelets of anyone in her office.

Even seemingly successful money managers can be tripped up by their money styles. Jessica runs a highly profitable unit of a major drug company with a firm hand. She applies the same techniques to her portfolio. Recently she bought 500 shares of an airline she reckoned would benefit from a drop in oil prices. It sank four points instead. As soon as the shares had recovered their ground, she sold the lot outright. The following week their price took off, just as she had originally predicted.

Different as their behavior is, all these women have one thing in common: they are letting deeply held feelings about themselves and their paychecks shape their financial decisions. Each woman's actions typify a pattern or style that flows from her convictions about what will happen to the money she makes and who, in the end, is responsible. The personalities are, respectively, the Nester, the Reacher, and the Driver.

You will learn more about these women and many others in the pages ahead. But already, their actions alone have signalled what makes them tick:

- **The Nester** wants nothing so much as security. Like Cathy, she views risk with a guarded eye. Her goal is to keep what she has, regardless of the price she pays in the process.
- **The Reacher** is bent on building, not holding, but refuses to work to do so. In fact, she often sets herself up to fail. Leslie and women like her secretly believe there's no need to try harder; something—or someone—will turn up. She sees money as a token of love and lavishes it on herself.

• **The Driver** is imbued with a sense of power. Like Jessica, she is willing to take risks to make money. Yet she is determined to control those risks by controlling her environment.

All of us, of course, have surprisingly complex feelings about money. Few individuals hold positions so extreme that they fall neatly into any category, no matter how broad. No woman can be pigeonholed into a single slot.

Yet at any given point in your life, your impulses will pull you sharply in one direction over another. **While you may hold the elements of many different money styles, one will predominate, and that is the tug you must strive to discern.** Without losing sight of their own unique identities, women can profit from seeing their characters writ large, as in a scrawl across a clean page. Learning what they are likely to do in a given money situation—and why—can help them learn how to act to get the results they seek.

Each of the women above could have profited from such insight. Cathy might have set a deadline on her research, promising herself to take whatever action seemed most sensible at the end of ten days. Leslie could set aside money for savings first, before spending anything else, and plan to reward herself with a special pin once she has added $1,000 to her kitty. Jessica could have trusted her own good judgment, and waited before she dumped her stock, instead of trying to show her shares who was boss.

Indeed, as these women show, there is a fine line between making decisions that reflect a deep understanding of your personal needs and letting unchecked emotions dictate your money moves. **To succeed financially, you must see why certain responses consistently appeal to you, determine whether they are the right ones, and if they are not, take other steps which would be more appropriate.** At the same time, you want to avoid deciding on a financial plan that is right for the woman you think you are, or would like to be, but has nothing to do with the person you actually are.

Because the woman you are right now is more than good

enough. In the next page or two we will start to learn more about money personalities and where you fit. But no matter where you find yourself, relax. You need not throw in the towel and trade your self in for a new one. **Each personality—Nester, Reacher, Driver—has its weaknesses, yes, but also deep and abiding strengths. As long as you balance the dominant traits in your personality with the talents of the others, you will do just fine.**

In fact, the perfect money manager is a combination of all three money personalities. All of us need a little nesting in our lives, a little reaching, and a measure of drive. By learning to recognize and to build on our own strengths and to use the strengths of others, we can become the best money managers we can be.

Knowing Yourself

Most women have no idea who they are or what it is they seek from their money. The evidence lies in the feelings they express:

"I work so hard for my money, but I don't seem to be getting anywhere."

"My bills are so high, I never manage to save."

"Every stock I buy goes down, and every one I sell goes up."

"I buy my children the best but feel guilty spending money on me."

"I'd like to get my finances in order, but I just don't have time."

"I feel good knowing I have more in the bank than my boss."

"I worry that I might run out of money someday."

Almost any working woman can add to these examples—faint concerns or nagging fears about the size of her bankroll, investment decisions that leave her paralyzed or blow up in her face, tax bills that threaten to swallow up her last raise.

To quell that kind of thinking and plan her finances wisely, her first task, and yours, is to know herself. **One of the greatest strengths we share as women is our ability to be in touch with our feelings. That knowledge can be a wellspring of financial strength.**

The woman who knows herself and is honest about who she is and what she wants is far more likely to be happy. By identifying her needs, she can take steps to meet them. And by recognizing her money personality, she is more likely to succeed with the measures she takes.

Money personalities involve far more than whether we feel comfortable with risk. In the pages ahead, you'll see that they also reflect the whole of your attitude toward life, yourself, and money as such, as well as your reaction to risk. For starters, however, let's see what they do *not* include.

Since girlhood, each of us has been honing an approach to life and to other people that we think of as our personality. Many women grew up shy and somewhat diffident. To this day they must steel themselves to get up in front of an audience. Others were far more outgoing, flirting at parties and speaking out at college seminars. Managers now, they confidently run a meeting or lunch with the chairman.

Whatever your social personality, put it aside for now. It has little or nothing to do with your money style. In fact, the two can just as easily be opposites. A woman who prefers a job in research to a slot on the sales force can be a hard-driving risk-taker when she tackles the stock market. And the most aggressive product manager might prefer conservative bank deposits for her private stash.

Nor does your money personality have much to do with your actual financial circumstances. Whether you are earning $25,000 or $125,000 makes no difference. Women manage to save a lot—or spend too much—on either income. **How you feel about money has more to do with how you feel about yourself than the number of digits in your bank balance.** Your goal is to get in touch with those feelings.

This isn't as easy as you might think. Money is at the core of the central conflict in American culture. Bombarded with exhortations from Macy's to spend and from Merrill Lynch to save, we want to do both and are totally comfortable with neither. All of us have seen men whose identities were tied to their earning power. They have blurred the distinction between money as a measure of economic value and money as a measure of personal worth.

As women pour into the work force, we confront the same questions head on. We are growing accustomed to *talking* about money—overseeing budgets, selling computers, defending marketing strategies. **Yet while our jobs have made us more sophisticated about the role money plays in business, we often are still confused about the way we *think* about money and the role we set it to play in our lives.**

Sorting it all out means making the effort to identify our deepest money feelings. Here is an exercise that can help you. Think of it as a way of scanning your features in a mirror, taking stock with an objective yet supportive eye. The questions spotlight the key traits that shape your money decisions. Answer each as frankly as you can.

TABLE 1.1

What's Your Money Personality?

1. The best description of your attitude toward saving is:
- **a.** The more I have in the bank, the better I feel.
- **b.** I am saving for a specific long-term goal.
- **c.** I have so many bills, there's nothing left.

2. When you find yourself splurging on a new dress, it's most often because:
- **a.** You feel good. You just got a promotion.
- **b.** You didn't get the promotion, and you figure a new dress will make you feel better.
- **c.** You need a softer image for your marketing presentation next week.

3. When your broker calls to suggest a stock, you:

a. Ask about its recent performance and whether she thinks another company might be an even better bet.

b. Agree to think about it. You never make a decision on the phone.

c. Go with her gut. If she is convinced it will move, you buy 500 shares.

4. You bought 200 shares of a farm equipment maker. The stock market has turned down sharply, and the value of those holdings with it. Nothing in the farm belt has changed. You would:

a. Buy more at the lower price.

b. Sit tight, but berate yourself for not having seen the correction coming.

c. Sell your shares before your losses mounted.

5. Which would make you feel worse?

a. Buying shares you expected to double and seeing them rise 40 percent.

b. Selling a stock after its value had dropped steadily since you purchased it, then seeing it go back to the price you paid and more.

c. Deciding not to buy a stock, and watching it triple.

6. You are preparing for an overnight business trip. All your expenses have been prepaid. You cash a check for:

a. $300.

b. $200. That seems like a lot, but you are not sure how much more you can charge on your credit cards.

c. $100, and plan to charge any unexpected bills.

7. You are out to lunch with several colleagues discussing office business. You might be able to put the meal on your expense account but are not sure. The waiter appears with the check. You:

a. Grab it. It makes you feel good to pick up the tab.

b. Reach for it if no one else offers. You will write it off on your federal tax bill if your boss questions it on your expense account.

c. Hesitate. You love it when someone else pays for anything.

8. Each of us aims to keep a certain minimum in her checking account. When your balance drops below that level, you:

a. Are not concerned unless it slips so low the bank will levy a penalty.
b. Feel very uncomfortable until you deposit more cash.
c. Are not sure what you would feel. You tend to wait to balance your checkbook until two or three months' worth of checks pile up.

9. You have read at least a dozen articles in the past year touting the tax breaks IRAs offer. You:
a. Think they sound like a good idea but awfully boring.
b. Opened one the first year they were available.
c. Plan to fund your retirement out of the capital you are building; $2,000 in an IRA is just small potatoes.

10. Your broker is urging you to open a margin account so you can borrow to buy a promising stock. The interest rate is relatively low, but you are playing with money that is not yours. You:
a. Jump at the chance. After all, the interest is probably deductible.
b. Ask more questions. Your decision will depend on your opinion of the stock.
c. Say no. The idea makes you uncomfortable.

11. Your ideal job would pay:
a. Salary only.
b. Salary and commission.
c. Commission only.

12. In order to save money, many women reuse plastic bags. You
a. Are one of them.
b. Wouldn't dream of it.
c. Can understand the reasoning but simply don't have the time.

To determine your money personality, look among the categories below to find the one that includes most of your answers. It is unlikely, of course, that all of your answers will fall under any one heading; we are each a mosaic of a number of money styles and may respond differently depending on whom we are with or how much money is involved. But your tendency to behave in one way rather than another often means that you share other impulses as well.

The Nester

Your answers: 1a, 2a, 3b, 4c, 5b, 6a, 7c, 8b, 9b, 10c, 11a, 12a

Such a woman is intrinsically conservative. Whether she had a lot of money as a child or barely enough, came easily to the money she now holds or scrambled for every cent, a Nester cares more about keeping what she has than trying to make it grow. **Given the chance to double her money or lose it all, she would pass the bet.**

Her feelings reflect a deep need for security. To feel safe, she is scrambling fast to build a formidable cache, penny by penny if need be. She nurtures her resources, stashing away money against an unknown and faintly threatening future, and derives immense satisfaction as she sees her coffers swell. She'll walk five blocks to save fifty cents on a tuna fish sandwich. Many Nesters save bags, washing out plastic and carefully folding brown paper, and feel proud for the money they don't have to spend.

Deep inside, the Nester believes no one else will take care of her. And at bottom, she also doubts her own ability to provide. Faced with a financial decision—how to invest an IRA or whether to buy a stock—she will research, think, compare. Sometimes endlessly. Many Nesters are stuck at the start-up phase of investing, crafting plan after plan that is never implemented.

Although they place great faith in what they see on paper, Nesters often question what they hear. Such women tend to avoid money managers, dismissing them as hucksters who will trick them into hazardous, and unwelcome, money deals.

For all their efforts, however, Nesters don't take very good care of themselves. **By and large, they park their funds in safe but painfully low-yielding accounts. Buying shares of a stock or a mutual fund would mean living with the prospect of loss, a vulnerability they find disturbing.** They rule out many investments without even considering them. Even presented with a lucrative investment opportunity, they can miss out; more comfortable gathering data than using it, they let the best deals slip away.

When they do edge forth into risk-laden ventures, their feelings still can do them in. All stocks bob up and down in value. When a Nester's sink, she is likely to panic and sell out at a loss, only to see her spurned holdings rebound and flourish. And the Nester never tries again.

On paper, such gun-shy behavior can seem the preserve of weak personalities. But all too many successful career women find their financial decisions dominated by a nesting mentality. Such women are good at their jobs, and often boast name-on-the-door clout and salaries on the balmy side of six figures. Their very commitment to career reinforces their conservative tendencies. In their eyes, they worked too hard for their money to risk losing any.

In the most debilitating strain, some Nesters even doubt their ability to keep what they have. **No matter how much they make or how much they save, they worry that an unseen hand will sweep it all away—and they will be unable to earn it back.**

Despite their skittishness, Nesters display many positive money characteristics. They have a strong sense of priorities and are willing to educate themselves and work for what they want. Their prudence will keep them from falling for ill-advised scams. For these women, the task is to press beyond their conservative bent and pump some risk into their portfolios.

The Reacher

Your answers: 1c, 2b, 3c, 4a, 5c, 6b, 7a, 8c, 9a, 10a, 11c, 12b

The Nester's opposite is the Reacher. Catching word of a hot stock at the office Christmas party, her reaction is "I want one."

That purchase would be added to dozens under the tree. A Reacher gets little satisfaction from putting cash aside. **She sees money as a tool only when it's being spent.** If she can fix a problem with money, she acts, now—whether she is hungry and needs to eat, tired and needs a vacation, depressed and needs a lift. To a Reacher, wealth is the ability to spend as much as she wants. Silk shirts grace her closet and a BMW her garage.

Many Reachers boast the high salaries that can pay their lofty bills. What they lack are savings accounts. Reachers are $50,000-a-year advertising executives with $500 in the bank. Or less well heeled but equally determined spenders who cannot find a way to save.

A Reacher often suffers from a fragile sense of self-esteem. What she owns, and what she does, tells her who she is. Her primary order of business is to pamper herself, and she buys the best because she's worth it. Anxious for approval in the eyes of the world, she gets a rush of well-being from picking up the tab at lunch and leaving a big tip.

Whatever their incomes, Reachers take risks in a concerted attempt to finance their lavish life-styles. Indeed, **Reachers often consider themselves sophisticated money managers because daredevil investments come easily.** With relatively little cash at hand, their deals are highly leveraged. And they are quick to applaud the wisdom of their ways because the interest is probably deductible.

Yet their moves are often reckless in ways they do not even understand. Driven to score, a Reacher fumes if she passes up a good buy. As a result, she is the classic sales prospect, trusting her advisors with blind, unquestioning faith. If her broker touts a stock as a winner, she buys 500 shares.

That done, however, she spends as little time as possible reviewing her decision. She prides herself on being laid back and dismisses more conscientious souls as rather boring. Her bank statements languish in a pile of mail to read another day. When she finally scans the stock listings, she can't believe how poorly her shares have performed.

A Reacher's mistakes can be inadvertent. She rarely takes the time to figure out her goals and choose priorities. Her lack of planning shows in a collection of ill-matched investments—all made on the spur of the moment.

While she may not admit it, many a Reacher secretly believes she is leading a charmed life. She is ever optimistic about what lies ahead, whether or not such sentiments are warranted. A vacation may clear all but $2,000 from her savings, but that's no problem: she'll work twice as hard when she returns, and get a raise.

Many of us start life as Reachers. We want it all so badly—clothes, career, success. Such longings are normal and often fuel our ambitions. The Reacher's task is to grow beyond those instincts into a money style that will let her achieve what she seeks. For all her flippant ways, a Reacher boasts strengths that will help. She does not clutch in the face of risk and will find it easier than her sisters to learn how to take wise ones. She is open to new choices and new experiences, and eager to take whatever steps are needed to preserve her life-style. With a more solid grip on her wallet, she will prosper.

The Driver

Your answers: 1b, 2c, 3a, 4b, 5a, 6c, 7b, 8a, 9c, 10b, 11b, 12c

At her best, the Driver is a paragon of money management. Whether or not she was trained in money matters or exposed to them as a child, she is convinced she can handle her finances as well as anyone else.

The hallmark of a Driver is her capacity to control. She expects her advisors to treat her seriously. One patronizing "let me worry about that," and she is on to another advisor. She asks tough questions until she hears answers that satisfy her. Although her show-me attitude makes forging relationships tough, she will stand by any pro who proves her value.

Unlike Reachers, who want it now, Drivers are content to wait. Their cravings are tempered by a commitment to larger goals. Their definition of wealth is what's in the bank, not in the garage. For these women, spending is usually for a purpose—a suit to enhance a professional image, a long-awaited vacation to recharge worn batteries. And a Driver's goals are equally specific—the down payment on a home of her own or a daughter's college education.

A Driver knows that losing money is part of investing. She focuses instead on how much she can make. **Confident in her ability to provide for herself, she feels comfortable putting some of her assets on the line. At the same time, she has faith in her decisions, so risks seem not threatening but welcome.**

As a result, a Driver is more likely than her peers to seek out risks. When the market is rising, Drivers can be counted on to phone their brokers and press for tips. Overall, in fact, a Driver may spend a great deal of time on money matters. If she owns stocks, she reads the stock pages. If she holds real estate, she checks the ads. For each investment she makes, she sets specific—often high—expectations. If it does not pan out, she is decisive about resolving the situation.

On the face of it, Drivers put aside their feelings in favor of making money. But **beneath the surface, emotions flourish here, too. A Driver is not so much riled by the ones that got away as frustrated by those that fail to meet her standards.** So programmed is she to be in control that if something goes wrong she can experience a profound sense of guilt and failure. Her sense of responsibility says she should have seen the market slump coming, or predicted the bad earnings report.

Taken to an extreme, a Driver's portfolio can become part of her identity. When the inevitable losses occur, she often takes them personally. For such women, selling securities for any reason can deflate their feelings like a leaky balloon.

Ironically, a Driver's overwhelming belief in herself can be her greatest weakness. **All too many Drivers think they know more than they do about the subject at hand—be it utility**

stocks, options, or tax shelters. Confident that their choices are wise, they are not worriers, and can be blind-sided by unexpected market shifts. Many a Driver does not spread her investment bets. She funnels all her assets into real estate because it proved so profitable in the past, or into shares of her company's stock because the management team is strong. Others pour their entire fortune into launching their own businesses and never seriously consider that they might fail.

Taking Stock of Yourself

Examined closely, each of these personalities consists of a particular combination of traits. Each trait, in turn, can be seen as a point on a band, with one extreme marking the full-blown presence of a given quality and the other the absence. The traits fall into four categories: how you see life (optimistic, realistic), how you see yourself (responsible, self-confident), how you see money (commodity, crutch) and how you see investing (risk, control).

As you read more about each quality, consider which personality best reflects your feelings on the subject. The chart on page 18 can help you organize your thoughts. **If you find many of your feelings bunched under one money style, your bent is reasonably clear. But pay close attention to maverick qualities that fall under another style entirely. They spotlight traits that may bubble up when you are faced with a stressful change or that may gain prominence as you grow older.**

How Do You See Life?

1. OPTIMISTIC ....PESSIMISTIC

The basis of all successful investing is a healthy sense of optimism. The ideal investor holds a bone-deep belief that

TABLE 1.2

Sizing Up Your Money Style

	Nester	Reacher	Driver
How You See Life	Pessimistic	Optimistic	Optimistic
	Somewhat unrealistic	Unrealistic	Realistic
How You See Yourself	Responsible	Dependent	Responsible
	Insecure	Insecure	Self-confident
How You See Money	Security	Love	Power
How You See Investing	Risk-adverse	Speculator	Risk-taker
	Procrastinator	Unconcerned	In control

everything will be all right. She views money positively and lays plans for the future with confidence.

At first glance, this seems an easy quality to gauge. But for many of us, it can be a tricky concept. Think for a minute of how you make money. What comes to mind?

A lot of women consciously or unconsciously believe that the way they make money is through their jobs, by pocketing paychecks, performing with skill and winning the promotions and raises that follow. Not so. Or at least, not enough. The first thing a woman must learn—and *believe*—is that she also makes money through her investments. As we make strides in the workplace, we must take a lesson from the capitalism that powers it.

Just as we have worked for our money, so must we put our money to work for us. **Very few of us will make enough in our lifetimes to meet financial goals by working. We need to supplement our paychecks with investing prowess.**

This is true for all individuals, but especially so for women. Historically, we have been equally as talented as men, but we have been paid less. These days women pocket little more than 63 cents for every dollar earned by men. We tend to pause in our careers to bear and raise children. We are more likely than men to leave our jobs to accommodate a partner or relocate to tend an ailing parent. As a result, a woman's saving and earning power often falls far short of that of the men in her life.

If managing her money is as important as earning it, the optimist believes staunchly in her ability to do both. And she is right. As long as she can work, she can take care of herself. Her life-style might change, and her investing program slow, but she will survive.

Women who lack this trait are shackled. Persistent doubt that their money can grow keeps many Nesters from getting the most from their hard-earned savings.

Veronica's main concern is to build a retirement kitty. She has funded her IRA each year since they were authorized, and now has more than $10,000 tucked away, all of it invested in money market funds. While they pumped out double-digit returns when interest rates were high, of late her investments have yielded far less. But because she believes that all her attempts to invest wisely will fail, she refuses to swing even a thousand dollars into a stock fund, or to commit any money to bank CDs lest interest rates rebound.

There's nothing wrong with a money market fund as such, of course. But Veronica's refusal to consider anything else is sorely limiting. Even if she would prefer to keep her retirement fund totally risk-free, and avoid stocks entirely, she could still put up to half of her money fund into a series of CDs that would help her stay ahead of inflation. By refusing to do either, she has condemned her savings to the least profitable spot for her money right now.

2. REALISTIC .... UNREALI' .IC

Optimism is not always a boon, however. There is a strain of this quality that holds women back because it belies reality. Like modern-day Scarlett O'Haras, such optimists bravely assert, "Tomorrow is another day. Tomorrow will take care of itself."

This conviction stems not from an honest, abiding belief in self but from blind faith. **Unlike Scarlett, however, who counted on herself, women who hold this view believe that the saving force when tomorrow comes will be someone—or something—else.**

Nowhere is this seen more clearly than among Reachers, who spend far more than they make. Outspending your pay is nothing less than a denial of reality. Yet the inveterate spender counts on next week's overtime or next month's commissions to help her carry an apartment she can't quite afford, or shrugs at the balance in her bankbook and pulls out her charge card because she *needs* a vacation. Even those who live within their budgets can bank on inheriting money from their parents to make up for years of failing to save. None of these women believes for a minute that she has to take care of herself.

Beneath the surface, unrealistic judgments and behavior are often pleas for something else. **What unrealistic women are really saying is they don't want to take responsibility for their own lives. They'd rather be dependent.**

How Do You See Yourself?

3. RESPONSIBLE .... DEPENDENT

There is an intense conflict in many women between dependence and independence. How you resolve this tug is one of the most important factors framing your money management style.

Part of the lure of dependence is simple: it's easier. Money matters can seem dauntingly complex and the choices so vast that many women simply surrender their power to think and question to somebody else, be it their father, their lover, or the woman down the hall. Letting someone else make the decisions and take the blame for making the wrong ones seems a painless way to avoid taking the rap for the ones that unravel.

But the appeal of dependency is more than a longing to pass the buck. After all, women make serious decisions on the job and are held accountable for those decisions every day. Our ambivalence about taking charge goes far deeper.

As young girls, we were taught to expect to play a supporting role. Everything was done for us. Food appeared on the table, clothes in the closet. If money showed up as well, it was most likely a present or an allowance doled out for no reason other than your presence in your father's home.

As we grew up, we sat back and watched as men continued to handle the cash. What we learned as a result can control us still: that managing money was masculine, dependency the natural feminine counterpart, that not knowing about money was part of being womanly, that having someone to handle it proved we were loved.

To this day, some women find dealing with money distasteful. Amanda has always enjoyed working with her hands. She finds needlework a welcome respite from her pressured job in the marketing department of a large bank. For years, the hallmark of her wardrobe has been hand-knit sweaters the equal of any in the most chic boutiques downtown. One day a friend suggested to Amanda that she start her own business producing and selling handmade goods. "Oh no, I couldn't," she exclaimed. "I knit for pleasure. I don't do this to make money."

Taken to the extreme, dependent women can recoil so completely from money responsibility that they become clingers. Such a woman does not trust her knowledge of money, much less her money management instincts. She avoids risk not so much because she is afraid of it as because she is scared of herself. She may be willing to undertake the routine work of money management, like balancing a checkbook, but she wants someone else on line when decisions must be made. This woman may promise, indeed may promise earnestly, to read the prospectus or write the will as soon as things ease up at work. But months pass, and she never follows through.

Nesters feel good when they build assets. Not so women who cling. Building a bank account is to admit that she alone is truly in charge of her life.

All women must learn that dependency is a dangerous trap. So long as you allow another person to give you security, you give that person the power to take it away.

4. SELF-CONFIDENT ....INSECURE

As women let go of their feelings of dependency, they allow their sense of self-confidence to blossom. For most women, the extent of their self-confidence is reflected in their attitude toward their pay. **While optimism is a diffuse trust in ultimate good fortune, self-confidence is a specific belief in yourself and in your ability to take care of yourself.**

This feeling is not as common as our progress in the work force would lead one to think. Despite years of experience, regular raises, and glowing performance evaluations, all too many women tend to view their salaries as rewards—tokens of esteem that are given gratuitously, not earned by dint of achievement. The distinction is subtle but vital. A reward is granted out of the largesse of the donor. It is optional, and well-mannered recipients are grateful. Earned income is another thing entirely. In such matters, the worker plays the pivotal role—she worked hard and *knows* she deserved every cent she got.

By definition, a gift is controlled by the giver. Bosses who feel threatened promote this feeling. **Women who view their paychecks as rewards inevitably come to think that someone else controls their access to money.** They manifest this belief in many ways. Some are reluctant to demand what they are worth or fail to do the necessary research to find out. Worse yet, others subconsciously make this line part of their world view. These are the women who doubt their own skills and think they are masquerading as managers only until their bosses find them out.

As a result, these women are never sure, absolutely sure, that they could get more money if what they have now were gone. **To protect themselves, they protect their funds, ferreting out the most conservative of investments.** If there's no more where that came from, they seem to say, we're going to make what we do have last.

Self-confident women don't think that way. They know their work is valuable, and that someone will always pay for it. That knowledge frees them to aim for getting ahead, not getting by.

How Do You See Money?

5. MONEY AS COMMODITY ....MONEY AS CRUTCH

Self-confidence allows women to see their money emotions for what they are.

Money is an emotional chameleon, taking on different shades of meaning from the way you see it. In most cases, the role you assign to money reflects your innermost needs. All of us need affirmation of the compliments we give ourselves. These longings can flow from a childlike need for praise or from an adult drive to dominate. **Whether you seek security, love, or power, the odds are long that you will see money as a tool to provide it.**

The Nester may think that money itself is what she's after. Martha certainly did not have much of it as a child. Today, despite a salary in the high 40's, she still feels a wave of disquiet whenever her rent goes up. She saves diligently, salting away 15 percent of her pay each month, and has managed to build a $20,000 account at her local bank. **Praise a Nester for**

efforts, however, and she belittles them. No amount of money on hand could ever be enough. As a result, Martha finds it hard to buy things for herself. She doesn't feel she's worth it. To her eye, money symbolizes security, and letting any of it slip away, even for a well-deserved vacation, is unsettling.

A Reacher, by contrast, sees money as a reflection of her self-esteem. Pauline was crushed when a fellow sales manager was promoted to a regional post she had secretly coveted. To soothe her disappointment, she bought two pairs of very expensive shoes on her way home, sending her credit card perilously close to the limit. Similarly, many working women feel vulnerable if they're not yet earning as much as their college roommates or the woman down the hall. But women who measure their self-worth in terms of their net worth will always feel wanting. Someone else will always earn more or have more in the bank.

Drivers are more likely to see money as a way to wield power. Carol buys frequent, often costly gifts for her friends in a bid to keep them close, even though her job does not allow nearly as many lunches as they used to share. In most instances, however, Carol recognizes that while she may want certain results from her actions, money cannot guarantee to buy them. She is at her most objective when she talks to her broker.

How Do You See Investing?

6. RISK-TAKER .... RISK-ADVERSE

Men are raised to take chances in pursuit of their dreams. Women's upbringing, by contrast, stresses security. Women are more likely to settle for less than they *might* get in favor of what they are sure they *will* get.

Until recently, their circumstances reinforced that attitude. With small salaries and even smaller savings, prudence suggested an investment course bent on preserving the little they had.

Women command vastly higher paychecks now, and are

managing to save more. Yet many of us are finding that the lessons of our formative years continue to sway our investing decisions. As a group, we find ourselves still playing the role of nurturer that we were taught by our mothers and society at large. That charter says to protect whatever is entrusted, and that goes for portfolios as well as for daughters.

Such thinking can be dangerous. **Many women seem to have forgotten that part of nurturing is fostering growth, however threatening that process might seem. It is only by living with the insecurity of at least a small amount of risk with our investments that we can win the financial security we seek.**

Today it is very popular for money experts to say: you don't need to invest in anything that makes you uncomfortable. You don't have to let any money decision keep you up at night.

This is simply untrue. What's comfortable is not always right. We must compare our goals with the means at hand. Not all people can live with high risk, and not all who can are wise to do so. But **if your means are limited, as so often women's are, you will need to take some risks to reach your goals.** In fact, it is as foolish to refuse to take risks you can comfortably afford as it is to shoulder those you cannot withstand.

The concept of risk is deceptive. What many women think of as secure investments pose far greater risks than those women perceive. Take bank CDs. You are guaranteed to get your investment back and more. But what will that sum be worth? Unless the interest you earn equals or exceeds inflation, its real value is *less* than it was when you started.

Not all women, of course, are chiefly powered by fear. A great many investors, including a disproportionate number of Reachers, fall prey to the flip side of fear—greed. This emotion is just as likely to skew their attitude toward risk-taking. An overzealous push to make a killing can blind investors to the real risks in their actions. **Wise decisions about risk flow neither from fear nor from greed but from a balance of the two.**

The best risk-takers are comfortable with risk because they

hold many other qualities of a strong money personality. They believe in their ability to make and use money, yet they have a realistic appreciation of the pitfalls in the attempt. To ensure success, however, risk-takers must also be willing to take control.

7. IN CONTROL .... UNCONCERNED

Only the very secure or the very rich have no fear of making money decisions. Most of the rest of us can suffer from bouts of indecisiveness severe enough to up-end the best financial plan. Strong as she may be on a job she knows well, a woman's lack of familiarity with money matters often summons up childlike feelings from the days when girls were taught to be tactful and deferential to authority.

Some women refuse to wield control because they want to be liked. Katlin would say yes to any recommendation from her broker, no matter how she felt about the idea, simply because she was unwilling to say no. Rebuffing a suggestion, she feared, would lead her broker to rebuff her.

Other women know their own minds well, but keep it a secret. They play a grown-up version of peek-a-boo with their money advisors, feigning interest in buying a stock or in writing a will when they have no intention of undertaking either. Still others will procrastinate, putting off buying that stock until so much time has passed that it's no longer a good buy.

Shrewd investors need to overcome their hesitation and act. The point is not to win friends, it is to make money. No money professional expects you to go along with every recommendation. If you have your doubts, say so, then go on to the next move. Successful investors must monitor their decisions, and act again if circumstances direct. Whether to take profits or cut losses or switch insurance agents, the best money managers stay involved.

If your hesitation is more fundamental, and your refusal to take control is just another way of refusing to act, remind yourself that **even money pros make mistakes.** Not all your investment choices will be good ones. Indeed, you can lose and lose again and still prosper.

Are You Working Toward Your Goals?

Never do your money feelings play a larger role than when it comes to naming the goals around which you will build your financial plan. Whether you long for an early retirement, a short commute, or to see Japan before you hit 40, you must identify your dreams in order to make them your accomplishments.

All good financial plans start with goals. Specific goals. Exactly how much money. Precisely when. To do just what. **The best goals are written down, not because that makes the list more authoritative, but because it forces the writer to be more concrete.**

For most of us, it is easier to think about how to get what we seek than to figure out what we want in the first place.

Many women shy away from framing financial goals because of the air of finality they carry. They flinch from specifics when they are young, when so much of their lives stands to change in ways as yet unknown. Choosing goals before they've lived their lives seems something akin to choosing a husband at age 22. They see no guarantees that either the goals or the mate will still be around when they turn 40.

As we age, goal-setting can grow harder yet. The years are taking their toll on opportunity. By choosing certain goals, you necessarily are passing others by. And the older we grow, the less easy it is to admit that only so much will be done, savored, experienced, owned, provided for.

Not to worry. Today's goals are the best we can muster now and can do no more than reflect today's priorities and our best vision of tomorrow's needs. While they may be written down, they are not chiseled in stone. **You always can change your goals and objectives. You cannot recapture time.**

To find the goals that really matter to you, sort your money-related concerns into a few broad categories. Here is one convenient format:

I am worried about I feel guilty about	I ought to	Safe to put off	Not important to me

Write down every thought that comes to mind, the more fanciful the better. Your aim is to uncover your most cherished hopes and the dreams you only conjure in private.

Questions to ponder include:

- What do you want for yourself?
- What do you need?
- Why are you working?
- What makes you happy?
- What, specifically, do you worry about when you think about losing your job?
- How, specifically, do you imagine yourself living if you could walk away from your desk tomorrow?
- How, specifically, do you imagine yourself living when you retire?
- Do you think you need more money or less money to be happy than you did five years ago?
- Do you think your feelings will continue moving in that direction?
- Whom do you love?
- What do you want to be able to do/and/or give to those persons?

Aim to get beyond fuzzy answers like "I want more money" to such concrete goals as "I want to save $10,000 in the next two years."

Then divide your concerns into short-, medium-, and long-range tasks. A short-range goal might be to pay for this summer's vacation in full, instead of in dribs and drabs on your

MasterCard for six months afterward. Classic long-range goals include buying a home, educating children, planning for retirement.

Look carefully at your list. The chief problem many women encounter in setting goals is failing to choose among them. Every goal is assigned the same priority. Every want is enshrined.

But only the richest among us can accomplish every goal at once. Check your plan with a sharp eye to see whether the ones you name are compatible. Consider tradeoffs. **In this era of skyrocketing costs, most of us will be able only to begin working toward our most important goals, and even those must be tackled in order. Chasing after too many may doom you to achieve none.**

Once you have your goals in hand, time management experts have wisdom to lend. In order to accomplish anything, you must break your goals down into components that you can deal with.

An important goal for all of us is retirement security. But labelling that as the target and moving on is like trying to climb a slippery learning curve. It must be more specific before we can even imagine accomplishing it.

Instead, block out specific objectives: to have an annual income equal to $50,000 when the year 2013 dawns, with a home and two college educations paid for.

Perhaps the most serious problem in setting goals arises when women cannot see their real needs. To lay any meaningful plans, you must have a thorough understanding of the steps to take to win financial security and how the steps interact.

The relationships can be complex. A single woman struggling to furnish an apartment must realize that the tax savings from owning her home can help free more cash to spend, and so set to work on building a down payment. A newlywed deciding to postpone motherhood must see that her decision will squeeze two of life's most costly tasks—paying for her child's college bills and saving for retirement—into a far more narrow time frame (both outlays probably occurring when she is in her fifties) so she must set to work now on one of them. Older women must see how inflation threatens to undo their lifetime efforts, and so structure their portfolios accordingly.

The next chapter gives an overview.

TWO

PLANNING FOR EVERY WOMAN: THE S-T-A-I-R TO FINANCIAL SUCCESS

I am often asked if good money advice is different for women than men. The answer is both no and yes.

Whatever an individual's money style, the right financial choices for any person flow from their place in life—their unique combination of goals, feelings, abilities, and needs. A man and a woman in identical situations with identical attributes would be right to pursue identical financial courses.

Men and women clearly aren't identical in many important ways. And that's what makes money management so different for us than for them.

Many women, of course, are relatively new to the process of money management, and that fact alone can separate our concerns from those of the men we see. Not only do our backgrounds diverge, we often hold different assumptions about what is important to us and strike out after vastly different goals.

More important, our *circumstances* are different. So far at least, women tend to be left holding the short end of the financial stick. We earn less but live longer. We have been given responsibilities but not taught how to handle them. All too often, we start to build wealth later than men with fewer dollars to work with.

As women, in fact, we have far more in common with one another than with any man we know. And the needs and goals we share as a group form our truest basis for good financial planning.

Just as women move through life in measured sequence, from girlhood to old age, they confront money questions in familiar stages, or lifelines, as this book calls them. Each stage holds distinctive, predictable challenges and carries with it the tools to meet them.

Unless we die at our desks, each of us will one day swap our paychecks and earning power for income from savings and investments. While we are working, then, we must use our pay to accumulate and build assets. A successful manager may boast a six-figure salary, but until she converts her income-based wealth into asset-based wealth she is not rich at all, just fortunate. **For most of us, that conversion from paycheck to portfolio is the single most important step in our financial plans.** At retirement, we will take back those assets and exchange them for income again.

Look again at the pattern. For each of us, there was a first job. In many instances, new graduates are just beginning to develop their money styles. Other women return to or join the work force in their thirties, forties, fifties, or even later as the demands of child-rearing end or the search for fulfillment takes hold. No matter the reason, such women need in short order to devise ways to save, build credit, boost assets and keep taxes at bay.

Many of us marry. That step alone vaults women into a new lifeline. They must scramble to mesh two households and often two conflicting sets of goals and priorities as well. Their combined incomes call for special tax and estate strategies. If they start a family, their money concerns grow nearly as fast as their offspring.

As women age, their need for money mushrooms. We reward our achievements, provide for our children, and often find ourselves acting as parents to our own parents. In later years our earnings end as we retire, and we begin to tap the fruit of our efforts.

Anywhere along this path, a woman might shift course abruptly. **For the hallmark of our lives as women is uncertainty. If single, we may fall in love and marry. If married now, we may leave our mate or find ourselves left. We may remarry, or we may not. We may choose a partner with children of his own. In later years, we are very likely to lose a spouse to death.**

The purpose of a financial plan is to steer you successfully through these shoals. As such, financial planning is a simple concept. Yet the process remains a nebulous one to most individuals. In part, that is because the term itself is flawed. What comes to mind when you close your eyes and imagine a financial plan? If you're like most investors, you draw a blank.

Financial planning means taking a series of specific steps to deal with specific issues to achieve a specific result. The best way to look at a financial plan is to imagine a stairway like the one in Table 2.1. Each step in the S-T-A-I-R represents an element of a good financial plan: Saving, Taxes, Assets, Insurance, and Retirement and estate planning.

Saving money comes first. Without cash to work with, you will never have assets. Your tax bill comes next. Paying less to Uncle Sam is among the best ways to save. No matter how little they may come to for now, savings represent assets. You need insurance to protect the income that produced them and the rewards of those efforts, whether a car, house, or fur. The last step of the stair is retirement and estate planning. Timely efforts here can win financial security for yourself in retirement or to pass along to those you love.

Like any staircase, we climb the financial planning S-T-A-I-R step by step. **Complete each phase, and you will reach the goals you set.** It is a methodical process that reflects the

TABLE 2.1

The Financial S - T - A - I - R

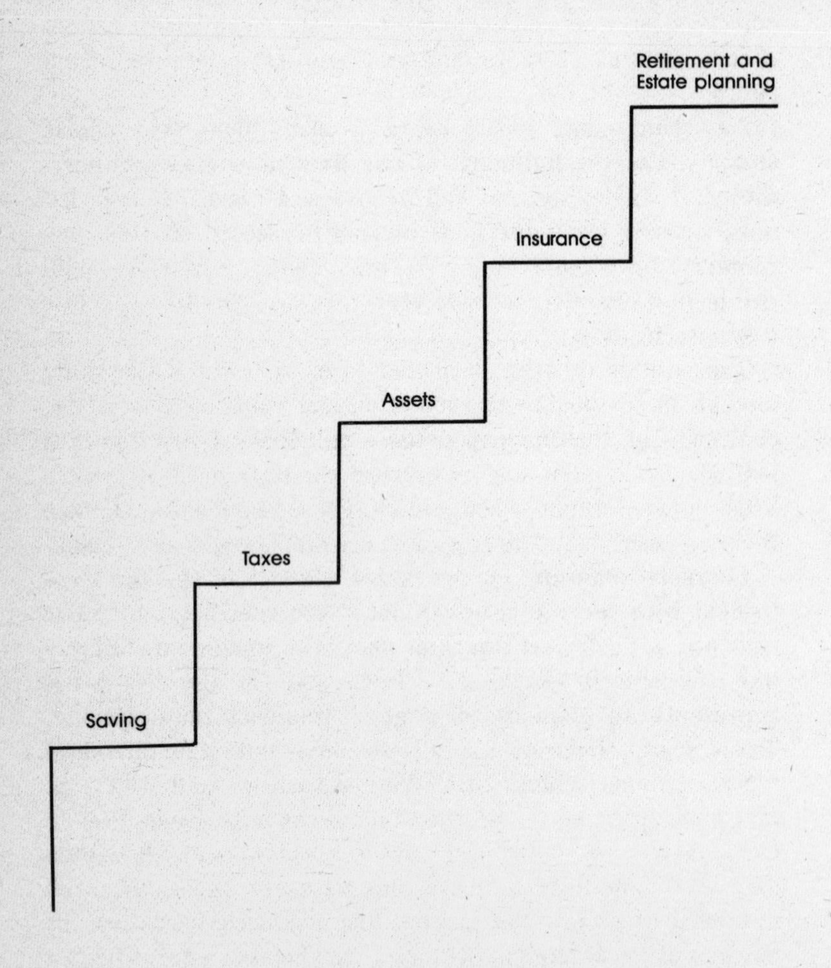

basically conservative nature of financial planning. The goal is to protect yourself with defensive measures that give you the base from which to take offensive action.

But beware. Skip a step, let down your defenses, and you'll suffer the consequences. You may stub your toe, and pay far more than you need in taxes. Or you may tumble and fall, winding up strapped for retirement cash or deep in debt.

Financial planning is a task almost all of us can do ourselves. As the pages ahead will show, you are your own best keeper: you know yourself, your goals, and your assets far better than anyone else. Even so, in some situations you can benefit from outside help. Many busy working women simply don't have the time or the inclination to do their own planning. As they grow more successful, they demand increasingly sophisticated products and more advice. A bountiful inheritance, fast-growing assets, or sudden fiscal complication also may call for a sharp professional eye.

Even then, however, you will help yourself best by growing familiar with each step of the financial planning process. Only then can you best evaluate and supervise your money pros, a task that is dealt with in detail in Chapter 11.

In the end, the specific elements of your plan will depend on a great many things: your money personality, to be sure, as well as your age, income now, future earning power, tax bracket, the number of years you expect to work, your current assets, family ties, chance for an inheritance, and willingness to live with risk. These and other issues are explored in detail, with specific advice, in Chapter 3 and in Part Two. For now, let's focus on the basics common to us all.

Saving

To create financial security, you need more than a good job. You need a well-honed plan for saving, investing, and managing what you earn.

Saving and investing are the only ways to build wealth. But many women try to skip the first step. Impatient to move to what they deem the far more glamorous task of investing, they pay too little attention to wringing the most out of their cash flow. But as working women, astonishing sums of money flow through our hands in a year and over a lifetime. **Other than not planning at all, the chief mistake most working women make is failing to spirit enough from their earnings into their bank accounts.**

A woman's financial security depends just as much on amassing capital as on what she chooses to do with it. **The younger you are, the more important saving is: early on, in fact, the fledgling worker's success actually depends *more* on making the proper spending/savings tradeoffs than on any investing decision.**

Think big. All too often, women condemn themselves to less by the modesty of their aspirations. Since what you make is the source of what you can save, set income goals for yourself. One compensation analyst dubbed her own pay goal 35/50. Translation: when she turned 35, she wanted to be earning $50,000. That goal may seem grandiose or far too modest for you. No matter. Setting your own target is what counts.

Then, take the steps needed to meet your target. If more schooling seems in line, spend the money and enroll or take a job that promises to reimburse the costs of acquiring new skills. Whatever you do, don't cheap out here. The most important investment you can make is in yourself.

Thinking big applies to other outlays. Establishing overall financial goals can help keep your actions focused. It's easy to dribble away your dollars on trivial things—manicures, movies, mousse—only to find no money left for bigger, more important aims like investing, vacations, homes.

Allocate a percentage of your income toward such long-term efforts and stick to it. Again, think big. **Ten percent of your gross income is the *minimum* to target toward savings.** Salt away more if you can.

Don't put the whole burden on your paycheck. Be alert for extra funds to stash away. A year-end bonus or income tax refund should be spirited into your cache. And when you win a big promotion, raise your savings target before you improve your life-style. Most women who have managed to sock away impressive sums have done so by putting off or pruning back purchases in their early years.

Taxes

Good tax planning has never been more important. **In fall 1986 Congress passed the most sweeping tax reform law in half a century. The new rules will change the way every woman should look at saving, investing, buying, borrowing—in fact, virtually every money move she makes.**

Though widely billed as tax simplification, tax reform does not make April 15 any easier for most of us. If anything, filling out one's 1040 may be even more difficult than in past years. That is because 1987 is a transitional year—one in which some changes take effect, other changes are phased in, still other tax breaks are phased out.

And even in 1988 and beyond, the welter of changes means you must pay more attention than ever to your 1040. In its diligence, Congress curbed or eliminated dozens of cherished deductions, ranging from interest on car loans to state sales taxes, instituted a slew of new rules for such time-honored tax breaks as IRAs and gifts to children, and completely rewrote the laws concerning stock trades and tax shelters. In sum, **the Tax Reform Act of 1986 makes it harder for you to take advantage of loopholes but makes it all the more important to seize the benefits from those you still can use.**

Even so, no single tax move or device will make an overwhelming difference in your tax bill. But a thoughtful combination of all the skills and techniques this book describes can slash your tax tab and boost your assets.

The first step is to identify, document, and file for every deduction you deserve. Research here is important even if you rely on a tax professional to prepare your return. Turn to Chapter 4 for a solid introduction, then watch for more tax tips in the life-style chapter that reflects your needs.

The greatest potential payoffs come with structuring your spending and investing in order to whittle down your bill. You'll learn how to succeed at this task, too, in the chapters ahead. While the information that follows is as up-to-date as was possible at the time, be sure to double check the fine points on any major tax decision with a professional before you act.

The starting point in all tax planning is your tax bracket. That represents the cut the IRS takes out of the *last* dollars you earn or your investments create. It tells you how much profit you actually pocket on a given investment, or how much you actually pay for a deductible expense. Most important, it applies only to the extent that you permit. Crafty scheming can cut your taxable income, hence your tax bracket, way down.

That can prove particularly valuable in 1987. **The most welcome part of the new tax bill is the progressive cut it mandates in marginal rates. The 1986 top tax bracket of 50 percent drops to 38.5 percent in 1987 and to a relatively gentle 33 percent in 1988 and beyond.** That means most taxpayers would benefit by taking as many deductions as they can in 1987, to offset the higher rates still in place, and pushing as much income as possible into the more lightly taxed 1988.

How to do that? Keep an eye out for every deduction mentioned in the pages ahead that you *can* take, and try to cram as many as possible into 1987. If you belong to a professional organization, for instance, pay 1988's dues in 1987. You'll read detailed tips in the chapters ahead. Self-employed persons will find it easiest to defer income. You can simply put off sending off any year-end bills until January 2. Even if you work for a corporation, however, a little finagling can still pay off. See if you can arrange to defer some of your salary or a year-end bonus, for instance, to 1988. And anyone can benefit by shifting earnings on investments, say the profit on the sale of a stock, into 1988.

Beyond that, **wise women now will cultivate a new mindset about taxes.** For the most part, the new law makes it pretty darn tough to shelter the income you earn from wages. But it still leaves relatively unscathed many of the classic strategies to shelter the income earned from investments, so-called unearned income.

Most important, **the drastic cut in marginal rates gives every working woman an even greater incentive to power ahead and earn money.** In the old order, with Uncle Sam skimming up to 50 cents in taxes out of the last dollars earned, it sometimes seemed pointless to win a raise or take a sideline job. Come 1988, the most you'll have to pay in federal taxes is 33 cents on every dollar—leaving you fully 67 cents on every extra buck you pocket.

Still, even 33 cents on a dollar is more than any of us wants to give up lightly. **The post-tax reform world offers several ways to structure your income in order to pay the least tax possible:**

- take steps to increase deductions—say, by buying a house
- eliminate taxes altogether by choosing investments that offer tax-free yield, if your tax bracket is high enough to make such moves worthwhile
- convert ordinary income to lower-taxed capital gains
- defer taxes to a later date
- shift income to relatives who are in lower brackets

By many measures, the best kind of income is tax-free. Payouts from municipal bonds and certain other investments are exempt from federal and, in some cases, state and local taxes. But such instruments usually pay lower rates than taxable deals. To see if tax-free income makes sense for you, find your 1987 taxable income (the sum you reckon you will report in 1987 after subtracting all deductions) on the chart in Table 2.2. The

TABLE 2.2

Taxable vs. Tax-Free Income

Your Taxable Income		1987 Marginal tax rate	To equal tax-free yields, you need taxable investments earning:						
Single return	Joint return		5% tax-free	6% tax-free	7% tax-free	8% tax-free	9% tax-free	10% tax-free	12% tax-free
Up to $1,800	Up to $3,000	11%	5.6	6.7	7.9	9.0	10.1	11.2	13.5
$ 1,800–$16,800	$ 3,000–$28,000	15	5.8	7.0	8.2	9.4	10.6	11.8	14.1
$16,800–$27,000	$28,000–$45,000	28	6.9	8.3	9.7	11.1	12.5	13.9	16.7
$27,000–$54,000	$45,000–$90,000	35	7.7	9.2	10.8	12.3	13.8	15.4	18.5
Above $54,000	Above $90,000	38.5	8.1	9.8	11.4	13.0	14.6	16.3	19.5
		1988 and beyond Marginal tax rate							
Up to $17,850	Up to $29,750	15%	5.8	7.0	8.2	9.4	10.1	11.2	13.5
$17,850–$43,150	$29,750–$71,900	28	6.9	8.3	9.7	11.1	12.5	13.9	16.7
$43,150–$89,560	$71,900–$149,250	33	7.5	9.0	10.4	11.9	13.4	14.9	17.9
Above $89,560	Above $149,250	28*	6.9	8.3	9.7	11.1	12.5	13.9	16.7

*Some income in this bracket will carry a 5% surcharge until the benefits of the personal exemption are phased out.

SOURCE: Public Securities Association

table shows what rate of tax-free return would equal or exceed that of a taxable investment for someone in your tax bracket.

Municipal bonds are expensive; most sell for $5,000 a clip. But investors can buy packages of bonds through municipal bond funds or unit investment trusts, a type of mutual fund that offers a preset portfolio maturing on a specific date. And many money market funds also specialize in tax-free securities.

Capital gains—the generous treatment of any long-term gain on a capital investment—also present a way to trim your bill. The profit on any investment purchased after June 22, 1984, and held for more than six months merits special tax treatment in 1987; only a maximum of 28 percent of the gain is taxed. By contrast, income from dividends, interest, and the profit on investments held less than six months is taxed at full rates.

After that, you can throw your calendar away. The Tax Reform Act ends the distinction between short-term and long-term capital gains. Any profit on the sale of a stock, bond, or other capital investment, no matter how long you own it, will be taxed as ordinary income starting January 1, 1988. For most of us, that will mean paying a higher tax on long-term capital gains.

The news is not all bad, however. Starting in 1987, you can deduct up to $3,000 in net capital losses (that is, losses after subtracting your gains, if any) dollar-for-dollar against your taxable income each year no matter how long you held the asset you sold. Hence your losses on one investment can be used to offset the increasingly stringent taxes on profits on more successful ones.

That's a big improvement over the previous state of affairs. While short-term losses always offset gains dollar-for-dollar, only 50 cents of every dollar in long-term losses could be deducted before 1987. And Uncle Sam still has pity on the most hapless of investors. Losses in excess of $3,000 can be hoarded and claimed as deductions in more prosperous years.

Still another effective tax-planning technique is to **defer taxes.** That strategy allows savers to gamble that certain income may be taxed less severely later. More important, it allows investors to leverage their holdings by using the before-tax rather than after-tax value of their funds. The most widely available ways to do so are IRAs and Keoghs.

Nearly every working woman should consider establishing an IRA, a special retirement plan that allows savers to set aside and in some cases defer taxes on up to $2,000 in earned income a year. Self-employed women or those who do sideline work such as consulting can swing part of that income into a similar plan called a Keogh. Keoghs are far more generous than IRAs. Individuals may deposit up to 20 percent, or $30,000, of their sideline income. Other corporate fringe benefits, discussed below, offer equal, or in some cases, more powerful lures. The most widely available is called a 401(k) program, named for the provision of the tax code that authorized it. These "salary deferral" plans allow workers to make tax-deductible contributions of as much as $7,000 a year. In many cases, you can get back some or all of those funds more easily than those in an IRA. Best of all, your company may match all or part of your contribution.

If they wish, women with families can turn their relatives into tax shelters of sorts. **One of the best ways for a high-earning professional to cut her bill is to whisk some income off her 1040 and onto that of someone less heavily taxed.** Whether she stockpiles for her children, helps out aging parents, or simply indulges a beloved niece, a woman can give any person up to $10,000 per year without incurring any federal gift taxes. Up to $1,000 in earnings on money held by children under 14, and all the income enjoyed by older children and adults, is taxed at the holder's often lower rates. This technique is discussed in detail in Chapter 6.

Assets

It's tempting to think that a formula can dictate the ideal combination of assets in your portfolio—the kind of rule that says, put 40 percent of your money in stocks, another 40 percent in bonds, the rest in cash and, presto! Retire in style. Nothing, of course, is that simple.

How you choose to invest your funds must reflect your money personality as well as your goals and circumstances. That done, the precise steps to take should flow from relative opportunities in the financial markets (explored in more detail in Chapter 9). Depending on the economic climate, the balance of assets you hold can change several, even dozens, of times in a year.

Deciding how to invest your funds may seem a forbidding task. **Relax. The exact mix of your assets is simply not critical. Over the long run, it probably won't make a bit of difference whether you allocate 20 percent, 25 percent, or even 30 percent to a given investment category.**

What *is* important is the direction you take. **To strike a successful portfolio balance, concentrate on getting the *relative* weightings in line.** A woman whose career is taking off may want the bulk of her assets in stocks. In that case, even 30 percent could be far too much money to assign to safety-first investments. On the other hand, if her life-style demands that she guard her holdings carefully, that same 30 percent may be too little for her needs.

The first rule in investing, then, is to decide what you want your money to do for you. Basically, the choice is to grow in value or to throw off income.

The answer may seem far from clear. Take the choices faced by a typical woman—increasing savings, helping her parents, planning for retirement. At first it seems she just wants one thing—more money.

A closer look, however, shows these needs break down quite simply into specific investment objectives—growth holdings to boost capital, income-producing securities to supplement her mother's income, and a long-term investment program to secure her old-age comfort. In a similar vein, you must start your investment program by examining your own goals and reducing them to income vs. growth choices.

A woman's portfolio will contain both growth and income

investments at every stage of her life. It is the relative size of these segments that varies to reflect your individual needs. And it is the purpose that dictates how they are to be deployed.

Every investment, whether an annuity or a zero coupon bond, is important to you only if it can perform a role in your portfolio. In that sense, **investments are best seen as tools. Like computers, some are multi-purpose. Others, such as the trusty stapler, focus on doing just one task well.** Knowing which roles each investment fills can help you choose among them and match them to your needs.

How well any one investment fills a given role depends on how it balances a set of investment characteristics. The most important are liquidity, return, and safety. **Liquidity** refers to the ease with which you can convert an investment to cash. **Return** measures the income you collect for your efforts. **Safety** reflects the risks incurred to get that return and the odds that the tool will not perform the task assigned.

A liquid investment fills a specific need; it can be converted to cash on short notice. But the yield you collect in the meantime may not be all that much. Long-term securities typically pay higher yields than short-term investments. That is because there is a greater risk that interest rates might rise, and investors lose out, before they repocket their principal.

Nowhere are tradeoffs more clear than with the question of risk. When they pan out, risky investments such as stocks tend to pay out far more than secure, easy-access investments such as bank CDs. Not always, of course. It is precisely that danger that requires a bigger potential payoff to lure investors' funds.

As you allocate your assets, you will take all three of these elements into account. Here are the steps to follow:

1. Pile up cash. No one should begin investing without a backup fund. Aim to set aside at least two months' expenses in an account you can raid at a moment's notice.

The exact size of the backstop you need depends on your circumstances. If your job is secure and your income steady, three months' worth of bills should be a fairly safe stash. Commission-based professionals and other women with erratic incomes are well advised to tuck away far more. The same holds true for those carving out careers in relatively low-demand fields who might need months to replace a lost job. In the same vein, the more other people depend on your income, the greater your need for cash.

So long as life seems promising, piling up money "just in case" calamity strikes hardly seems an urgent task. **It helps to remember that your cash reserve is not for emergencies only. That is the hoard you will tap to seize unexpected opportunities.** Without a cash cushion, for instance, you could miss the chance to lock in lush yields when interest rates hit record levels. More dire, you might be forced to sell off stocks at a loss if their value skidded just as you needed cash to cover an uninsured medical bill.

The smallest nest eggs—$500 or less—are best shunted into an ordinary bank checking account. While you earn no interest on those funds, beefing up your checking balance can help reduce or wipe out bank service charges. Avoid passbook or other standard savings accounts, however. The meager interest paid on most such accounts could easily be topped by the fees involved.

As you pile up funds, consider bank money market accounts. Many banks will open such accounts for $1,000 or less. Such limits are set by each bank. Shop around to find the smallest minimum. One type of account resembles a savings acount, with a limited number of transactions permitted per month. A more flexible version, sometimes called a Super-NOW, functions much like a conventional checking plan. But banks tend to charge more for and pay less interest on Super-NOWs.

Mutual funds also offer money market accounts. They sometimes accept smaller opening antes than banks, but limit checks to a certain minimum, often $250 or more. Most working women would do better keeping their cash in a bank. While the interest they earn may be slightly less, they will begin to forge a relationship with a banker. Ultimately, that tie could prove far more valuable than a percentage point or so in additional interest. Banks are the chief source of the credit most women need to unfurl their plans (see Chapters 4 and 12).

2. Diversify. Cushion-plumped, you are ready to broaden your base. The most important task is to diversify your assets. A wide range of holdings lessens the risk that one bum choice will derail your plans.

The specific ratio of cash to stocks to other assets—the portfolio mix—you seek depends on your goals and how long you have to reach them. **Broadly speaking, if you value safety or need income, you will want to steer the bulk of your assets into income-oriented deals—money market funds, bank CDs, Treasury securities, bonds, and the like. If you are looking for growth, and can shoulder risk, seek out more speculative plays—stocks, real estate, gold, and so forth—that hold out the chance for capital appreciation.**

Specific portfolio suggestions follow in the chapters ahead. Table 2.3 offers a preview. It illustrates **the seven stages of a typical woman's portfolio** as she shuttles back and forth between conservative and risky investments, seeking the balance best suited to her situation at the time.

As we have seen, a woman's first investments should be super-secure, with just about all her funds nestled safely in a cash reserve (1). Once they have built a stockpile, however, most women should bounce toward the other extreme (2) and add some risky investments to their holdings. With fewer responsibilities, they can afford to gamble in the hopes of building a financial stake. But not too much. Any assets saved are precious now and rebounding from a loss would take time. Women with children or older women approaching retirement but just beginning to work would wisely keep a greater share of their funds in investments where the principal is guaranteed.

As her assets swell, a woman's next moves should cushion the growing number of speculative investments in stocks and the

TABLE 2.3

The Seven Stages of a Woman's Portfolio

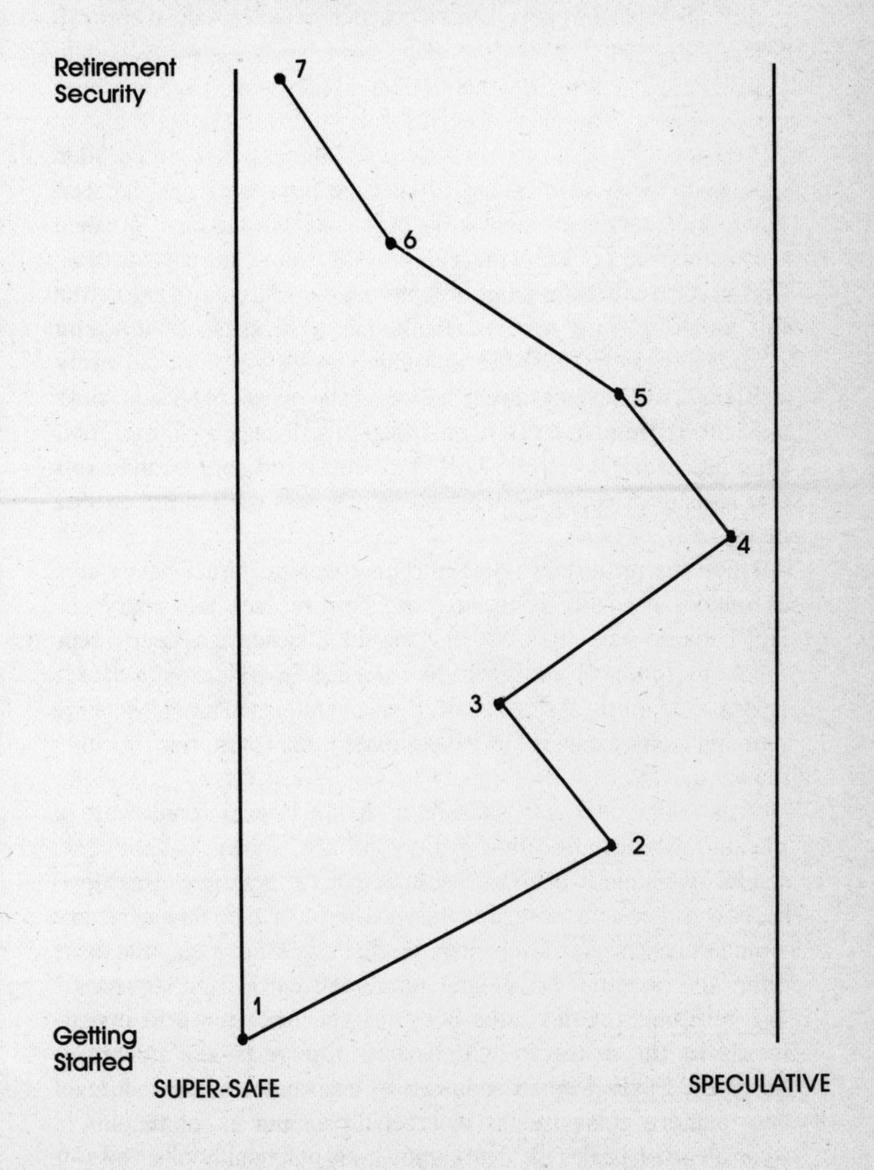

like with another chunk of relatively secure holdings such as bank CDs. Her aim is to keep a balance between safety and risk (3).

Still later in life, a woman likely will barrel into her peak earning years. The greater her income, the less impact a loss of capital would pose to her life-style and the easier it would be to replace those funds. Hence, their high-pay years are the time when most women can strike the riskiest balance in their portfolios. They will swing again to the right, farther than their first speculative forays but still not to the extreme (4). Even at this point a wise woman maintains a measure of low-risk investments to balance her holdings.

Should she have children (5), or as she grows older and looks ahead to retirement (6), a woman again will seek a change. This time her overall portfolio will shift to a more conservative mix that aims to protect a growing share of assets for a child's or her own use.

Once she retires, her portfolio may well feature a heavy slug of income-oriented investments to help replace the salary she left behind. Nonetheless, she should continue to keep some funds in holdings designed to increase in value as a hedge against inflation. As a result, her overall investment posture remains somewhat more risk-oriented (7) than her opening moves (1).

This route contrasts sharply with the conventional way of illustrating asset allocation. That approach, shown in Table 2.4, stacks investments from safe to speculative. It shows, graphically, how super-safe investments should form the base of every woman's portfolio. Each step up the pyramid after that base offers the potential for greater return but carries higher risks.

It's important to remember that you need not add investments in the order in which they appear in the pyramid, however. Many women should leap from base-building in level one to more gutsy moves in level three. But all of us should steer clear of peak-risk deals until both our bankbooks and our stomachs can handle the chance of loss.

TABLE 2.4

The Investment Pyramid

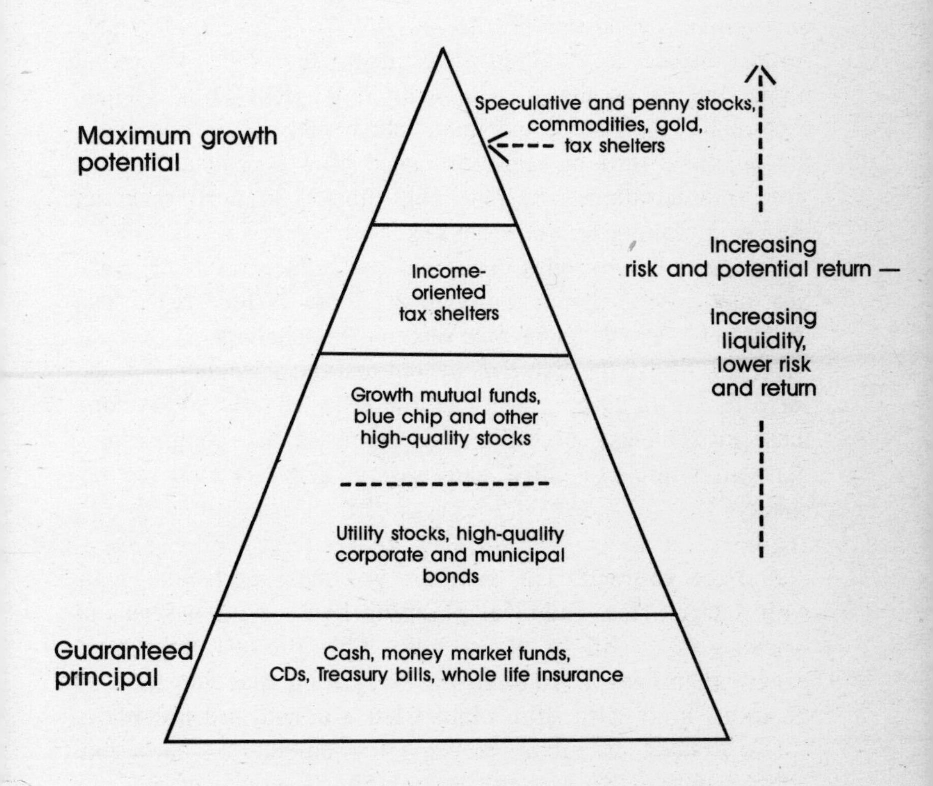

The most conservative investments anchor the pyramid's base. Money market funds, CDs, Treasury bills, and the like are geared to preserve capital and pay out income. Whole life insurance commonly is listed here as well. Bear in mind that only part of your premium represents an investment, and not necessarily a good one at that.

The middle layers hold investments that offer somewhat higher income at the price of a bit more risk. These include high-quality corporate and municipal bonds and utility stocks that fluctuate little in value. So-called growth vehicles such as stock mutual funds and blue chip stocks, in turn, seek out growth by taking on yet more risk.

The next tier bunches deals that can reduce taxable income but may pose a threat to principal. These include real estate investments and other income-oriented tax shelters.

At the tip of the pyramid lie out-and-out speculative deals. Here the rewards are great but the risks equally so. Among these instruments: speculative and penny stocks, commodities, gold and other so-called hard assets, and a variety of tax shelters.

3. Pace yourself. This is where you must mesh your goals with reality. **Most financial planning books have a series of worksheets to fill in about now. This doesn't. For most practical purposes, you can do everything that you have to do in an hour with little more than a pencil and notepad.**

You'll need to put a precise dollar amount on each goal you've set, whether a week's vacation in Bermuda next summer or college tuition for your five-year-old. The chart on page 224 can help you.

Then tote up all your assets (cash, investments, and the like) and subtract your debts (student loans, outstanding credit card charges, a mortgage, and so on). The difference between them is **net worth**—what you can show for all your hard work until now. That in turn tells you how much you have to work with to achieve your goals and how close—or far—you are from achieving them.

The first question to ask yourself as you look at a goal is how much time you have to reach it. Refer back to the targets you set in Chapter 1 and see which fall as short-, mid-, or long-range needs. A young woman planning to quit work at 65 has more time to build a nest egg than a 55-year-old eyeing early retirement. But she may also be concerned about a 14-year-old daughter who will need college tuition soon.

If a chief goal is to save for a short-term need, say a down payment on a house in two years, you'll want to keep that money safe and easy to tap. Funnelling the money into the stock market makes no sense here; chances are too great that you could lose some or hit a market lull just when you need the cash. By contrast, you have far more flexibility with your long-term needs. **When goals are down the road, you can adopt a more long-term horizon. That means you can take on more risk.** Over the years, speculative investments like stocks tend to even out—if not exceed—the performance of super-safe investments. If the worst happens and you lose a bundle, you still have the time to earn it back.

Then, reflect on how important the goal is to you. Regardless of how near at hand, the more significant it is, the less risk you can afford to take to reach it.

The key question to determine, however, is whether you are on line with your plans. Some goals simply cannot be met through your investing program. The sooner you need the money, the less time there is available for investments to grow. If you want cash for retirement in three years and have not saved enough, hold off on any thoughts of trying to double your stash in two years. That effort could leave you poorer, not richer. In such cases, you must either lower your expectations or increase the amount you have available to invest by saving more or finding another source of income.

4. Use your employer's plans fully. Take advantage of any company savings plan or other investment program that will bolster your own firepower. Some corporate plans, for instance, will match any contributions you make, giving you an immediate profit on your investment. Others hold out lucrative tax advantages. **Because any contribution you make to some plans is subtracted from your taxable income, you are investing with the full, not after-tax, power of your earnings. Only after tapping all such offerings to the fullest should you consider a personal investing program.**

5. Weigh tax consequences. No investment decision is complete until you've asked yourself two questions: what are the tax consequences of this move? could I accomplish the same goal with a more lightly taxed investment?

Though they may not be much of a consideration now, taxes should play an increasingly pivotal role in your investment decisions. As a rule, the higher your tax bracket, the more likely that tax-free or tax-advantaged investments will provide a greater return than holdings that throw off ordinary income. And as tax rates skid in future years, income-producing investments such as bonds and high-yielding stocks may prove more attractive than small-growth issues that pay no dividends. At a time when the tax laws are changing dramatically, the key to winning the greatest after-tax return is to know the ground rules.

6. View your assets as a whole. Here, too, the idea is to think big. **To properly diversify your assets, you must take all of them into account.** That includes corporate fringe benefit programs, IRAs, your home and other real estate, as well as your investment portfolio. A woman whose corporate pension plan is invested in low-yielding but secure fixed-rate instruments, for instance, might prefer to throw some or all of her IRA savings into a growth stock mutual fund.

Once you've determined the mix of income and growth-oriented investments that seems right for you, take the process one step further. **Be sure that you also diversify your holdings with various types of investments.**

To spread out your stock holdings among many companies, the best and easiest way is to buy shares in a mutual fund. If you do select individual stocks, buy shares of companies in a broad range of industries. Check that each responds in a different way to economic shifts. Different as they may seem, for instance, both banks and utilities tend to suffer when interest rates rise because the profits to each are tied to the cost of money.

This approach is equally important with fixed-income investments such as CDs, Treasury securities, and bonds. The way to diversify here, however, is not among different kinds of investments but rather by distributing your purchases among instruments with different maturities. Consider a Treasury bill. Aside from its slightly favored tax treatment (income earned is free from state and local, although not federal, taxes) and a slightly greater degree of safety (such funds are backed by the full authority of the U.S. Government), a six-month T-bill is very little different from a six-month CD.

The real differences among fixed-rate investments flow from how long they run. Six-month, one-year and five-year vehicles will pay sharply different rates. **No matter how alluring one might seem, resist the notion to channel too much of your money into a single maturity. A rate that seems lofty now may look puny in five years if inflation resurges.**

More important, you will *lose* money if you must sell the investment before it comes due. Instead, buy a series of issues in rolling maturities, that is, with securities coming due in sequence, starting in a few months and stretching over the next few years. If you were right, and rates drop, you still have most of your money at work even though the securities with the shortest terms will have matured. If you were wrong, and rates rise, you will get some of your cash back regularly to reinvest at new, higher levels.

INSURANCE

Insurance is a natural partner to your assets. The size of your nest egg influences how much protection you need against unexpected loss of income, whether through disability or death, or loss of the asset itself due to fire or other accident.

Women who have not yet built a solid cash reserve need insurance as a backstop. Those whose savings are fat enough, by contrast, have little need for hedging.

No matter how much or how little you have in the bank, to buy insurance wisely you must practice astute risk management. **The key word here is management. None of us can or should eliminate all risk from life. The potential reward is just not worth the stiff cost involved.** The trick is to protect yourself againt the big blows that could upend your planning. Count on your fallback fund to help you deal with smaller losses as they arise.

Do You Need Life Insurance?

The role of life insurance is to make up for lost time. It helps out those who need your support if you die before you have had the chance to provide it fully. It is not a replacement for you or a way around the grief death brings. It is merely a means of managing the loss of income that follows.

How much insurance you need depends on what your income would have provided and for how long. If you are working, you may be making a key—if not the sole—contribution to the family income. That contribution needs to be replaced. A single woman might not have anyone depending on her pay and so can skip buying life insurance entirely now. On the other hand, she may owe sizeable debts—student or car loans, for instance—and might want to hold insurance that would repay them if she died.

To determine your life insurance needs, you must figure out how much it would cost to provide income for those you have a responsibility to protect, for as long as you wish to protect them. Bear in mind that expenses might rise and fall over the years, as parents' health costs mount or children finish school. Then total up the resources available—Social Security benefits, IRAs, pension benefits, and other assets. In some cases, your dependents may be able to work and bring in income.

TABLE 2.5

How Much Insurance Do You Need?

A.	Final expenses	$ 10,000
B.	Debts (excluding mortgage)	
C.	Education fund ($25,000 per child)	
D.	Emergency fund (two months' gross income)	
E.	Total annual expenses	
F.	Surviving spouse income	
G.	Income needed to meet expenses (E − F = G)	
H.	Insurance to cover expenses (add a zero to G)*	
I.	TOTAL INSURANCE NEEDS (add A through D + H)	

*When invested at 10 percent, this sum will throw off the amount needed. Bear in mind that in a period of relatively high interest rates you may be able to earn more income on that sum, and in times of lower rates you likely will pocket less.

SOURCE: Financial Strategies Inc., Washington, D.C.

Compare what your dependents would need with what they would have. Table 2.5 can help you make a rough calculation.

The shortfall, if any, represents the gap you want life insurance to fill. If it is small, you may choose to fund it outright. More likely, you are seeking a sum that, invested wisely, will throw off the income you seek.

Once you determine that sum, you next must decide the role you want insurance to play in your financial plan. The simplest is strictly pragmatic: insurance as protection. That sort of coverage is known as term—that is, a policy that promises to pay a specific benefit over a specific length of time. **Term insurance is cheap while you're young. And that, fortunately, is precisely when you are most likely to face the biggest gap between what your heirs require and what you have saved so far.** When term insurance expires, so does the protection, unless it is renewed. To do so will cost steadily more as you grow older and more likely to die.

In comparing term policies, check prices first. Some carriers charge twice and more what a competitor asks for precisely the same coverage. Be sure to look beyond the first year's premiums. Rates on all policies will rise, but some will rise more steeply than others. Check the table for the cost of coverage five and ten years hence. And be sure to get renewable term, so you'll have the chance to pay that bill. By definition, term insurance is of limited duration. If you want to extend it, look for a clause allowing you to renew your policy to age 65 regardless of your health.

Insurance also can serve as an investment vehicle. It is this function that most insurance agents tout. What they are referring to is the traditional form of insurance known as ordinary or whole life insurance. **As their name suggests, whole life policies are designed to protect you until you die. They combine a fixed insurance benefit with a savings, or cash reserve, plan.** To build that kitty, the premiums kick in at a far higher rate than those for a comparable amount of term, but they remain level over the life of the policy. The main benefit of building assets within a life insurance policy rather than your personal portfolio is that the earnings on those assets are not taxed until you withdraw them. That helps your money grow faster.

You can get at the cash value of your policy before you die, either by borrowing against the amount that has accumulated or by surrendering the policy outright. But cash value generally does not start to build at all until about the third year after the policy has been in force, and it grows handsomely only after the 10th or 15th year. So the longer you keep a whole life policy, the more attractive an investment it becomes.

As investments go, however, conventional whole life policies have tended to pay below-market rates. **If you are thinking about buying a whole life policy, be sure to look at how the return on the investment portion of your policy compares with other investment options, and at the conditions under which the investment return might change.**

Many savvy shoppers began deserting such policies in droves. As a result, insurers are trotting out a draft of new policies to lure yield-conscious buyers. These are designed to offer either a heftier return or the ability to fine-tune coverage.

Universal life is one example. It combines a simple term insurance program with an accumulation fund on the side. Your annual premium funds both the cost of your insurance and a savings account that is sheltered from taxes until withdrawn. Once you have paid the initial premium, you often can change both the amount you pay and the coverage you buy. Funds in the savings portion, invested by the insurer, pay interest that is closely tied to rates for shorter-term bonds. But the guaranteed minimum rate of return can be as low as 3 to 4 percent after the insurer takes its cut.

Variable life, as the name suggests, is more akin to a roller coaster than a standard insurance policy. Both its cash value and death benefits vary. The fluctuations come because, as with universal life policies, some of the premium you invested is in a side fund. Unlike universal life, however, you determine how those funds will be put to work. Some of the investments you can make, like stocks, do carry risk. If you have chosen that option, and the market value of your shares drops, your cash value sinks along with it. That also could mean that you would receive a smaller death benefit, though never less than the minimum specified when you signed on. If you do well, both the death benefit and the cash value will spurt ahead faster than traditional policies. The premiums cannot be changed.

Insuring Your Greatest Asset: Your Ability to Work

So long as you *have* to work, you need disability insurance. If you need a salary to survive, your ability to earn it is your most precious asset.

It is in far more jeopardy than you might think. Until you reach age 65, the odds that you will suffer disability that prevents you from working for at least three months are far greater than that you will die. In fact, while you are in your thirties and forties, you are more than three times as likely to be disabled as to die.

If you are a working woman, your employer may have already provided a measure of disability coverage that will pay off if you're out of action. But that level often is minimal and may not be enough to maintain your standard of living for more than a few months. Social Security might chip in, but only if you are severely disabled.

Look to see how much protection you hold now. Then consider taking out a policy on your own to boost your coverage to between 50 percent and 60 percent of your gross earnings. The money you pocket from a plan you pay for is tax-free.

The most important item to check is whether you will collect at all for most injuries. What is the policy's definition of disability? The "loss of hand or eye" means just that, not the loss of the *use* of one. Look for a policy where you can set your own job description and determine your own definition of disabled. Check to see that the policy can be renewed—at the same rate—through age 65. You can keep down the cost of such protection by agreeing to a longer waiting period between the onset of disability and the time the first check would appear. But be sure that you can afford to wait that long.

Most women are well served by the health policies that come with their paychecks. As you grow older, your needs may change. Issues to weigh then are discussed in Chapter 7.

How Much Do Your Possessions Mean to You?

Once you own a home, you must carry insurance to cover loss. The best policy is dubbed HO-5, which covers the broadest range of damage. For any policy to pay off, however, you must insure your home for at least 80 percent of its value (that is because the insurer assumes the land itself will not be destroyed).

That does not mean that your insurance will pay out enough to replace your home and its contents. Normally, homeowner's insurance only covers the present value, or actual cash value, of damaged goods—the cost to replace minus an allowance for depreciation and use. That could mean you'd collect as little as a few dollars for old but still useful items.

If your furnishings would be far more costly to buy new than they are now worth, and you could not easily cover the difference on your own, **consider taking out a so-called replacement cost policy,** available at a higher fee, that will fix whatever you have or pay the cost of brand-new goods. Failing that, be sure to line up sufficient coverage for big-ticket items. Many policies set limits on the amount they will pay for loss of jewelry, silver, and the like, unless the policy includes an additional clause to cover them.

Most homeowner's policies also provide protection against claims by those injured on or off your property—again, up to a limit. But recent trends in court awards have far exceeded the funds most such plans offer. **Wise women should consider buying a so-called umbrella or excess liability policy.** Such policies commonly provide one million dollars or more in coverage for as little as $100.

Even if you do not own your home, track down a renter's policy that covers its contents.

RETIREMENT AND ESTATE PLANNING

The reason underlying all financial planning is not so much what happens now as what happens then. For most of us, the most costly and long-lasting "then" is our own retirement—the rainbow's end of a nine-to-five—or nine-to-nine—career.

To enjoy a comfortable old age, however, your efforts must take into account the twin realities of women's lives today: women live longer (78 years to a man's 71, by the most recent tally), and inflation is ever poised to nip away at your steps.

All too often, working women continue to work because they cannot afford to retire, or are forced to trade satisfying jobs for a sharply diminished life-style. Two out of three older Americans living in poverty are women. Fully 60 percent of unmarried or widowed women over age 65 have no income other than Social Security and nearly half the 5 million women who live alone have yearly incomes of $3,000 or less.

Whether your retirement is decades away or very close, when your paychecks stop you will rely on one of three kinds of income. As a working woman, you are likely entitled to Social Security benefits based on your years on the job. In addition, those who have worked steadily at one job may collect a pension. Every woman should be familiar with the terms and features of her plan and should know *exactly* when she will be guaranteed a check.

What she may not have any idea of is how large it will be. The most common type of plan, known as a **defined benefit plan,** promises an employee a specific amount at retirement. The amount is generally a certain percentage of your last several years' salary, depending on how long you have been with the company. A growing number of companies, however, are adopting an alternative scheme known as a **defined contribution plan.** In these instances, the company agrees to put in a fixed amount each year, based on a percentage of your salary. They do not guarantee a specific payout when you retire. The size of your check will depend on how well those assets are invested over the years, the number of years you worked, and your salary. In many cases you can add your own contributions to the plan.

For many of us, however, the bulk of our income may have to

come from our own personal savings. Fortunately, there is a wealth of vehicles to help build that cache. Every working woman should consider an IRA, discussed in more detail later, as a must reward for all her hard work.

An increasingly popular program known as a 401(k) should also be explored. In order for you to join one, your employer must offer such a plan. A 401(k) allows an investor to shelter far more than an IRA under similar terms: contributions are deducted from your income, so you pay no tax on the money you deposit and all earnings grow tax-free until you take out the cash. **If you cannot fund both, a 401(k) often has the edge over an IRA.** For one thing, your total contribution is deductible. In addition, there is no $2,000 limit. You can set aside as much as 25 percent of your salary, up to $7,000. And the most generous of employers usually match some or all of your ante.

What's more, you can get at your money far more easily than in an IRA. Pry open an IRA before age 59½, and you will owe a 10 percent tax penalty plus taxes at your current rates on some or all of those funds. With a 401(k), by contrast, you often can get back your funds at no penalty if you retire early or borrow against your account at attractive terms. And just as with IRAs, you generally can withdraw your own contributions to help pay a child's college bills, buy a home, or meet a financial emergency, but you will have to pay a 10 percent tax penalty on top of any income tax owed. Your employer sets the rules, so read the plan description carefully before you sign up.

To lay your retirement-planning strategy, you will need a specific idea of how much income you want when you step down and how much capital you'll need to produce it. A more thorough discussion of how to plan appears in Chapter 7.

Just as every woman needs to plan for retirement security, every woman should have her own will. **Whether her income is large or small, her holdings substantial or modest, whether she is single, married, divorced or widowed, a mother, a daughter, or a friend, she needs a will to make her wishes clear.**

Writing a will is a compliment to yourself and to those you love. It is the summing up of a lifetime of responsible financial planning. Properly crafted, it will see that those you care for are taken care of when you die.

Failing to write one, however, could lead to just the opposite course. If you do not prepare a will, the state will do it for you. While each state's laws are different, the results may be far from what you had in mind. If you are single, your parents may collect assets better directed to your brothers and sisters. If you are married, but have no children, your parents may pocket funds you would prefer to see passed on to your spouse. **Only through a will can you say precisely who gets how much and when, provide for a lover, see that someone you trust will care for your children, leave your favorite ring to a close friend or your stock portfolio to your alma mater.**

What's more, only a will can see to it that Uncle Sam collects the tiniest possible share of your holdings. Many women believe that their assets are so modest, no taxes would be owed. Up to a point, that is true. Wives can give their husbands an unlimited sum tax-free upon their deaths. In addition, under current law you can pass along up to $600,000 without incurring any federal estate taxes.

But many career women boast assets greater than that amount already. **Almost everything you own is subject to tax upon your death. Just the proceeds from your life insurance and home—assets you often don't touch in your lifetime—can easily push your estate into high-tax territory.** To reckon your worth, be sure to include your car, home, art, jewelry, silver, savings, investments, life insurance holdings (taxed in your estate even though paid out to the beneficiary you named), pension and profit sharing plans, and half of any assets you own jointly with your spouse. If toting up these items places you near or above the tax-free limit, consult a lawyer to discuss tax strategies.

Other, more personal concerns also can present compelling reasons to write a will. If you wish to leave property to someone who won't—or can't—manage it herself, you can make special arrangement in your will.

Taken together, these elements form the base for every woman's financial plan. To see how the specific steps you might choose can best reflect your money personality, read on.

THREE

BUILDING YOUR OWN MONEY S-T-A-I-R

Matching your money personality to your financial plan is a bit like playing rummy. You can pick up a card now or let it go, perhaps with the hope that you can get it back later. Whether you choose to draw or pass depends on how you perceive your needs.

If your idea of a hot investment is a biotech firm poised to announce a cure for cancer, you are not likely to pay much attention to a portfolio stuffed with bank CDs. You might not even have one to your name. But some kind of safety-first security could be precisely the investment needed to lend valuable balance to your daredevil holdings.

Nester, Reacher, or Driver, with a little soul-searching you can determine how you are likely to behave in certain circumstances. The real choice you face is to decide whether to let yourself respond in character—and pass the card—or take other steps, and pick it up.

The best financial plans address this quandary with a two-pronged approach. They shore up weak spots you might have been inclined to overlook. And they build on the strong points in your money style to help ensure success of those moves. In reviewing the steps in the last chapter, you may well have identified areas where your present practices fall short. This chapter can help you recognize why you find some steps difficult and see how to act instead to achieve financial success.

That may involve rethinking your money style. Many of us are like the girl with the curl of Mother Goose fame. When we are good we are very, very good. At times, in fact, too good. Some financial snags are the result of practicing an admirable, even laudable trait to a fault. One of your biggest stumbling blocks may not, technically speaking, be a weakness at all. Yet taken to excess, even positive qualities can hold you back.

SAVING

Few women will prove such intrepid investors that they can quit their jobs to bask on the beach. But each of us has the chance to be comfortably rich one day because we managed our spending wisely.

Many women find it next to impossible to save. For them, the challenge is to restyle their spending patterns to have some money left at the end of the month. But even women who find saving easy must examine their outlays closely, lest their coffers end up full but not quite full enough.

Nesters, for one, have a lot at stake. They want nothing more than to build their wealth. But because their stress on security tends to make them conservative investors as well, they probably reap the most modest of returns on their assets. **As a result, Nesters need to set far more money to work to produce the same results enjoyed on average by their more speculative sisters.**

Both Heather and Jill got $10,000 bonuses last January. Heather salted away her stash in a money market fund paying 8 percent. That means her savings pumped out $800 last year before taxes. By contrast, Jill poured her funds into an aggressive stock mutual fund that boasted a 15 percent rise. Her before-tax take came to $1,500, nearly double what Heather pocketed. To do as well as Jill, Heather would have had to invest nearly $20,000.

Jill has a challenge, too. She and other women like her must plump their savings cushions, too. **Drivers need a fat cash backstop. At any minute, one of the speculative deals they thrive on can become unglued, dragging their savings down with it.** In short, no matter what kinds of investments she seeks, every woman would do well to save more than she already does.

No woman can help herself pack away more unless she knows where her money goes now. A few know instinctively. These are the shoppers who can peg a box of detergent or pair of pantyhose to the penny—as well as how many of each they use a month. But most of us are far less precise. We know our food bills are high, for instance, but would be hard-pressed to put numbers on the grocery store bills, the deli, the dinners out. **By and large, most women can account for only three-quarters of their spending.**

The best way to see what is going on is to put it on paper. Draw up a chart that shows how much you spend on what. Most of the numbers already lie in your checkbook and credit card statements. A scan of those records will reveal your basic spending patterns in a few hours. To be sure to capture one-shot tabs like Christmas gifts and auto insurance premiums, go back at least a year.

If you are like most women, this exercise will leave you with a fat category called "cash." Behind its anonymous facade lurk such elusive items as paperback bestsellers and a bunch of spring tulips. If you are truly to master your spending, that is the next area to tackle.

Your aim: to record every cash purchase for a month or two. Carry a small notebook and jot down purchases and prices as you make them. Or get receipts for every penny you spend and pop them into an envelope to deal with later. Either way will work as long as you follow through. Tote up your records at the end of your trial period, and feed that data into your spending outline.

The totals you see play a searchlight on your money behavior and values. Are the checks you write to boutiques bigger than those you write to your bank? How much do you save, anyway? Is the total a five-digit number? four? three? What percentage is it of your total pretax income? Your minimum goal should be at *least* 10 percent.

The chart you have created is, of course, the budget that flows from your money style. And **just like any other aspect of your financial plan, your spending patterns can be changed. If you do not like what you see, try out another style on paper.** You may find the new pattern more appealing than your current one. Move the numbers around until you can find a configuration you like and can live with.

The words ''live with'' are important. **Budgets are documents, not straightjackets.** The best reflect an understanding of where you are most likely to spend and why.

No one needs to tell a Nester how to save. She knows. The way you save money is by not spending it. For Reachers and Drivers, however, the situation is more complex.

At first glance, Reachers seem to spend, period. Examined more closely, however, they tend to display one of two distinct styles. The escaper is careless, the enjoyer carefree.

A woman who spends to escape is negative, and often self-destructive. She spends out of low self-esteem or to boost a flagging self-image. Marilyn thinks of herself as the kind of woman who buys only the best. The $75 or so she spends each month on fresh flowers makes her feel strictly first class. Susceptible to pressure, she finds herself wearing the latest fads in clothes and never questions friends who want to go to a more costly restaurant than she might prefer. But the lift she feels with a new dress in the closet can fade abruptly. In fact, anger at herself for buying something that has failed to give her joy can make her feel worse. She often goes out and spends yet more, piling up far more debt than she can comfortably repay.

Other Reachers operate on a more straightforward plane.

Paying for what they buy is no problem: these women pull down high salaries and keep their purchases within strict limits. Their careers have given them money to enjoy and they are bent on savoring the fruits of their success. But while they can pay their bills, they are not getting ahead.

Both kinds of Reachers have a problem. **Unless they marry a man who will do their saving for them, inherit a bundle, or reform, they will never have any assets to speak of. They will have spent them all.**

To guard against this, Reachers must protect themselves from themselves. Aching after a disappointing day, they need to plan to walk to the park, not the shoe store. Or buy a new shade of lipstick instead of a dress.

Reachers have a second goal: to guard against pruning their spending so severely that they end up feeling sorry for themselves. Self-pity is the very emotion that got them into so much trouble in the first place. They must strike a delicate balance. Unless they are so deeply in debt that any outlays are foolish, too strict a budget will do them in.

To lay their plans, Reachers might use the chart on the opposite page. List all the things you buy that give you joy, a feeling of escape or simple self-indulgence. Star the ones with tiny price tags. They offer the greatest pleasure payoff for your cash.

Reachers can be highly motivated, but rarely by the process of saving itself. Though they get scant pleasure from watching their nest eggs grow week by week, many perform well when they set up goals for things to *have*: the down payment on a new house, for instance. The chart on page 70 can boost their resolve; it shows how fast diligent savings can grow.

When she strays beyond the bounds she sets, a Reacher must press to be kind to herself. Blowing her budget represents a blow to her self-esteem as well. Instead of lambasting herself, she must praise her efforts to date and encourage herself to try again.

If despite her best efforts she cannot discipline herself, a Reacher's only way out is to get someone else to do it for her.

TABLE 3.1

Finding What's Fun in Your Budget

List the items you spend money on, then rate them according to the pleasure they give you. Things that mean a lot to you should be squeezed in—and those offering less satisfaction should be dropped.

Expense	Very High	High	Fair	Low
Dinner out	_______	_______	_______	_______
A massage	_______	_______	_______	_______
New hardback book	_______	_______	_______	_______
New running shoes	_______	_______	_______	_______
Fresh flowers	_______	_______	_______	_______
A makeover	_______	_______	_______	_______
_______________	_______	_______	_______	_______
_______________	_______	_______	_______	_______
_______________	_______	_______	_______	_______
_______________	_______	_______	_______	_______
_______________	_______	_______	_______	_______

Every woman who has trouble saving should take advantage of the devices that whisk funds out of her paycheck before she even pockets it. Many employers offer savings plans or 401(k)

TABLE 3.2

Steady Savings Pay Off

(Compounded growth of $1 invested annually)

Year	5%	6%	7%	8%	10%	12%
1	1.00	1.00	1.00	1.00	1.00	1.00
2	2.05	2.06	2.07	2.08	2.10	2.12
3	3.15	3.18	3.21	3.25	3.31	3.37
4	4.31	4.37	4.44	4.51	4.64	4.78
5	5.53	5.64	5.75	5.87	6.11	6.35
6	6.80	6.98	7.15	7.34	7.72	8.12
7	8.14	8.39	8.65	8.92	9.49	10.09
8	9.55	9.90	10.26	10.64	11.44	12.30
9	11.03	11.49	11.98	12.49	13.58	14.78
10	12.58	13.18	13.82	14.49	15.94	17.55
15	21.58	23.28	25.13	27.15	31.77	37.28
20	33.07	36.79	41.00	45.76	57.28	72.05
25	47.73	54.86	63.25	73.11	98.35	133.33
30	66.44	79.06	94.46	113.28	164.49	241.33
35	90.32	111.43	138.24	172.32	271.02	431.66
40	120.80	154.76	199.63	259.06	442.59	767.09

Even if you set aside just a small amount each year, your efforts will add up. This chart shows how much a $1 investment compounded yearly will grow to over time. Say you put aside $500 a year in an investment earning 7%. At the end of ten years, your nest egg would total $6,910 ($500 × 13.82).

programs that automatically deduct the amount you specify from your pay. Banks can be allies as well. Most are willing to transfer a fixed sum each month or pay period from your checking account into the plan you select. Some Reachers also find it effective to enlist a friend or money professional who can be counted on to applaud warmly each time she adds to her mutual fund. A good financial planner, for instance, will celebrate every step you take to build your reserve.

While Reachers see spending as a way to provide something they lack, Drivers often use money to celebrate what they have. Gail would never buy herself a new dress if she lost a valued client or gained ten pounds. She would feel she didn't deserve it. Instead, she buys when she feels wonderful, whether a hammered brass plate picked up on a trip to Mexico or a piece of good jewelry to commemorate her promotion to V.P.

The problem is that such rewards come dear. Once in a while, a pat on the back is fine, but too many can soak up vital cash for other needs. A good business outfit can easily top $400. A closetful can set her back thousands, all in the name of professionalism. Even on smaller purchases, perspective is easily skewed. Twenty-five dollars used to be a lot to spend on a wallet. Now $50 seems like a bargain.

Many Drivers save best when they harness their sense of anticipation. They can stash away huge chunks of their funds as long as they know they can treat themselves afterward. A regular reward can be pure bliss for some. One software designer buys a bouquet of pink flowers on her way home from work each Friday as nothing more than a celebration of surviving another week. For others, an unexpected splurge adds zing. That means deciding to buy three pints of raspberries, for breakfast, lunch, and dinner, when the first crop appears.

But little treats won't do the job when the reward you seek is big, and that is where Drivers can face their stiffest challenge. At a recent time management seminar, the leader asked a group of women executives what they would do with more time. "Read a book." "Take a walk." "Sleep in." From the back of the room a voice shouted, "Go shopping"—and the women broke into applause and laughter. That nearly everyone agreed says something about the life-style of the successful manager. Many see the chance to spend the day at Saks as the sweetest reward of all.

Women who recoil at the thought of setting spending limits should consider their budget as a means of authorizing spending—in fact, authorizing spending without guilt. If you have identified and earmarked $400 to spend this month on clothes, or $2,000 for next summer's vacation, you know the money is there for that as well as other needs. That allows you to go ahead and spend without repercussion, and enjoy it while you are doing it.

At times, enjoyment itself can be the problem. That often occurs when shopping takes the place of a hobby. Hard-driving women may not have taken time to develop other interests. Mastering the art of French cooking takes years and is not a pastime well suited to someone who eats half her meals out with clients. Learning how to drive a golf ball or smash a tennis serve also requires the kind of time often in scarce supply among successful career women.

If you find you cannot keep your spending in line with your goals, skip a season and take a class instead. Get a personal shopping service to line up choices of any outfits you must add, and steer clear of the stores until you've learned all there is to know about Bordeaux.

TAXES

Busy working women tend to overpay their taxes because they underplan. Some tactics come harder to some money styles than others, but all women harbor qualities that they can use to help cut their bills.

A Nester has the potential to be an excellent tax planner. Acutely aware that every dollar paid to Uncle Sam leaves one fewer for herself, she accepts the need for the kind of record-keeping that nails down write-offs. She will faithfully tally spending on business periodicals, client dinners, and other deductions, down to the cost of the stamps used to mail in her return.

But many Nesters are uncomfortable using the ammunition their records provide. A successful public relations manager of a Fortune 500 firm, Susan opened her own consulting firm on the side. She ran the business from a spare room off the kitchen and kept a meticulous log of phone calls, car mileage, and other deductible business expenses. When she filed her first year's 1040, however, she only reported half of those costs in order to make sure she showed a profit. Reporting a loss, she feared, might trigger an IRS audit.

Like Susan, many Nesters find just the thought of an audit profoundly disturbing. For the IRS to question their tax return is akin to doubting their integrity.

At the same time, such women would rather undress in public than turn over their books to a stranger. The loss of privacy would be too much. Then there's the matter of the deductions themselves. No matter how detailed their records or solid their advice, Nesters often question whether they are entitled to those deductions. They fret that they've overlooked a vital receipt or an obscure condition that excludes their case.

This reluctance to assert their rights costs Nesters money they can ill afford to lose. Any woman who finds it hard to prune her tax bill should recall the counsel of Learned Hand, the respected Appeals Court judge. Said he: "There is nothing sinister in so arranging one's affairs as to keep taxes as low as possible. Nobody owes any public duty to pay more than the law demands."

Nesters can be far too generous with Uncle Sam in other areas. Their employers often withhold a sizeable chunk of their pay for the IRS. Nesters don't mind the skimpy cash flow because they like what it buys: a fat income tax refund. But it makes far more sense to close the year entitled to just $100 or so. Any more than that amounts to an interest-free loan that robs you of the chance to earn income on those funds yourself.

This problem, at least, is easy to fix. Change the number of allowances you claim by filing a new W-4 form with your employers. So long as you pay at least 90 percent of your tax bill or the amount you owed last year, you will owe no penalties on your scheme.

Like Nesters, Reachers often pay too much in taxes. But the

reason for their folly is far different. **While Nesters are afraid to plan too well lest they provoke an audit, Reachers tend to stumble out of neglect.** Many take a measure of pride in complaining about the fact that they pay so much. Five-figure tax bills are a perverse affirmation of their financial clout.

Workhorse tactics to whittle down those bills, such as investing in municipal bonds and IRAs, strike many Reachers as boring. Not surprisingly, they have little patience for the kind of careful record-keeping that can yield noticeable tax savings. Lynn bought her first home three years ago—an aging Victorian townhouse. She poured thousands into renovations—roof repairs, rewiring, a new bathroom—and threw every receipt away. When she goes to sell the house, she plans to use her purchase price as the benchmark in figuring any taxable gain. If she had good records, however, she could add the cost of any home improvements to that sum, and be liable for far less tax.

A Reacher's real interest lies in a big killing and exotic moves. Tax shelters like those she hears about at cocktail parties hold an appeal she often finds irresistible. The larger the write-off and flashier the deal, the greater the lure.

This tendency works well for women whose holdings are suited to such moves. But many Reachers snatch up shelters far too early in their lifelines, before they've built a foundation of productive assets. At the same time, their penchant to trust all financial pros, even hard-charging salesmen, means they often are "sold" a deal of questionable value. In the worst case, a Reacher loses her investment, her deductions are disallowed, and she faces back taxes on the deductions she took.

Drivers too may need to temper their zeal for cutting taxes with a measure of reality. Many are just as aggressive at tax time as they are when the market is moving up. Barbara *knows* that she spent a lot entertaining clients last year for which she was not reimbursed. With or without the records to back her, she'll take the sum she feels entitled to write off. Her feeling is that she will reconstruct the evidence somehow if her return is ever questioned.

Drivers and all women who are active investors should be sure to pick up on all deductions that flow from their investment programs. The more you make, the harder that is to do in the wake of tax reform. Starting in 1987, you can deduct only those investment, business-related, and miscellaneous expenses that exceed 2 percent of your so-called adjusted gross income (which essentially is the same as your total income, less any deductible contributions you make to an IRA or Keogh). But no one should rule out the possibility. Expenses that fall into this category include the cost of phone calls to her broker, subscriptions to newspapers and magazines offering investment advice, rental of safe deposit box used to store securities, fees paid in connection with her IRA or to a financial planner. (A more complete rundown follows in Chapter 4.)

But she should be on guard lest, taken too seriously, tax strategy fouls up her investing goals. Some Drivers hold on to stock otherwise marked for selling just to get the benefit of long-term capital gains treatment. But in the interim the stock goes down so much they would have been better off selling it and paying the short-term capital gain.

No matter what their money styles, a great many women are so anxious to avoid paying taxes they will go to questionable lengths to avoid them. Such women seek out tax-free investments such as municipal bonds even if not in a high enough tax bracket to benefit. Before lining up any tax-free investment, every woman should consult the table on page 40 to see if tax-free income really puts her ahead.

Any woman who suspects she might be missing out on legitimate deductions should make a date to brainstorm with a good tax planner. Tips on how to locate one appear in Chapter 12. Bring your last three years' returns for clues to what you might have done better and could try to do now.

ASSETS

Matching your portfolio to your personality is a complex process. Economic circumstances—your age, income, family status, and other factors explored in Chapter 2—tell you how well you can withstand financial loss. Equally important, however, is to assess how much loss you can handle emotionally.

A woman who fears losing money worries no matter how much she has. But the greater her fear, the fewer her options. In the extreme case, Nesters close off whole categories of profitable investments. That forces their remaining choices to do yeoman's work against high odds. By their nature, income-producing vehicles are limited in the return they can offer.

To use her style well, a Nester must push herself to take on risks to boost her overall yield and protect her purchasing power. One way to do so is to put a number on how much she *needs* in the bank to feel safe. What would it cost her to live for a few months? $3,000? $6,000? $10,000?

Whatever the sum, Nesters should respect their feelings and set it aside. That done, they can deal with the balance of their holdings in a more aggressive fashion. The exercises in Table 3.3 can help.

Women who value security need look no further than bank CDs, Treasury securities, and bonds for income. So long as they are prepared to hold these investments to maturity, they will be rewarded with current market yields and peaceful dreams.

All operate on the same philosophy: the buyer lends the issuer a fixed sum of money, gets it back at a preset date and in the meantime pockets a steady stream of income. To reflect this condition, these instruments are referred to as **fixed-rate investments.** So long as at least part of her funds are in an easy-access spot such as a money fund, most women are wise to boost their income from idle funds by steering part into short-term CDs. Precisely because such investments cannot be tapped at a moment's notice, CDs tend to pay higher rates than money funds.

TABLE 3.3

Taking the Risk Out of Risk-Taking

If you would like to invest in stocks but shy from the risk, the following techniques can help. These tactics also are useful for women who are comfortable with risk but who recognize the need to plump their portfolios with income-producing investments.

- **Relax.** If you have gone to school, opened a bank account, or bought a home, investing is something you have done before. What you are considering now is nothing more than a new way to do so.
- **Ask "what if?"** Anticipate the worst and write it down. Sample: "I could invest $5,000 in shares of this company only to see it go belly-up tomorrow. I would lose the money." Then look at the consequences. You are not talking about losing all your money, just the funds in this particular deal. Viewed objectively, many risks do not seem so threatening.
- **Limit your anxiety.** If you're investing for the long-term, you can afford to sit out most of the market's daily shifts. Unless stock prices rise or fall sharply, plan to worry about your investments at a specific time each day or week. After work or Saturday morning are good slots. If you find worries creeping in at other moments, tell yourself you'll consider them at the appointed time.
- **Get smart.** While your anxious feelings are very real, they may stem more from ignorance than reality. Be sure you understand any investment thoroughly before you sign on.
- **Diversify.** No matter what your money style, diversifying your assets will help keep them safe. For Nesters and other gun-shy investors, this means buying more than one or two stocks that you reckon are good plays. An easy way to spread out your money fast is by buying shares in a mutual fund. Women who seek out more daredevil holdings should likewise put some of their money in safe positions as a backstop.
- **Invest regularly.** Plan to invest a fixed amount of new money at regular intervals—weekly, monthly, quarterly—regardless of the investment's price or general market conditions. Mutual funds are the ideal vehicle for this strategy; they will accept steady contributions of just about any amount you set. In this fashion, you will lower the average cost of the shares you buy since you will pick up more shares when

the market is down, and fewer as prices rise. This strategy is often called dollar-cost averaging.

• **Look for the familiar.** If you own your own home and are attuned to its changing value, you may feel more comfortable with other investments relating to real estate. Or using your work-related expertise, you might choose to buy shares in other companies in your field. If you opt for a mutual fund, scan the prospectus for the names of firms whose business you know professionally or that make products you like. Anything that helps you feel at ease about your investment will help you get the most out of it.

• **Hedge your bets.** If a stock you hold goes up, you can use options to protect your gain. Discussed in more detail in Chapter 10, a "put" that gives you the right to sell shares at a preset price can lock in your profit if your shares fall below that level. An easier technique is to set a limit, known as a stop-loss order, to how much you will let a stock's value fall before bailing out.

• **Prepare for setbacks.** Often, the initial consequence of your decision is disappointing, even painful. A stock may slither sideways or plunge in value. Decide in advance how you will react. Consider setting a floor below which you will sell out.

• **Stay loose.** Aside from tax shelters and other long-term deals, few decisions are irreversible. If you have made a mistake, you can always change your mind.

The drawback of all fixed-rate deals, whether CDs, Treasury securities or bonds, is precisely that: the income they pay is fixed and is not adjusted to reflect current market conditions. If interest rates spiral up, as they did in the early 1980s, owners are stuck with relatively meager returns.

More important, every time interest rates change, the resale value of all fixed-rate securities changes. If interest rates fall, the instrument immediately becomes more desirable; after all, it is paying more than the rate offered by new issues. Hence its price would rise. On the other hand, if rates shoot up, the market value of the security falls. While you are not likely to sell a CD before it matures, you could face a problem if you hold bonds. The reason is simple. No one is willing to pay $1,000 for bonds paying out 10 percent if the going rate on new issues is 13 percent. As a result, such investments will fetch less—perhaps far less—than the face amount if the holder decides to sell before it matures.

Even short-term CDs impose fees for cashing in early, the familiar penalty for premature withdrawal. But the risk is greatest in long-term investments. While prices don't change much on issues coming due in less than five years, the swings on long-term securities can be dramatic.

Bonds are structured like any other fixed-rate investment—a fixed rate of payment (usually twice a year) until maturity. But in addition to the interest rate or market risk, bonds pose another, that of security. Bonds are only as good as the seller's ability to repay. The longer until the bond matures, the more difficult the risk is to assess. The outlook for a company's health ten or twenty years down the road is hazy at best.

To supplement your assessment, check with rating agencies such as Standard & Poor's and Moody's. The highest grades they issue to bonds are AAA and AA or Aaa and Aa, respectively. Anything below BBB or Baa is not considered investment quality.

No matter how deep their need for security, however, Nesters should close out their passbook savings plans. The painfully low yields paid on such accounts make them suitable only for sums of $500 or less—and then only if holders already keep a fat balance in their checking accounts.

For many Nesters, breaking out of such holdings is tough. Megan wanted to try. She steeled herself, then called a broker who suggested several stocks she thought were takeover targets. Megan poured $5,000 into the two she thought most promising. But neither was bought up, and one stock's value plunged after the company reported poor third quarter earnings. A few weeks later, she sold out both positions.

Just as she feared she would, Megan lost money on her venture—$2,000, to be exact. And the sting of that loss makes it unlikely she will invest in stocks again for some time. But what her moves told Megan and the lessons that they offer to wiser women are two different things. Megan thought the problem was in buying risky stocks. But the real lesson concerned the way she went about it. She failed to follow **the prime tenets of investing: hedge your bets and edge into risk slowly.** The same goes for any security-conscious investor.

The easiest way to do both is to pick up shares in two or more **mutual funds.** With each purchase, owners receive a stake in dozens of issues. Middle-of-the-road choices include growth-and-income funds that aim for consistent returns in bull and bear markets and growth funds that emphasize long-term performance.

If individual shares hold more appeal, Nesters should hew to securities with a reputation for pumping out high, continuous dividends. Such issues limit risk in two ways: they tend to trade within a fairly narrow range, reducing the risk of loss of principal. And their steady payouts mean owners enjoy at least some return even if the share price tumbles. Investment services such as Standard & Poor's The Outlook run regular lists of stocks with unbroken records of dividend increases.

Some Nesters may find that so-called **convertible securities**—bonds or preferred stocks that are convertible into common shares—offer the best of both worlds. (Common stocks, of course, are the familiar securities that represent an ownership share in a company. Preferred stock also gives the holder an ownership stake. Its name is derived from the fact that it has a preference over common stock when the company issues dividends and if it falls into bankruptcy.) Convertible securities tend to pay higher income than the dividends offered by the company's common stocks and their prices swing less dramatically. Yet because owners are entitled to exchange, or "convert," their holdings for a set number of shares, they have the chance to cash in on the profits if the underlying stock climbs in value.

When it comes to risk-taking, a Nester's greatest strength is her ability to tackle long-term goals. The best way to

profit from any investment in equities is over the long haul, when market reversals can be more than offset by prosperous years. But a Nester must be sure not to confuse the long term with taking a long time. Her biggest risk is missing opportunities by dawdling over her choices. One technique to weigh: setting deadlines. If her broker calls with a suggestion, for instance, she might promise a decision by the end of a day or so. Or she can set her own target date for funding an IRA.

Once in the market, Nesters must keep their cool. Such women especially must remind themselves that all investments, however stellar, slide as well as soar. If need be, she should avoid looking at the stock pages daily. Irresponsible as that sounds, it is better than jumping in response to the market's every flutter. She can ask her broker to call if one of her holdings falls below an agreed-upon limit or she can plan to check the price of shares bought for long-term appreciation just once a week.

While Nesters must push themselves to take risks, aggressive moves are second nature to Drivers. **Drivers flourish when they are involved with their investments.** While building a financial cushion, they should take an active role in seeking out lofty yields. In the case of CDs, for instance, their quest might take them to **out-of-state banks** offering juicy returns to attract funds from a wider market. At the same time, Drivers can tuck a bare minimum of their cash reserve into such prosaic vehicles and steer the balance into relatively secure but more glamorous income-payers such as bond funds.

Investors willing to accept moderate fluctuation in the value of their holdings to pocket a higher yield than money market funds provide can consider **short-term-bond funds.** These funds buy fixed-income securities maturing in one to four years. Thus, they benefit from higher rates without running too great a risk of loss in underlying value.

Some corporate and municipal bond funds sport still higher yields by dealing largely in low-quality issues, coined **"junk" bonds.** These might include older bonds of companies whose credit ratings have slipped or newly issued securities offered by equally shaky companies that offer top rates to attract buyers. Again, high yields come with high risk. If the issuing company goes under, so will your investment.

Still another high-yielding investment is known as a **Ginnie Mae.** That's the nickname for certain fixed-income securities as well as the government agency that sells them, the Government National Mortgage Association. As a rule, these securities tend to pay a point or two more in interest than Treasury securities that run the same term. Ginnie Maes consist of mortgages bought from banks and other lenders and repackaged for sale to individual investors. As mortgage holders pay back their debt, Ginnie Mae holders receive regular checks that return part of the principal along with interest. Like bonds, their market value can drop if interest rates rise.

Once they have parked a suitable slice of their funds in income-producing investments, Drivers can and should seek other deals that fill their need for more high-flying investments. Instead of the growth or growth-and-income funds that play to a Nester's preference, Drivers can snap up **aggressive stock funds** when the markets are strong. Such funds stretch for maximum capital gains by pumping money into speculative stocks. So-called sector funds also heighten an investor's risk by limiting investments to companies in a single sector of the economy, such as energy or defense. Because their focus is more narrow, they will falter or fly far more than the market as a whole. In the same vein, international stock funds offer the spice of foreign intrigue.

Investors who are willing to shrug off the safety of numbers held out by mutual funds can tailor portfolios of their own. So long as they ante up the $20,000 or so needed to spread their bets wisely, Drivers can seize control of their own investment courses. The most daring can borrow money on margin, trade in options, or use other techniques discussed in Chapter 11 to leverage their funds and boost the potential for profit and loss.

The skills that help a Driver succeed at investing can also

hold her back. Many a Driver thinks she is infallible. That means she can unwittingly ride a falling stock down to the bottom, convinced that its value will one day recover. While Nesters tend to sell off too soon, Drivers need the courage to bail out if their choices turn out to have been flawed.

And even if she sits tight while a favored stock is falling, a Driver still can err if she comes to feel like a woman spurned. Once a laggard stock clambers back to the price at which she bought it, many a Driver takes revenge—and dumps the stock—without considering if it will go yet higher.

Every serious investor should ask herself how much time she is willing to devote to her holdings. By definition, aggressive ventures demand closer surveillance than cautious ones because of the greater risk of loss. Many also demand near-precision timing of buying and selling as well.

Women for whom involvement is not a bother but rather the point often are traders. They are mesmerized by the excitement of buying and selling. Sharon works with two brokers and compares the suggestions of each before she acts. She often makes five or six calls a day to her pros. When her stock picks soar, she feels a rush of accomplishment; but even a good day at the office can be tainted if her holdings tumble.

Another breed of Driver is a holder. Such a woman buys and holds for the long haul. Her success or failure means little to her demeanor and even less to her life-style; she would not dream of spending any of her capital and even windfall profits would not prompt the urge to splurge.

This woman's laid-back posture will help her make the most of the long term. Yet to use her style well, she must realize that no investment flares forever. When markets change, she should consider reshuffling part of her assets along the lines discussed in Chapter 10.

Although their money styles are vastly different in many ways, Reachers share with Drivers a love of flashy money moves. They hold the seeds of the pure risk-taker who will make and lose a great deal of money over her lifetime.

But **unlike Drivers, who are bent on building wealth, Reachers at times must trick themselves into investing.** Sensible arguments about the merits of emergency funds and IRAs may sway them for a moment, but their resolve to take hold of their money affairs tends to melt away in a few days. To capture her attention, a Reacher requires an emotional hook.

One of the most powerful is an appeal to her pleasure in rewards. **A Reacher's interest in investing quickens when she sees it as a way of being good to herself. A Reacher's biggest problem is that she often has nothing in the bank when she comes to this conclusion.** Many of the investments she finds most appealing—tax shelters, individual stocks, and the like—command higher initial payouts than she can afford or are best suited to taxpayers who already boast hefty income from investments. What's more, such options would heighten her risk of loss by failing to spread her bets. Her wisest course is to buy into mutual funds that accept regular deposits. That way she can build her assets steadily. Depending on market conditions, growth or aggressive growth stock funds, international issues, or high-yielding bond funds will satisfy her need for distinctive holdings.

Once she has saved more capital, a Reacher often enjoys owning investments whose status enhances her self-image. Among them are the classic **blue-chip stocks,** well-known companies with a record of steady growth such as General Motors.

By the same token, many Reachers are attracted to **gold**'s glitter for their portfolios as well as their wrists. This tendency, however, should be tempered. Long considered an enduring source of wealth, gold of late has been hostage to world psychology: when international tensions rise, it tends to shoot up, then sink back when tensions ease. Thus, its investment value is hard to predict. Gold can provide a last-ditch hedge against a roaring spate of inflation. But in the interim, most gold investments offer no return on their holdings. If the allure is irresistible, consider buying shares in a mutual fund that specializes in gold.

INSURANCE

Of all financial decisions, insurance is the most businesslike. Buyers pay a fixed fee, or premium, for a guaranteed payoff upon a guaranteed event. But few aspects of financial planning stir more emotion.

Insurance agents know this well. For years, they have tailored their sales pitch to buyers' psychological needs. If you love your spouse, your child, your sister, they argue, you will want insurance to protect them. If you truly have their welfare at heart, you will buy enough so they need never work again. And the more you care, the sooner you'll buy it, lest later on you find you can't.

As these arguments show, many of the factors that guided your investing moves lurk behind your insurance plans. The most important of these is your feeling about risk. **Consciously or unconsciously, many a woman's insurance decisions reflect nothing more than the extent to which she is a gambler. As a result, the danger most women face is twofold: buying too much or not buying at all.**

Nesters tend to be well aware of their feelings on the subject. Afraid of risk and loss, they latch onto insurance as a way to keep safe. No matter what demands come up, a Nester will rarely let her coverage lapse; she'll borrow, if need be, to pay the premium. If anything, Nesters are likely to carry too much insurance, even as they wonder if they hold enough.

Not surprisingly, a few Reachers use insurance as a tool to boost self-esteem. When she was named executive vice president of her firm, Kim promptly signed up for a term life policy of half a million dollars. She smiles secretly to herself every time she thinks of the fact that she's "worth" that much.

More often, however, Reachers avoid insurance. For one thing, they find it boring. Real estate, or stocks, or options offer far more excitement. And many find their "me-first" strain tends to discourage spending on anything from which they themselves will not benefit.

Many Drivers likewise make a deliberate decision to forgo insurance. They have always expected to work hard themselves, and see no reason why others should not have to do the same—with or without them. Buying insurance strikes them as a passive, defensive act that is inconsistent with their decidedly offensive game plan. Such women carry little if any coverage unless a child is involved. Even then they are likely to name a small amount and expect their offspring to work or skimp if they outlive her. This, of course, is a questionable approach. After all, they can bet wrong: Nesters are not the only ones who die. But it at least has the benefit of being consciously decided.

Drivers must be careful not to let themselves be ruled by unexamined instincts. Risk-takers in the investment world, they carry those instincts to their insurance dealings. While young, they don't see insurance as a good bet so they skip it. They don't for a minute think they are going to die. But, taking big risks only works when you know what you are doing and can withstand the loss.

Sizing up your money style can prove helpful when choosing not just how much insurance to buy but also which kind.

If, like many Reachers, a woman has trouble saving, she might consider buying a whole life policy. Although not the best financial value, it is a crutch, and a useful one at that, if she otherwise is simply not putting anything aside. Over the years, the policy will build cash value she can pocket or borrow against. Eventually the dividends it pays may be set to work to pay the premium itself, freeing that payment for other investments.

Drivers who prefer investments they can control might look into variable life policies. Such programs allow them to dictate how the savings portion of whole life is invested. At the same time, they often are best off buying term and pumping the money they save into their personal portfolios.

Nesters might opt for term as well. Such policies offer the greatest coverage for the least cost. This addresses both their need for security and their reluctance to spend money. The most cautious Nesters might feel good owning a small whole life policy to make certain they will enjoy a measure of lifetime protection.

RETIREMENT AND ESTATE PLANNING

When it comes to retirement planning, Reachers have the most to lose. Few feel any sense of urgency about preparing for their later years until those years loom close. Unless curbed, their natural tendency to count on someone or something to bail them out can leave them the most vulnerable women of all. This is one place where Reachers must reject their styles, and in essence, mastermind a 180 degree about-face. They must settle down and earn a pension or settle down and save—preferably both.

The same tactics that can inspire them to begin investing often can prove successful here. **Rather than view a retirement kitty as savings, Reachers should think of these funds as deferred spending.**

Few Nesters, by contrast, need a pep talk to take retirement seriously. Security in their old age is the issue underlying most of their money moves. But Reachers, Drivers, and Nesters alike can be reluctant to commit their funds to special retirement plans. Putting money in an IRA can seem tantamount to stashing funds in a vault and throwing away the key.

Such women need to reexamine the thinking behind their concerns. True enough, all women should aim to keep their IRAs intact until they retire or turn 59½. But, subject to taxes and a 10 percent penalty, you can withdraw all or part of your funds any time before that. And for many women earning in the highest brackets, the tax benefits of IRAs are so powerful that many people break even even if they are later forced to cash out early. Taken together, the benefits of tax deductions and tax-free compounding can outweigh the tax penalties after as little as ten or so years. The higher a woman's tax bracket, the earlier this takes place.

In investing their IRAs, Reachers must examine their first instincts carefully. Attracted as they may be to high-flying investments like computer stocks, they should adopt a conservative posture. Until they manage to accumulate a fat savings cushion, all Reachers should view IRAs as the closest thing they've got to a safety net and shield their contents from risk.

Nesters, too, may need to rethink their retirement investments. Stashing away money is only part of the task. To reap the most from their efforts, they need to press to earn the highest possible return.

Of all women, Nesters are most likely to start IRAs early and sign on for other retirement savings plans at work. This gives them a solid savings base. Their instinct, however, is to see *all* these funds as vital to their future. Ginny felt this way, and she kept her entire cache in the safest of deposits—money market funds, bank CDs, and the like. There, of course, is also where the bulk of her other assets lay.

There is nothing wrong with Ginny's portfolio per se. But her approach is limiting. Blessed with a growing cash cushion, wise Nesters can consider directing part of those funds into stocks that stand to grow in value over the long haul. At minimum, they should make sure their holdings reflect the fact that IRAs are a long-term proposition.

So long as interest rates are relatively stable or falling, Nesters must overcome their tendency to keep the bulk of their funds in easy-access investments. No matter how great an aversion they have to long-term investments, such investments make good sense for this task. By and large, long-term securities pay higher yields. Because taxes on income earned in IRAs are deferred until the funds are withdrawn, the greater the yield, the more the investor will benefit from the compounding of those yields.

Many Drivers find all of this talk about retirement somewhat alien. Committed to their work, they cannot imagine themselves ever stopping. For these women, the more appropriate question is not when they want to retire but when they want to achieve financial independence, and be able to quit even if they do not choose to do so.

This approach puts retirement into a framework Drivers find makes sense. In their own way, their push to build wealth is just another way of looking at the task of providing long-term financial security.

According to those terms, many are doing a fine job already. What is easy for them to overlook, however, are the many ways to advance this cause, and the power of multiple efforts. Many Drivers tend to shrug off the value of IRAs, for instance, dismissing the $2,000 contribution as meaningless. As the chart on page 90 shows, however, even seemingly small contributions can blossom over years. More important, piggy-backing IRAs, 401(k)s, and other tax-deferred plans can create a plump cushion to backstop any risky investments the Driver might eye down the road.

For all their differences, most women have one thing in common: regardless of what they read or have been told or even secretly believe, they don't like wills. No one wants to think about her eventual death. Planning an estate means dealing with the fact that we are not immortal and that something could happen to us well before we pass our prime.

A Nester finds it easiest to overcome her aversion and at least plan a will. She sees it as another way to care for those she loves. Just as she values her own security, she wants to give security to others.

Yet a great deal of time can pass before the job is actually done. She may spend a long while thinking about whether she should give her sister her pearls or bequeath them to her best friend. She might hesitate to go forward unless she feels that every detail is just as she would prefer and that the end result precisely reflects the way she wishes herself to be remembered. If she and her husband cannot agree on a guardian for their children, or if she feels lukewarm about the most obvious choice, she can let her need for perfection keep her from making any arrangements at all.

TABLE 3.4

How an Individual Retirement Account Blossoms

Current Age	Total Contribution	Annual Interest Rate 8%	10%	12%	14%
		Total Value at age 65			
25	$80,000	$559,562	$973,704	$1,718,285	$3,059,816
30	70,000	372,204	596,254	966,926	1,581,345
35	60,000	244,692	316,887	540,585	813.474
40	50,000	157,908	216,363	298,667	414,665
45	40,000	98,846	126,005	161,397	207,536
50	30,000	58,648	69,899	83,506	91,960
55	20,000	31,291	35,062	39,309	44,089
60	10,000	12,672	13,431	14,230	15,071

Reachers put off wills as well but usually for different reasons. Often they are afraid to let a lawyer see how little they have managed to save. Or they would rather not be bothered. Writing a will reminds them that their carefree days are numbered.

Macabre as it sounds, Reachers often can press themselves to act by reflecting for a moment on what others will think of them after they are gone. Pulling together a thoughtful will can go a long way toward seeing that they will be remembered fondly.

Drivers may not relish the prospect of drawing up a will, but they often take the step most readily. At bottom they see it as a way to retain control over their affairs even when they will obviously no longer be in charge. Allocating assets among relatives, channelling money into trusts, naming guardians and executors all appeal to the Driver's wish to exercise the greatest possible power over events. In some instances, Drivers opt for elaborate wills because they deem their heirs incapable of wisely handling the wealth they have built.

II

REAL MONEY STORIES OF THE '80s—

From First Job to Career Peak to Retirement Security

If financial advice is really to work, it must be custom-tuned. As you create your own financial plan, you are not just a particular money personality—a woman who is comfortable with risk, overly optimistic, or a cautious soul. You are a single woman making critical choices about her retirement assets, or a newlywed trying to mesh money goals with her spouse, or a mother struggling to set aside funds for a daughter's education.

To determine a plan that fits your needs, you must look closely at your situation. The precise steps you will take spring from your place in life.

The six chapters that follow form the core of this book. They take a woman through her money lifeline, starting with her first concerns as a fledgling investor through to the challenges of managing a retirement nest egg or deploying an inheritance.

FOUR

FROM COLLEGE TO CAREER

In many ways, our first job is what we have all been waiting for: the chance to show our stuff, to make a contribution, and at long last to earn a paycheck for our efforts.

Most women in the start-out stage in life don't have much money—and so they assume they have little to gain from financial planning. But nothing could be more wrong. **Some of the most important money decisions you will ever make are your first ones. No matter how little you have, the right financial moves can help you stay out of trouble and build a solid base that will serve you well over the coming years.** It is not a minute too soon to make a financial plan, following the Money S-T-A-I-R outlined in Part One. The pages that follow will show you the specific steps to take.

Setting up a solid savings program, planning spending wisely, laying the foundation for a gilt-edge credit record, making the first down payment on long-term retirement security, and putting in place the insurance programs that can protect you against financial disasters—all of these steps will pay off solidly now and even more handsomely later. Those who begin saving and investing methodically in their twenties, and persevere, can without a doubt achieve financial independence.

If the promise of future rewards is not enough to inspire your efforts, look at the flip side. **The *less* money you have, the more vital it is to plan—and the more you stand to lose if you don't.** Without a cash base, you court disaster if you do not have insurance to bail you out of a sudden loss of a job or other downspin. And only a well-honed strategy can make the most of every cent in your checking and savings accounts.

Your Most Precious Asset: Time

Make no mistake: whatever your salary and whatever your situation, you *do* have assets worthy of your very best attention. In addition to your power to earn a living and to learn how to make and implement wise investment decisions, you have the most precious power of all—time.

Time can multiply even the smallest of salaries. **Because money, like all green things, can grow over time, any woman who puts her money to work—now—stands to come out far ahead of those who only get to work later.** One of the most significant steps you can take is to put time to work for you right now. **You can always make up for money lost through financial mistakes. You can never, never regain the value of lost time.**

Let's put it yet more strongly: **act wisely now, and you can almost guarantee future financial security.**

When you first begin to work, your path in the years ahead is hazy at best. It's not yet clear where you will settle, if you will marry, what career you will follow, how successful you will be. Those uncertainties paralyze many otherwise forceful women. They delay starting life lest they interfere with something that is yet to be determined by what *might* happen. They put off furnishing an apartment because they fear their tastes might change. They put off buying a house in case they later decide to marry or move. They wait to buy stocks or bonds or real estate until they are older and somehow, magically, wiser.

Men don't wait. They assume the choices that they make now will fit with what they want later—or that they can change whatever they've decided now to mesh with their new plans. And so should you. Set your course as if life as you know it now will remain that way. If your path changes dramatically, you can always retool your plan.

Saving Is Your Most Important Target

For now, saving money takes precedence over any other money task. Unless you build a cash base, you cannot weather rough financial storms and will never have the money to put to work in investments.

Targets first. **No matter what your age or salary, aim to scrape together $1,000 just as soon as possible.** That is the bare minimum you'll need to field such unexpected expenses as an emergency trip home to tend an ailing parent. To get a grand, resolve to put a specific percentage of your pay away each month. **Shoot to save at least 10 percent of your gross.** That may seem steep, but it *is* doable. If you pay low rent or live at home, set your sights even higher—20 percent to 25 percent of your pretax pay is not too lofty an aim. Whatever sum you set, take it off the top—and salt it safely away before you pay any other bills.

Be sure, too, that you have a clear idea of what "savings" really are. **There is a big difference between accumulating money to spend on clothes and a trip to Bermuda and amassing capital for long-term goals.**

Natalie, a 22-year-old management trainee at a Chicago department store, was proud of her ability to put aside $300 each and every month, starting with her first paycheck. A half a year later, however, she realized that her bankbook was not nearly as fat as she expected. A closer look revealed that the money went out of her account almost as fast as it went in. In June, she laid out $500 on a share in a summer house. In September, she signed up for a wine-tasting course. The next month, she picked up a new winter coat on sale.

Reachers, of course, fall into such traps most readily. But every money personality must battle the budget gap now. **The years when you are young and free are the perfect time to save. But they are precisely the time when most of us also confront the greatest temptation to spend.**

Just the purchases needed to set up housekeeping are formidable. Recent graduates start housekeeping with little more than a beat-up chair and clock radio to their names. Even before they move into their first apartments, their landlords demand a month or more rent as a security deposit. Add to that the costs of a sofa to sit on and a bed to sleep in and you are quickly talking big bucks. And that doesn't even begin to cover the cost of sprucing up a classroom wardrobe for an office entrance.

The upshot is clear: to even begin to make a paycheck stretch to cover the multitude of demands, careful planning will be needed. No matter if you have been budgeting pennies for all the years you were in school and are sick of it now. **To meet your money goals, you will have to be every bit as careful of the money you now earn as you were with the smaller sums you managed as a student.**

Frustrated at her inability to build any savings, Natalie decided to see where her money *was* going. That's a good starting point for any budgeter-to-be.

As discussed in Chapter 3, Natalie began by keeping a written spending record. Her goal was to search for the soft underbelly of her spending—what she bought that she could do without. Natalie had put out $250 for the coat. But she wore it every day, and it made her feel like a million. Even if she had to do it over again, she decided, she would make the same decision.

That kind of thinking makes sense. Few of us regret money

that we have invested in basic purchases that we use often. Even an occasional luxury is not a bad idea.

But Natalie had second thoughts about some of her other spending decisions. The share in the summer home, she realized, had cost far more than she expected. She ended up spending more than $20 each weekend to travel back and forth, and while she was there she found herself spending astonishing sums of money to pick up meals on the run or keep up with her friends' free-spending ways.

In fact, Natalie spent a lot of money on food, period. Exhausted when she came home from work, she often picked up Chinese carry-out at $10 a dinner or reheated a frozen casserole. And when she was perfectly honest with herself, she couldn't even remember most of what she had eaten a month ago.

For Natalie, as for most young women, the best decision was to cut back on anything she could not see, taste, or hold after 24 hours. That meant taking buses or subways instead of cabs no matter how weary she felt, and spending part of every Sunday making roasts, casseroles, or spaghetti sauce that she could raid at home on tired evenings. Much as she enjoyed her gossipy lunches out with friends, she limited them to a few a week and brought a brown bag lunch from home. She also bought a hot pot she uses to boil water for midafternoon tea breaks.

If you take the time, as Natalie did, to look over your spending patterns, you will likely see similar areas where you can cut day-to-day operating expenses. Other women have managed to keep to a tight budget by walking instead of taking a train to work, cutting down on running shoes and other expensive exercise clothes, and cutting back on long-distance phone calls.

If a lot of your money goes into a few pricey purchases, don't stop them entirely. But consider saving them for a once-a-month treat or a reward for a particularly good job on a tough work assignment. If you cringe at the thought of never buying tulips in the spring, then plan to stop at the florist after you finish the report that's due the first of next month.

The next area to tackle is the furnishing agenda. Unless you keep a handle on such outlays, they can easily overwhelm any efforts you make to keep daily outlays in line.

Make the most of your budget by cutting corners where they don't count or won't show. Comb secondhand shops, flea markets, and garage sales for finds and patronize discount centers. Try to cadge furniture, kitchen gear, and the like off parents, older siblings, and other family members. And if you haven't given it a try, you may be surprised to find how satisfying it is to repaint an old table or wallpaper your own bathroom.

Comes now the question of your wardrobe. Flea market finds will only get you so far at the company's monthly sales meeting. Face it, in many fields you *are* what you wear and you need to dress the part.

Money spent to improve yourself or your image is the single exception to the overall rule of save, save, save. Although it does not appear on your net worth statement, your most valuable investment now is yourself. Invest in a good haircut and set of cosmetics. If needed in your field, buy a few good suits and a leather briefcase.

But don't buy them in Gucci's. You still can try to keep your expenses in line. Haunt discount clothing stores for good buys. Buy two or three pieces of good jewelry and wear them to death as a trademark.

The same is true for education and networking that will help you in your field. Join professional organizations, read publications in your field, attend seminars. If your career would benefit from your going back to school, take time now to think of when and how to return. Passing up the chance to boost your lifetime earning power for the sake of saving a few thousand dollars now is the wrong choice.

Where to Find Money

Some of the best cash-building opportunities come in disguise. You need to recognize and seize them when you get a chance.

• **Small change adds up.** Make a habit of emptying your wallet each night. Put all the nickels, dimes and quarters into a box or old-fashioned piggy bank. Having less around can help you avoid small-ticket items like candy bars. And over a few months, you can easily accumulate another $100.

• **Extra checks**—for birthday or an income tax refund—are prize opportunities for savings. Take a third and blow it if you must, but speed the bulk into savings.

• **Each and every raise** is a chance to boost your monthly savings target. After all, you've been living on less up until now. Try to keep on the same budget, and hustle your new income into savings.

No matter *what* you're earning, however, you're not earning enough. "I don't want to sound like I'm greedy for tons of money," says one recent graduate earning $12,500, "but it's very, very hard to make ends meet on what I am paid now."

No wonder. That is not much money for anyone to live on, let alone for a young woman in one of the country's big cities. And that underlines a basic point: greed is not the issue. The only way to be sure you will ever get the money you need is to focus now, early on, on your job outlook.

All too many women fail to consider their long-term financial needs soon enough in their careers. They choose fields they love without once looking to see if they can survive, let alone prosper, on the starting salaries offered. Then they stick out the lean years without making the tough decisions on how to escape the ties that hold them down.

If getting along seems next to impossible now, and making enough to flourish is a marginal prospect at best, start now to

TABLE 4.1

How to Get on Track and Stay There

- **Be sure your goals make you happy.** If the idea of saving $1,000 for its own sake is as appealing as going to the dentist, frame another target. Perhaps you want to take a trip to Europe in two years or buy a home of your own in four. Think of each savings installment as another step to that specific goal.
- **Save room for treats.** If you just adore chocolate truffles, and your waistline doesn't seem to mind, allow some room in your budget for out-and-out self-indulgence. You'll never stick to a regime that makes you feel sorry for yourself. And judicious rewards for meeting savings goals—even when the rewards themselves cost money—can boost your motivation for the long haul.
- **Look for free rewards.** All of us enjoy things that don't cost money. If you have a passion for books, begin to haunt the local library or start a book swap with friends or your colleagues at work. If movies are more your style, share cable with a friend or look for theaters that offer off-hours specials.
- **Be honest with yourself.** If you always weaken when you go by the local gourmet shop, drive or walk a different route and do your regular shopping someplace else.
- **Check your progress.** Every three months, take stock of your spending patterns again. Be sure you are keeping to the decisions that you've made. Then look at the balance in your bankbook. If the results are there, you'll *know* you're on track.

---

consider how you will ever get the money you need. Sweeping changes may be in order.

For starters, look at the long-term prospects for your line of work. If they are not bright, investigate whether a related area might be more promising. If you can arrange for a lateral move within your organization, consider that now. If you think you would need more schooling to switch, look into courses. You may be better off working for someone who would pay for part or all of any continuing education you seek.

Lining Up Credit

Whether to help finance schools or sofas, working women can and should tap another source of money: credit. A prime task of these early years is to create the ability to borrow big bucks one day, even if you do not need the money now. It won't come automatically. You must take steps to *prove* you are a good credit risk. When you need a loan to buy your first car, you should not need to confess you've never borrowed a cent in your life.

For better or worse, it's never been easier to get credit. And put any lurking doubts to rest at once: it's no liability to be a woman. In fact, some of the nation's most powerful credit card companies are actively courting the lucrative market that working women represent. And in some instances, it's not even a drawback to be a recent graduate. Some concerns offer to shortcut the credit application process for promising managers. The credit card company or your local bank can give you details.

Even without special programs, however, you can build your credit record on your own. **Lenders basically care about just one thing—themselves. They want to be sure you will give back whatever they give out.** To call that shot, they look at your income to see if it is enough to handle the bills they imagine. In addition to seeing *whether* you can repay your debts, they aim to find out how *likely* you are to do so. That means how likely you are to continue collecting your paycheck. A few years on the job will help to encourage that opinion. But so long as you stay in the same career field and advance steadily, even relatively frequent job changes will not be held against you.

To prove to a lender that you are a good prospect, you'll need to show that you can use credit wisely. **First off, ask your bank to extend so-called overdraft privileges on your checking account. That allows you to write out a check (or withdraw**

money from a cash machine) for more than the balance in your account, up to a preset amount. You won't get into any trouble. The bank will automatically extend a loan to cover the overdraft.

Then use that feature. If you have a $500 line of credit, put off depositing your paycheck for a few days and overdraw your account by $100 or so. Presto. You have just written yourself a loan. Deposit your paycheck a day or two later, pay back the loan and pat yourself on the back. You are on your way to showing a banker you can manage credit wisely. Do the same thing again in a few months. **Each time you take out a loan and repay it promptly, you are building a track record that says that you are a reliable credit risk.**

Be sure you move quickly to pay back the loan. Interest rates on these accounts are high, and banks start charging interest immediately. Remember that in most instances, just adding more money to your account does not wipe out the loan. Ask the bank how much you owe (if you wait, they will send you a bill automatically, much like a charge account bill). Then write out a check specifically to repay the amount you owe.

Your next credit-building step is to apply for a charge account at a local department store. **Because they have relatively few branches, department stores can cut off credit quickly if a customer overspends. As a result, they tend to use more lenient credit standards than national credit card companies whose cards are accepted by thousands of outlets.** At the same time, if you own a car, sign up for an oil company credit card. That tells a prospective lender you are well heeled enough to have a car of your own.

After a year or so, step up to a national card such as MasterCard, Visa, or American Express. **MasterCard and Visa offer revolving credit, which allows users to pay off their bills in installments if they like. American Express and other so-called T & E (travel and entertainment) cards, by contrast, do not extend credit as such for more than a few days.** By their rules, you must pay off your balance in full each month.

If you are refused a national credit card, however, don't fret. "No" is rarely the last word. Visa and MasterCard provide cards through banks, and different banks have different credit standards. While the bank closest to your office may have turned you down, the one around the corner might consider you a fine credit prospect.

If you simply don't have a good enough credit record to get a card, consider asking a parent or other relative to co-sign for you. That should assure most bankers that the bills *will* be paid. Your credit file will show that you got credit with a co-signer. After a year or so of steady payments, however, you can ask for a card issued on the strength of your own record.

Any time you have been turned down for a loan, you should check your credit record with the company that tracks such information in your area. These outfits, known as credit bureaus, are a powerful force in the lending industry. While they do not issue ratings as such, they collect and distribute the information banks and other lenders use in order to determine if you are a good credit risk.

As middlemen in the credit granting process, they compile millions of reports on who paid what bill when. In turn, they will send a copy of your file to a lender who is considering granting you credit. By law, you are entitled to see that file as well.

To find out which credit bureau does business in your area, ask a local bank or department store which bureau it uses. Check your local phone directory for a number and give them a call. Often you'll hear a recorded message explaining how to get a copy of your report. In the main, you'll need to send a letter stating the obvious—name, address, year of birth, Social Security number—along with your signature. If you have been turned down for credit within the past 30 days, there is no charge for a copy of the report. Otherwise, expect to pay $10 or so for a copy.

Read it over closely. **If you disagree with any information in the file, say so.** By law the bureau must then investigate your side of the story. If they find they have made a mistake, they will change the report. No matter what the outcome, however, you can add a statement of up to 100 words explaining any facts that do not reflect well on you. If you missed a few bills because you lost a job, for instance, note that information to your file. A lender is more likely to excuse such a lapse if it knows the reasons it happened.

Chances are you will find lenders more than willing to extend credit. Your real challenge as an up-and-coming professional is to know when to say no. **It's easy to think a wallet bulging with credit cards shows your money clout. But even if you do not use it, too much credit can backfire.**

Here's why. When lenders consider a request for credit, say for a car loan, they aim to determine whether you can carry the loan. To do so, they look at how well you could manage with the debt you carry now—*and* what you would owe if you charged to the limit on each card you now hold. While you may have no intention of running up such bills, the lender has no way of knowing that. **If the amount of credit you *could* tap is high enough, a lender may deny your request just to play safe.** Until you establish a rock-solid credit rating, the best way to avoid such problems is to limit your cards.

Whatever cards you have, use them regularly. To build a credit history, you must make and repay many purchases.

Within reason, of course. One college senior bought a $250 suit to wear to her job interviews and a second for her first day of work. After a week on the job, which pays $16,000, she decided nothing in her school wardrobe conveyed the right professional image and ran up another $1,800 in bills.

This woman needs to slow down. **Even when your closet and cupboards are bare, call a time-out when your charges top 15 percent of your take-home pay.** Much more than that, and you may start to have trouble repaying your bills. Not only do you want to avoid getting bogged down in debt, you want to clamp a lid on the cost of borrowing. Interest on charge accounts is among the most expensive forms of credit, often approaching 20 percent. What's more, money spent on repaying last year's binges saps your ability to build next year's nest egg.

TABLE 4.2

How to Choose the Best Credit Card for You

No consumer should be grateful just to get a credit card. At the same time a lender is looking you over, take time to scrutizine the lender's offerings. Bank cards differ in the terms and privileges they offer. Check them out thoroughly before you sign on. Here are key questions to ask about any card you consider:

Ask the lender:

• **What is the interest rate on unpaid balances?** Last year some banks charged more than 20 percent while others charged less than 13 percent.

• **How does it decide how much you owe in interest?** Again, procedures vary. Some lenders base your charges on the previous month's total balance. This is the most costly approach, since you do not get credit for payments made during the month. Others base their bills on what you really owe. Check, too, when your interest charges begin. Some lenders charge from the date you made the purchase, while others charge from the date they issued the bill.

• **What is the annual fee?** Fees for credit cards vary from nothing to $50 or more. Of course, you'll want to look for the card with the lowest fee. But remember: there's no free lunch. Often banks that lure consumers with bargain-basement fees sock it to them with high interest charges.

Ask yourself:

• **How often do you plan to use the card?** If you need a card you will use often, go with the national cards that are accepted widely.

• **Who are you trying to impress?** Credit card companies are pushing prestige plastic—gold and even platinum cards that tell the world their holder meets exacting credit standards. This form of cachet, however, does not come free. Expect to pay from $10 to $200 more for a gilt-edge product.

• **What extra services would you use?** In addition to the cachet they confer, such cards often come with a host of special services such as travel insurance, discount shopping services, even credit for every purchase you make. You may find deals like these useful, but be sure that the bank is not charging an extremely high fee to pay for them.

• **Do you need records of your purchases?** T & E cards return copies of your receipts with your monthly statements, which can prove useful if you have lost the originals and need backup for your expense account or personal records.

• **How many cards do you really need?** Increasingly, department stores and gas stations are accepting national cards. You will find your life simpler—and the consequences of a lost wallet less wrenching—if you limit your local cards to the two or three you use most often.

The same goes for national cards. For the most part, you will pay $15 to $25 for each card you hold. Consider limiting yourself to one—or two at the most—for now.

• **Do you need a card for convenience or for credit?** If you plan to buy items in installments, stick with conventional credit cards. But find out how much interest you are paying for this privilege. In many instances, the bank that issues you a credit card can also give you a personal loan for the same purchase at a lower rate.

Taking Stock of Taxes

No one likes to pay taxes, of course. But women just starting out need patience more than they need an accountant. The bottom line is, there is not all that much that first-time workers can do to save on taxes. Serious tax planning and tax sheltering pay off best when you are earning a bit more.

That does not mean you can write the IRS out of your life. Build a foundation now for tax cuts later.

Your first step is to learn as much as you can about the tax code. **Even if you end up using an accountant one day, your knowledge will prove useful. Unless your tax preparer is a mind reader in addition to her other talents, *you* must alert her to every tax break you deserve and provide the records to back up your claims.** In the rush to fill out hundreds of returns each April, few tax pros can take the time to review every potential deduction with you. And unlike a court of law, it's up to you to *prove* you merit each deduction you take.

Tax breaks come in two forms—deductions, or amounts that Congress has determined taxpayers can subtract when computing their taxable income, and out-and-out tax credits, which you can subtract directly from the tax you owe.

Looking back at Congress's work, it is hard to see a clear line of reasoning behind some of their decisions. You can get an investment tax credit on a cow or a race horse, for instance, but not on a saddle horse.

That means that the only way you can truly learn the rules is by studying them. Sounds boring, but remember—every dollar you don't ship to Uncle Sam is another dollar for you.

Never in recent memory has this task been more necessary. The wide-ranging tax bill enacted in fall 1986 completely rewrote the book on many commonplace deductions. Table 4.3 and the paragraphs that follow highlight some of the most widely used ones, also known as write-offs. Many others will be introduced and explained in later chapters. As long as you itemize your deductions, you can subtract from the amount of income you report to Uncle Sam all unreimbursed expenses that qualify in these areas.

One of the biggest changes under the new tax law hits precisely at the deductions career women prize—**business expenses.** The IRS usually lets you write off the cost of belonging to professional organizations, subscriptions to "must-read" magazines in your field, even a briefcase or carry-on bag you use solely for business. Under the new tax law, however, business expenses are included with other miscellaneous expenses. You would get a deduction only for the amount of the miscellaneous category total that exceeds 2 percent of your adjusted gross income. For most of us, adjusted gross income is the same as gross income—that is, all your earnings, whether from wages and salary or income from taxable investments. But you can "adjust" your gross by subtracting any deductible IRA or Keogh pay-ins.

Finding write-offs may be easier than you think. In addition to the business expenses mentioned above, check the list in Table 4.3. What's more, you may also be able to write off the costs of **job hunting** in your field. While the search for your first job will not qualify, later expenses will. This includes money spent on your resume, mailings, phone calls, employment agency fees, travel costs to interviews, and the like—whether or not you actually changed positions. Even a cross-country trip can be a deduction if you went for an important job interview. Start keeping track now of any job-related expenses that may prove useful at year-end.

After-hours time also offers opportunities to edge above that 2 percent floor for write-offs. For starters, you can include much of the costs of making money through your **investments.** The IRS usually gives a green light for: money spent for investment advice, whether through a financial planner, magazine, or this book; postage and phone calls to your broker and the cost of a safe deposit box used to store income-producing assets such as stocks and bonds or rental property records.

A mixed bag of other **miscellaneous expenses** can also be thrown into your totals to see if you merit a deduction. They include everything from certain legal fees to the cost of hiring someone to wade through all the rules and prepare your tax return.

Tot up all the money you spent on these items. Then see how you compare. If, for instance, your adjusted gross income comes to $22,000, you can deduct any miscellaneous or business expenses that exceed $440 (2 percent of $22,000). If your total spending on such items comes to $520, you can write off $80.

Working women also are entitled to other **career-oriented tax breaks.** The biggest, of course, is an **IRA,** discussed more thoroughly later in this chapter. In addition, if you change jobs down the road, and must move to accept the new position, unreimbursed **relocation costs** can reduce your taxes as well. There are, however, certain requirements and limits. If the situation comes up, check with a tax pro on the details.

Uncle Sam also likes to encourage our better natures. Write off any donations you make to your church, alma mater, or other recognized **charity**—whether in cash or by check. In addition, you can deduct any *out-of-pocket* expenses incurred in volunteering for a church, medical research group, or other official charity, including mileage, tolls, parking, postage, photocopying, and other costs. Buy a batch of chocolate chip cookies to take to the Girl Scout meeting, and you can write off the cost. *Make* the cookies at home and you can deduct the cost of whatever you spent on ingredients, down to the last chocolate chip.

In a less welcome move, the new tax law also swept away or restricted many time-honored tax breaks. Big spenders used to be able to write off the money they spent on state and local sales taxes. No more. In addition, while mortgage interest is still deductible, Congress cut back the write-off you can take for interest paid on **consumer loans** (student, car, credit card, and other borrowing for personal reasons), after a phase-out period. Sixty-five percent of interest would be deductible in 1987; 40 percent in 1988; 20 percent in 1989; 10 percent in 1990; and nothing after that. The law left one loophole for those who own their own home: loans secured by a house you own still qualify under certain circumstances. A more detailed discussion of home equity loans follows in Chapter 6.

For these and other expenses, your best bet is to keep good records. **Generous as he is, Uncle Sam will not simply take your word for the fact that you baked cookies, attended meetings, drove to a company in the next state for a job interview. You need proof.** Cancelled checks and store receipts, of course, are best. But you can also make a good case for smaller expenses if you keep a written record of your spending as you incur expenses.

First-time taxpayers likely won't have many deductions. As

your career progresses, however, you can hope to do better. **The tax law in effect allows you a certain number of deductions automatically, known as the standard deduction. Once your write-offs exceed that level ($2,540 for single individuals and $3,760 for married persons filing jointly in 1987, then $3,000 for singles and $5,000 for couples in 1988), you can save money by claiming your deductions.**

Despite your best efforts, you may not come up with enough deductions to itemize on an annual basis at first. But careful planning may make it possible to top that limit every other year. Susan, a bank trainee, contributes $100 each year to her alma mater. She can make two gifts, or a total of $200, on December 31 in order to bunch both checks in the same tax year. This tactic can be used with any deductible payment whose timing you control, including work-related expenses such as subscriptions and professional dues.

A common tax problem among first-time workers is **over-withholding.** Based on the number of exemptions you took when you signed your payroll papers, the personnel office calculates how much you will owe over the course of the year. That sum is deducted in equal installments each pay period.

If you won't be working a full year (for instance, if you started your job in June), however, you won't be earning a full year's pay. In most instances, that means that you will owe less in taxes. If that is true in your case, you can cut your withholding and get more of that money now.

To find out, do a rough calculation of how much you will owe this year. Figure approximately how much you will earn from wages and other income such as bank account interest. Then add up how much you expect in deductions. If low write-offs keep you from itemizing, your task is simple. Look up your taxable income on the table that appears on page 40 and do a quick calculation to see roughly how much you'll owe. If it is less than the amount that your employer will withhold this year, talk with a personnel officer to see how you can lower your withholding.

TABLE 4.3

A Wealth of Deductions to Cut Your Tax Bill

Here is a sampling of the many write-offs you can take as long as you itemize. Of course, you can take only deductions you actually incurred, and you cannot deduct any expenses your employer later reimburses.

CHARITABLE

• Fair market value of clothing, household articles, and other items donated to Goodwill, the Salvation Army, a church, or other recognized charity. (If the value of a single item of donated property exceeds $5,000, you must attach an independent appraiser's statement of the item's value to your return.)

• Out-of-pocket expenses on behalf of recognized charitable activities, such as Scout leader's uniforms, or the cost of postage, photocopying, supplies, and the like.

• Mileage (12 cents a mile in 1986), parking fees, and tolls for church, school, scouting, and other volunteer activities.

• Charitable percent of National Geographic Society, Smithsonian Institution, and similar organizational dues in excess of the cost of complimentary subscriptions received.

MEDICAL

As long as the total unreimbursed amount is more than 7½ percent of your adjusted gross income, you can include:

• Cost of eyeglasses and contact lens replacement insurance.

• Cost of traveling to and from a physician, dentist, or hospital.

• Health club dues if prescribed by a doctor to treat a specific medical condition.

INTEREST

The deduction for consumer borrowing is being phased out. In 1987, you can write off 65 percent (in 1988, 40 percent; in 1989, 20 percent; and in 1990, 10 percent) of the interest on personal loans such as:

• Credit card finance charges.
• Interest on student loans, car loans, and other borrowing.
• Penalties on premature withdrawals of cash from bank CDs.
• Mortgage prepayment penalties.
• Points paid on loans for your principal residence, if customary in your area.

MISCELLANEOUS

You can write off any spending in the following categories that exceeds 2 percent of your adjusted gross income:

Business Expenses

• Part of annual dues for credit cards used for business purposes.
• Dues, tuition, and other fees related to membership in professional organizations. Enrollment in courses and seminars associated with current trade or business.
• Business gifts, up to $25 per person.
• Business calls charged to your home phone.
• Cost of passport used for business.
• Briefcases and suitcases used exclusively for business travel.
• Office supplies such as pen-and-pencil sets.
• Costs of attending a trade or business convention.
• Costs of technical magazines, journals, and newspapers relating to business.
• Business-related educational expenses that do not qualify you for a new trade or business.
• Travel expenses for a second job if you go directly from the first to the second.
• Resumes, employment agency fees, and other costs of looking for a new job in your current field—whether or not you get one.

Investments

• Fee for safe deposit box holding stocks, bonds, or other income-producing assets.
• IRA or Keogh account start-up costs and custodian fees if billed and paid for separately.

• Fees for investment or financial planning advice.

• The cost of books, magazines, and newsletters providing investment advice, including the cost of this book.

Other

• Cost of preparing your tax return, including postage and photocopying and fees paid to an accountant or other tax preparer.

• Portion of legal fees related to tax advice.

Based on data from Price Waterhouse, Commerce Clearing House

If you have enough deductions to itemize, the procedure is similar. Subtract your deductions from your income to determine your taxable income. Then turn to the tax tables for itemized returns to compute your tax. Again, if that amount is less than the total your employer will pull from your paychecks this year, an employee benefits officer can help you calculate what you *should* be withholding, and you can take home the extra in your paycheck each month.

Building a Bankbook

If your first planning task is to build a fallback fund, your first investing task is to park it somewhere. The best place for such easy access funds is a money market fund, discussed in Chapter 2. The first money funds were offered by mutual funds, and today they remain a popular place to park cash. Except for those affiliated with brokerage firms, most do business by mail or toll-free phone numbers. You'll see ads for dozens in the financial pages of *The Wall Street Journal*, your local newspaper, or financial publications.

To open an account, call the firm to ask for an application form. Send it in with a check and you're in business. Most require at least $1,000 up front, but a few will open an account with less. If you'd like to be able to write checks on the balance, say so, and you will receive a set of checks. In most instances, however, your check must come to at least $500.

Convenient as money market mutual funds are, however, most working women should stick closer to home. Banks also offer money market funds, and they can be a better deal overall. The reason: unlike mutual funds, banks offer many of the products and services you will need in your financial future—lines of credit, car and home loans, home equity loans. In the long run, you will benefit from having a close relationship with a bank. There's no better time to start to build it than now.

Your first step is to find a bank that values your business and offers good products in return. That means shopping around. **Bank products, rates, and fees vary widely, even in the same community—and on the same block.** Take the time to compare the offerings of at least five in your area. For questions to ask, see Table 4.4.

Once you have targeted a good bank, make the effort to build a relationship with one banker. We'll talk more about how to cultivate her friendship in Chapter 12. In the meantime, remember that she is just as anxious to succeed in her career as you are in yours. Help her, and you will win a friend for life as well as special courtesies when you need them. Bring her new business, whether your IRA or car loan application or three friends from the office. She in turn will be delighted to speed through your loan request, counsel you on how she sees interest rates changing, and call you when the bank runs a special promotion on CD rates.

Most women just starting out, then, should funnel their rainy day cash into a money fund. Their portfolios look like this:

GETTING STARTED	
Money fund	100%

Pretty plain, yes? That's what beginning is all about. **Most of the money management mistakes in this world are made because we seek out the dazzle of alluring investments before we do the plain-Jane work of building a secure base.** For now, your prime—in fact, sole—concern for this money is to keep it absolutely safe, utterly secure and available, instantly, when you need it. A money market account is *the* best place to use.

If the idea seems boring or their rates stodgy, have heart. Once you save a bit more cash, you will be able to squeeze out a higher yield on these funds and still keep yourself well-protected. The next chapter will show you how.

There's one big catch in this advice, however. Although the U.S. Government no longer limits how much you must have to open a money market account, many banks impose their own minimums. With less than $500, you may not be able to open a money fund in the bank you prefer.

In that case, check the rates and fees on two options—a regular checking account and conventional savings account—to see which offers the better deal. If your bank will even accept small savings accounts, check the fees it charges to maintain one. In all too many instances, banks are demanding up to $3 and more a month to service low-balance accounts and charging a fee if you use the account more than a few times a month. That means that you can end up paying more in fees than you collect in interest. No deal there. Worse yet, small-balance checking accounts can also soak you on fees—and you won't get even a cent in interest to offset them.

The only way to get around that is to add your savings nest egg to your regular checking account. But careful here. Do it only with the firm understanding that it is money to be saved, not spent. If you think you will be tempted to spend, don't add the amount to the total in your checkbook register. And open a money market account just as soon as you have the minimum needed to do so.

Lines of Credit. Building any kind of cash reserve takes time.

Until you have accumulated a fallback fund, consider asking your bank for a line of credit to use in an emergency. **A line of credit allows you to get cash, no questions asked, up to a preset amount.** Banks package them in one of three ways: as part of your regular checking account, as a separate account, or as part of the limit you can charge on a national credit card. When you need money, you simply write yourself a check against your bank account or take out a cash advance against your credit card.

Lines of credit make sense. If you ever need to tap one in an emergency, you will be protected. But **respect that money. Don't even consider tapping it for anything less than an emergency.** A trip to Nassau is not an emergency, no matter how tired you feel.

Learning About Investing. While your investment needs are simple now, you should start to prepare for more sophisticated moves. If, like many women who have entered the work force in the past five years, you never learned from Daddy how to wheel and deal, now is the time to educate yourself.

Reading this book is a solid first step. Money basics will seem second-nature when you're done. You can also gain insight on current market trends by attending one or more of the many money seminars sponsored by banks, brokerage firms, and financial planners. For the price of a phone call and an evening, you can get answers to individual questions and cart home a truckload of brochures.

Just remember *why* seminar sponsors are doing this. To win your business, of course. That means they will be pitching hard for follow-up appointments and may be tempted to gloss over some of the negatives involved in whatever product they are trying to sell. **The key point to keep in mind at such meetings: you have no obligation whatever to tell the sponsors anything, sign up for anything, or buy anything.**

You may be better off attending money management programs offered by local high schools, colleges, or professional or civic groups. Although they may charge a fee, the best courses will be less biased.

TABLE 4.4

How to Find the Best Bank for You

There's more to choosing a bank than finding the one with the most automatic teller machines (ATMs). Although those units can be blessings to time-pressed professionals, the backup behind the machines is far more important to a successful banking relationship. Here's how to size up a bank:

- **Compare rates.** You'll find an astonishing difference on what banks pay for money market accounts, CDs, and other savings products, even among banks in the same part of town. Start with a series of phone calls to the half-dozen or so banks that advertise most widely. Chances are, they are actively seeking new deposits—and so might tend to offer consistently attractive rates. Get a rundown on the accounts that interest you most.

Wait a few weeks and look again. Banks also can offer come-on rates far higher than their normal payouts. That is especially true when they are introducing new products or trying to win new business, say, at IRA season. Unfortunately for you, they will soon drop their rates to more normal levels.

Bear in mind that a high number on a rate does not necessarily pack the biggest total return. The way a bank calculates, or "compounds," interest on deposits is even more important than the rate it pays. The more frequently a bank compounds interest, the more you will earn on your investment.

Here's an example. The annual yield on a one-year CD paying 12 percent simple interest is 12 percent. But if the rate is compounded daily, the yield you actually receive jumps to nearly 13 percent. The best way to compare rates is to ask how much $100 would be worth at the end of the term.

- **Visit the most promising.** Look around. How many teller windows are open? How long are the lines? Are bank officers available to answer questions? Does the bank prominently display its money market, CD, IRA, and loan rates?
- **Ask about fees.** Deregulation has allowed banks to pay higher interest on their deposits. In turn, they now impose stiffer fees for most services. To keep from getting hosed, be sure to check costs. Last year, for instance, you could pay anywhere from $9 to $12 to bounce

a check in one east coast city, or $10 to $15 to stop a check in a midwest capital.

How do you find out? A good bank will provide a list of fees if you ask. Pay careful attention to the costs of the services you use most often. Is there a charge, for instance, to use an ATM? In addition, find out how much you must keep in a checking account to avoid a monthly service charge. What are the penalties if you run too low? How many checks can you write at no cost? What is the fee per check after that? Will you receive your cancelled checks at the end of each month for free? Ask whether you can cut a better deal if you also open an IRA or bring in other deposits.

• **Consider what's convenient for you.** Banking can take up a lot of time if you're not careful. Is the bank open evenings, weekends, or other times that suit your needs? Are its ATMs located near your home, office, and other places where you spend time? Does the bank belong to a national ATM network so you can get cash when you are on the road?

• **Take home a pile of brochures.** Then read them carefully. Can you understand the explanations?

• **Scrutinize services.** Does the bank seem genuinely to want your business? Will it help to make your banking affairs easier? Can you deposit a check and withdraw cash from it immediately? How long does it take an out-of-state check to clear—three days or three weeks?

Can the bank grow as you do? Does it offer preferred customer lines or other special perks for high depositors? Does it offer a range of investments for IRAs, or just money market accounts and CDs? If you plan to buy a home, check that it is active in the home mortgage market. If you plan to invest in the stock market, ask whether it offers discount brokerage services.

• **Look for a personal touch.** Sit down with a bank officer to discuss opening an account. Listen for reasons you would *want* to do business there. Sample: the banker asks about you, and the kinds of services you need. Her institution regularly rolls out new products and tries to stay competitive in rates.

The most important thing a bank can do is employ workers who are willing to talk to you and help you find the best products for your needs. If your first attempts to talk to a banker are rebuffed, take your business elsewhere.

If you don't have time right now for courses or seminars, try to read *The Wall Street Journal* and the business section of your local paper regularly. You'll grow familiar with business and investing terms and the ways in which economic conditions change over time. More guidance on how to make sense of financial news follows in Chapter 10.

Backstop Yourself With Insurance

With your first paycheck comes your first insurance coverage. **Unless an elderly parent or disabled relative is dependent on you for support, or you have a great many debts, the life insurance policy your employer provides should be all the coverage you need for now.**

Even so, you may find yourself assiduously wooed by life insurance agents. Dismiss them. While you can lock in lower rates on whole life policies by signing up when you are young, those so-called savings are no bargain if you do not need insurance in the first place. You are far better off saving the premiums you would have paid and, if need be, using the income earned on that money to pay higher premiums later.

A far more important concern is protecting your earning power with disability insurance. **At this stage in life, your ability to work is your most important asset.**

Chapter 3 outlined some of your key concerns in sizing up disability policies: how much they would pay, how soon, and how long. Most likely you already have some sort of coverage from your employer. Find out precisely what it offers; many company plans offer minimal, short-term coverage. If the checks would not be enough to tide you through a loss, supplement that coverage with another policy.

Chances are you can get your best deal through the company that provides your employer's coverage. It can sell you a policy that picks up where your present policy leaves off. If you cannot find a good deal there, many life insurance agents also sell disability policies, and some specialize in disability alone. Compare the terms and costs of several before you sign up.

Thinking Long-Term

Most young women don't think about retirement at all. The future *is* far away, and present needs soak up the little cash on hand. But early, consistent efforts, no matter how small, can play a critical role in creating your long-term financial security.

As a single woman, you need higher-than-average retirement savings. They will be the buttress of your security, and may have to last a long while. The average life expectancy for a woman today is 78. **Almost as soon as they start working, single women must begin to think about what they will live on when they stop.**

Despite the widely trumpeted problems of the Social Security Administration, the system has been put on a sound financial footing. Even the youngest of today's career women can look forward to receiving some sort of payout. In 1986, the average retired worker collected $478 per month. Your take, of course, depends on how much you earn over the years and how long you eventually decide to work.

A typical woman in her thirties earning $16,000 today might expect to pocket the equivalent of $540 a month in today's dollars at age 65. That would represent about 40 percent of her current salary. Someone the same age earning $31,000 stands to collect $775 per month—or just 30 percent of her gross—if she works steadily and wins average pay increases. Unless she can slash her expenses to that level, she must come up with another source of income, period. That means either her employer's pension and retirement savings programs, or herself.

It will help immeasurably if you are employed by a company with a generous pension program and work there long enough to qualify for a piece of it. By now, you may have a hazy idea of how likely it is to happen—or whether you have any plans of being around that long.

No matter what your intentions, however, for the moment you cannot count on it. Many companies do not irrevocably guarantee, or "vest," a pension right until an employee works at least ten years (although some grant rights to a portion sooner). Down the road, the new tax laws will help ease this problem. Starting in January 1989, most companies will have to give workers the absolute right to all their pension benefits in five to seven years. That will be immensely useful to women who shift jobs steadily to work their way up the career ladders or who bow out for a time to raise a family. But that remains a long way off for women now in the job force. **Take time now to explore the terms of your employer's plan and be sure you understand how long you need to stay before you would receive any money at all.**

The less likely you are to pocket a corporate pension, the more concerned you must be with building your own. One of the surest ways is to open an IRA as soon as you can. Funded over the full length of a woman's career, it can swell to formidable proportions. As the table on page 90 shows, $2,000 set aside each year for 40 years earning just 10 percent will come to fully $973,704.

IRAs work because they put time to work for you. As soon as your funds start earning interest or otherwise growing, then those returns themselves begin to grow and accumulate interest. **The value of time is so powerful that you can start an IRA, stop it cold a few years later, and still laugh your way to the bank.**

Say you put $2,000 into an IRA each year from age 22 until you turn 28 and never add another cent. The following year, the woman in the next office gets around to making her first IRA $2,000 contribution at age 29 and contributes that sum faithfully through age 65. Then you both retire. Assuming that both investments grew at 12 percent a year, your six years' worth of early-bird contributions and your colleague's belated 36 years' of investing would be worth almost the same amount.

So do it now, if you possibly can.

Another key reason to start an IRA now is the fact that

you stand to lose part of its lucrative tax breaks as your career picks up steam. Here's the deal. Every worker can salt away up to $2,000 of her pay and postpone paying taxes on every cent of its *earnings* until she withdraws the funds. And as long as you are not covered by an employer-sponsored pension plan or a Keogh, you also can deduct the *contribution* from the income you report to Uncle Sam, and hence put off those taxes, too, until later years.

But any worker building just about any kind of pension benefit will see her IRA deduction drop as her income rises. Under the new tax law, only single persons with less than $25,000 in salary and married couples reporting less than $40,000 jointly retain the full $2,000 deduction. Folks pulling in larger salaries will find their write-off trimmed progressively until it peters out entirely for singles earning $35,000 and married couples earning $50,000.

Regrettably, your first paychecks stand to come in safely under those limits. But think positive. It is highly likely that you will lose the deduction on your contribution in just a few years as your income spurts ahead. **That means you should press to pump the largest sum possible into an IRA now, while you still can reap the maximum rewards for your virtue.**

There is one catch. Uncle Sam gives out very few favors with *no* strings attached. **To make sure you aim to save for retirement, not a trip to Rio, the law generally imposes penalties if you pull out your funds before age 59½, unless you become ill or disabled.** Pry into an IRA early and you must pony up a 10 percent penalty as well as taxes at your present rate on any deductible contributions plus all earnings that have built up.

Even so, as long as you allow your IRA to grow for a while, you stand to come out ahead even after paying taxes and penalties. **And pesky as they are, early withdrawal penalties can help you toe the line. Knowing you'll be zapped if you raid the account, you may decide to leave your IRA intact after all.**

Of course, depositing the full $2,000 may be more than you can manage. After all, your primary goal *is* to build a fallback fund. Don't fret. You can still benefit from an IRA. **All the lavish publicity about the $2,000 write-off tends to obscure the fact that as an investor you can contribute any amount you want.** Some banks and mutual funds will open IRAs with $50 and less.

That little bit of money will not go far, of course. But it does establish an account that you can add to anytime over the course of the year up to the date your tax return is due. And if you can manage to squeeze out as little as $500, or about $9.62 a week, you are going places. If those funds earn an average of 10 percent, at the end of 40 years you'll boast a fat $243,426.

You may be sold on the idea of an IRA but totally confused about where to invest your contribution. That's not surprising. In the five years since IRAs were made available to every working person, the number of choices has mushroomed. They all boil down, however, to two main choices: income-producing investments such as CDs, bonds, and the like, and investments that aim for growth such as stocks or real estate. **Income-producing investments tend to offer security, although you will lose out if interest rates shoot up sharply, except with money market accounts. Growth investments offer the chance for higher returns but at the risk of losing some or all of your principal.** Table 4.5 runs through some of the questions to ask before investing.

The only thing that comes close to competing with an IRA at this stage in your life is a company retirement savings program that matches some or all of your contribution. That's free money, and any time you can get free money, you ought to look into it. Company-sponsored retirement plans like 401(k)s make sense if the company will vest its contributions fairly quickly so you can be sure you will work there long enough to win them for keeps and if the terms of the plan allow you to withdraw your contributions under conditions acceptable to you.

Women just out of school are among the few who proba-

bly do not need wills. Even they, however, should draw up a letter of instruction that would ease the task for those who would have to sort out their affairs should they die. Make a list noting your bank accounts (bank names and numbers), insurance policies, credit card information, investments, names of any money professionals such as accountants and lawyers, as well as your Social Security number. Keep it in a desk drawer at home and let one or two people close to you know where to find it.

TABLE 4.5

How to Choose an IRA Investment

With the many choices available to IRA holders today, a little shopping can pay off big. Here are questions to ask yourself before choosing the type of investment you seek. That done, screen the organizations that want your account with the second set of questions.

Ask yourself:

- **What are your goals?** Do I want my money to remain safe, even if I have to settle for a relatively low return on my investment? Or am I willing to risk some of these funds, even though I stand the chance to lose some or all of them? Careful here. Unlike other investments, you cannot replace IRA losses. Once the money is gone, it is gone.
- **How long until you retire?** The younger you are, the more comfortable you can feel taking risk. Older women should be increasingly cautious with their IRA funds lest they blow the money they spent so long saving.
- **Is your IRA the cornerstone of your retirement?** Women who have not earned a corporate pension or funded a Keogh or other personal pension plan must rely more heavily on their IRA accounts than women who have other retirement programs in place. That means they should adopt a relatively more cautious stance with the funds.
- **How is your other money invested?** By and large, you want to spread your assets among many types of investments. If you play the stock market or seek out other aggressive investments with your non-IRA money, consider parking your IRA funds in safer fields, such as CDs or Treasury securities.

  If you have invested the bulk of your non-retirement money in fixed-income investments, you might want to consider putting some of your IRA funds in stocks. And now that the favorable capital gains tax treatment on stocks is ended, you no longer forfeit a tax break by putting them into an IRA. (The IRS taxes all money withdrawn from IRAs at ordinary income rates, regardless of how the money was invested.)
- **How much have you set aside?** Each year, of course, you can

salt away up to $2,000. Once you boast a five-figure sum, you can consider opening a so-called self-directed account that will let you diversify your funds among a variety of investments under one umbrella plan. It's usually not worth it to open one earlier, because the cost of commissions can eat up your early profits.

Ask about the organization:

- **What is the fee to set up an account?** A few organizations, notably mutual funds and brokerage firms, charge start-up fees.
- **Is there an annual custodial fee?** Remember, annual fees recur every year. Look for a low-cost operation. Many banks do not charge annual fees.
- **How easily can you switch investments?** Mutual funds and brokerage firms let you move money fairly easily among their products. Banks also are willing to let you move around, but many offer a more limited choice of IRA products—money market funds and CDs. A handful of banks sell mutual funds.
- **What will it cost you to switch investments?** Watch out for charges each time you move from one investment to another.
- **What will it cost to close the account?** A few organizations slap on fees of up to $60 to close your account. Avoid them. IRAs are long-term investments, and you are likely to want to change organizations at least once over the life of the account.

FIVE

THE SINGLE LIFE: INDEPENDENCE AND RESPONSIBILITY

Being independent means being free. For the single woman, the decisions she makes and the priorities she sets are hers alone. Single women pay a stiff price for their independence, however, and that is responsibility.

When it comes to financial planning, singles are a very special category. Corporate executive, entrepreneur, or professional woman, all face the task of building financial security alone. No husband helps to fatten the savings pool, or lends advice (welcome or no) on what to do with the money.

At the same time, single women *need* that security more than other women. **A single is truly on her own.** If she loses her job, she's lost her entire income, not just part of it. There's no husband or lover to lean on in an emergency and no child to take her in in her old age.

As a result, wise singles put themselves where they belong on their list of priorities, at the very top. That can mean buckling down to build capital instead of buying yourself a fur. But over the long run, sound priorities ensure financial control and self-sufficiency.

UP AND COMING

Getting a cash reserve together takes time. But by dint of hard effort and a spate of welcome raises, most young women eventually pull together a solid savings base. Once they reach that point, single women can afford to begin a more aggressive investing program—and should.

Adding Pow to Your Portfolio

Start by revving up the income you collect on your fallback fund. **With more cash on hand, you no longer need *all* your funds available at a moment's notice.** Consider parking just two months' expenses in a money fund and channeling the rest into three- or six-month bank CDs. That way, you can win the higher yields that come as a reward for locking up cash for a longer term. Look for a quarter- or a half-point or so in extra interest for your bravery. See Table 5.1 for questions to ask when considering CD investments.

That done, consider shifting your other assets around a bit. **Unless you plan to buy a new car or make another major purchase soon, you likely will not need to use that money right away. That means you can ease your emphasis on income-producing assets in favor of those that will help your money grow.** And you probably should. For one thing, any interest you collect is taxable at rates that could get pesky as your income rises. More important, you now are entering stage two of the asset allocation cycle outlined in Chapter 2. A wise woman's emphasis shifts to taking a measure of risk to fire up her assets.

The hardest part about risk-taking is getting started. Stock listings seem little more than a gray wash of ciphers. The financial pages throw around a dictionaryful of unfamiliar terms. The market seems to lurch erratically from good day to bad, offering no clues to what to do and when.

TABLE 5.1

A CD Checklist

You'll feel more comfortable shopping for CDs if you think through the answers to these questions:

- **How much do you plan to invest?** If you can spare just a few hundred dollars, do not lock it up for a long time. If something comes up and you need the cash, you will pay a penalty (generally by forfeiting some or all of the promised interest) to get it. Stick with CDs that run for six months or less.

If you have a thousand dollars or more, consider committing your cash for as long as several years. Before you do, however, break up your funds into several small units of, say, $500 each. That way, you can cash in just one or two in a pinch and limit your penalties for early withdrawals.

- **Are you saving for a specific goal?** If you know you need money at a certain time, say next summer when you go on vacation, you often can tailor the due date of the CD to fit that schedule. Banks can write CDs for any length of time—days, weeks, months—although not all are that flexible.
- **How much income do you want?** By and large, the longer you park your money, the more the bank will pay you for it. That can tempt income-hungry investors to choose the longest maturity. Before you do, ask yourself:
- **Are interest rates going up or down?** Granted, it's hard to tell. Chapter 10 gives you a few good clues. Read it first, then decide what *you* think interest rates will do.

If you think that rates are likely to spring up, keep your cash in CDs of three months or less. That way you can reinvest at steadily higher rates as the certificates come due. If rates are in a downward spiral, aim to lock in a good rate now. Guess right, and you could be collecting 10 percent or more when market rates fall to single-digit levels.

If you just plain don't know, mix it up. Invest some of your funds for a year or more, the balance for a shorter term. If rates go up, you will be able to reinvest the latter soon enough, and the yield on your longer-term funds will probably not look so bad. If rates edge downward, you will at least have some of your capital pumping out an attractive return.

• **How do your bank's rates compare with those of its rivals?** Once you have begun to work with a good bank and a helpful banker, you should not mind if the bank down the street pays a quarter-point more on CDs from time to time. It is more important to stick to one bank and build a relationship there. On the other hand, take note. If your bank *consistently* pays less than its rivals, that may be a sign that its other services are also below par. In that case, consider shopping for a new bank.

Don't cringe. **Once you make your first investment moves, much of the mystique will fall away.** To get started, look back at the discussion of assets in Chapter 3. That outlines the basics of what a stock is. The glossary at the end of the book can help you decipher any tricky terms. Then, take a few weeks to practice on paper.

Start by picking a few stocks that you think might do well and would invest in if you had money to spare. Likely candidates might include your own company or another corporation in your field or one whose products you know from the supermarket or hardware store.

Follow–the stocks' performance for a month or so. You can track **the stock listings** in the financial pages of your local paper or *The Wall Street Journal*. The first entry, to the left of the stock's name, is a pair of numbers showing the stock's high and low over the past 52 weeks. This gives you an idea of whether the issue is trading near the upper or lower level of its value in the past year.

After the name of the stock itself you'll see another series of numbers. The **dividend (Div.)** shows how much per share is paid out to holders in dividends each year. That figure can be important to you if you are looking for income. Next in line, the **yield (Yld.)** shows you how much that dividend represents as a percentage of the stock's price—in other words, what your return is on the investment.

After that, **the p/e ratio (PE)** compares the annual earnings of the company per share with the stock's price on that day. This widely used measure can help you compare a stock's price with those of other issues. All things being equal, a stock with a low p/e is a better value than one with a high p/e.

The last lines show a stock's trading pattern over the day. You'll see the stock's highest and lowest selling price, the closing price, and finally the change in price—up or down—since the previous close.

Follow the listings daily and you'll soon become an old hand at the stock pages. While you're at it, look over the reports on the performance of the market as a whole. The most familiar barometer is **the Dow Jones Industrial Average.** This reflects the rise or fall in the value of a group of 30 blue-chip industrial stocks. Though the market of course is far broader than this, the Dow is widely seen as a shorthand for the market as a whole.

After you have followed the market's vagaries for a few weeks, you are ready to start investing on your own. The precise way you should do so depends on how much money you have right now. **With less than $10,000, steer clear of individual stocks.** On that kind of budget, it's hard to buy enough *different* issues to be sure you are hedging your bets.

A better choice would be shares in a solid mutual fund. Each dollar you tender goes into a pool that is invested by the fund's managers in a wide range of securities, whether stocks, bonds, gold or other assets. That gives your dollars enormous firepower. **It would take a portfolio of $50,000 to give you the same kind of diversification you'll be getting with each mutual funds share.** Many funds will open accounts for $1,000 or less.

If that sounds appealing, **the best way to choose a fund is by identifying your financial goals, then finding a fund that shares them.** For investors and funds alike, the basic question is whether you want to earn steady income now or can afford to take the chance of making even more money later—or losing some of what you have.

Risk-takers will find stock mutual funds in all stripes. **Ag-**

gressive growth funds are out-and-out risky plays. Many pay no dividends at all and focus on highly speculative issues. You may win big, or lose big. Less venturesome stock funds include **growth funds** looking to build assets over the long haul and **growth-and-income funds** that try to pay out dividends along with increasing the value of underlying shares.

Investors more interested in income can choose from a variety of **bond funds. The higher the return promised by the fund, the riskier the investment will be. While bond funds aim to keep your principal safe, their shares fluctuate in value and can be risky in times of rising interest rates.**

Once you know the kind of fund you're after, you are ready to track down the best fund in that category. Table 5.2 offers a checklist for your hunt.

Growth funds are a long-term investment. Don't count on fast appreciation the first year. But aggressive moves demand you keep a sharp eye on the overall market. If it begins to falter, you must cash in your holdings to keep your profits. Consult the advice in Chapter 10 on how to spot a change before it arrives.

Once their income spurts, many women also should consider buying a home of their own. **Real estate** can shelter their growing paychecks as well as their possessions. Over the years, the rise in real estate prices has proven a good bet against the rising cost of living. In some areas, in fact, the key question has been whether you can save money as fast or faster than property values are rising.

It's not clear how long that trend will last. Housing values resurged in the mid-'80s when mortgage interest rates dropped. But a sharp rate run-up could dampen the market again. **The best rule of thumb for now is this: do not consider your home an investment unless the market in your area is strong and stands to continue so. But prize its value as a tax deduction.** Homeowners who itemize deductions can write off the cost of the interest they pay on their mortgage and state and local property taxes as well. And when you sell the property, you can put off paying tax on any profit you make as long as

TABLE 5.2

Meeting Your Match in a Mutual Fund

There are dozens of different funds in every fund category. But whether you are interested in a growth fund, bond fund, gold fund, or other fund, the following questions can help you choose the best one for you:

• **What is its track record over time?** Your best bet may *not* be the fund that topped the charts last year. Funds that post the greatest gains often do so by focusing narrowly, and an investment that sparkles one year may not shine the next.

Unless you plan on hopping from fund to fund every few months, you want to find a fund that has performed well consistently. Many magazines, including *Business Week, Changing Times, Forbes,* and *Money,* report on both the recent and the historical performance of funds on a regular basis. Check to see how well a fund has performed over the past year as well as the past five years and ten years. The better a fund's long-term performance, the less likely it will stumble badly in any given year.

• **Are the managers who notched that performance still around?** As in any profession, fund managers move around. Ask a fund representative (many have toll-free 800 phone numbers you can use) who managed the fund over the years and whether he or she still calls the shots.

• **How much will it cost you to invest?** All funds charge an annual fee to cover their costs and time in managing the fund's assets. In addition, however, funds sold by brokers charge sales commissions as high as 8½ percent to invest. Unless you need a broker to help you choose a fund or to tell you when to move from one fund to another, you are better off focusing on funds that are sold with little or no commissions, known as no-load funds. You can deal with these funds by mail or over the telephone.

• **Will you also pay a fee to get out?** A growing number of funds are adding fees to redeem your shares that can be as high as 5 percent if you sell within a year.

• **Is the fund a member of a family of funds?** As its name implies, a fund family is a group of sister funds managed by one organization. Such families offer the benefits you might expect from close-knit clans. As a rule, you can switch all or part of your money from one fund to another at any time, often just through a phone call. That can help you profit from fast-changing markets with a minimum of effort. With that in mind, check to see if the family includes the kinds of funds you think you might be interested in down the road.

---

you buy another residence at least equal in price within two years.

As long as you are planning to stay in the same community, a shift from renter to owner status can make sense. But **be wary of buying if you suspect you might want to relocate.** It likely will take a few years' appreciation to recover the bank fees and other costs entailed in taking out a mortgage and buying a home. And if you cannot sell the house quickly when you are ready to leave, you might not be able to afford housing in your new community. If you want to go ahead, the best ways to finance the deal are discussed in Chapter 11.

No one should launch any investment program unless she has a fallback fund of at least two months' expenses in place. Women who are saving for a down payment should keep most of their cash in secure income-producing investments such as short-term CDs and Treasury securities. Those who set their sights on growth might consider a plan that looks like this instead:

UP AND COMING

Cash (Fallback fund)	5% - 50%
CDs, Treasuries, bond funds	10% - 20%
Growth stock mutual funds	15% - 25%
Second growth stock fund	10% - 20%
Aggressive growth fund	5% - 10%
Growth-and-income fund	10% - 20%

Planning for Tomorrow

It is not too soon to begin to think about next century's needs. That is, *your* needs when 2001 is here and gone and your income-earning days are history as well. While you will not be attending your retirement party for a long time, you will need every one of those years to lay the foundation to enjoy your old age. **If you're smart, you've been putting at least $500 into an IRA each year. If you can, this is the time to increase your contribution.** Invested wisely, every additional dollar you manage to salt away will multiply several-fold by the time you retire.

If your adjusted gross income has zipped past $25,000, you are faced with one of the first downsides of a growing paycheck. **As long as you are covered by another employer-sponsored penson plan or a Keogh, you'll not be able to write off the full $2,000 on your tax form.** Instead, the sum you can deduct is phased out as your income rises. If it tops $35,000, you lose the write-off entirely.

To see how much you can deduct, take 20 percent of any adjusted gross income between $25,000 and $35,000. Subtract that from the $2,000 maximum. The result is the amount you can write off. Say you're earning $28,000. Twenty percent of $3,000 (the difference between $25,000 and $28,000) is $600. Subtract that from $2,000. In this case, you could write off $1,200 of your contribution.

Not the full deduction, but a bargain still. The fact that an IRA can grow tax-free is the *real* advantage of having one and always has been. No matter how much—or how little—of your ante you can write off now, the money you stash away stands to billow dramatically because no taxes are siphoned off.

Say you're in the 28 percent tax bracket, which begins at just $17,850 in taxable income in 1988. If you save $2,000 a year and invest the after-tax proceeds in an account paying 10 percent annually, your money would be worth $139,563 at the end of 25 years. Sheltered in an IRA, however, where all the earnings grow tax-free, your nest egg would swell to $216,364 over the same period—a difference of $76,801. Deduction or no, **IRAs now represent one of the few ways left in the post-tax reform world that hard-pressed workers can shelter income. That makes them all the more valuable as your earnings increase.**

And don't lose heart. **There is one not-so-small benefit to making a non-deductible contribution. Because you must pay taxes on the money you kick in, you won't have to pay taxes on those funds if you are forced to pull them out early one day.** You will, of course, owe taxes and penalties on any deductible pay-ins as well as earnings that have accumulated tax-free.

Keeping track of what you *do* owe taxes on and what you don't stands to be an accounting nightmare. Your best course of action is to keep separate IRAs—one funded with contributions for which you have taken deductions and one holding funds on which you have already paid taxes and received no deduction.

As a working woman's assets multiply, they give rise to serious estate planning questions. With no one directly dependent upon her, the single executive may have less of a sense of urgency about providing for matters after her death. But often her concerns are just as real as those of her married colleagues. **In most instances, she can no longer postpone writing a will.** Wills are the only way to make special arrangements tailored exactly to your individual needs.

Many young women assume they want everything to go to their parents. That may not be wise. **If your folks are comfortable, leaving them money if you die first runs the risk of running up extra estate taxes.** If their own holdings are large, your assets may be taxed twice—once when you die and again when they die—before they are passed to other members of the family.

Even if your parents could use the money, you may still want to make special arrangements for them. They may not have much experience handling large sums, for instance. Should you leave them a hefty inheritance outright, they may not know how to manage it. Or they may grow feeble, and unable to handle money issues.

In either case, a trust might be in order. **A trust is a legal arrangement by which property is passed to a beneficiary but the control and management of the property are held by another person.** To protect parents with few money skills, a trust would see that a competent manager took over all management tasks. In the case of well-to-do parents, a trust could make it possible for them to pocket the income from some or all of your assets while the principal itself would be passed to another—brother, sister, or other loved one—after their death. Such a strategy would ensure that they did not have to pay taxes on your holdings. Or you might prefer to leave your holdings to a brother or sister who needs the money more.

If you have no close family ties, think of those who have been helpful in the past or supportive in the present. If you want them to have any of your belongings when you die, make an appointment to see a lawyer now.

UP AND RUNNING

Just when many working women finally have some income to invest, they stand to blow it all if they're not careful. Pouring all their energies into their jobs and often trying to build a relationship as well, all too many can find themselves tending to the bottom line at work and at home—but not in their bankbooks.

If You're Running Behind, Don't Panic

If you have not already gotten started, now is the time. But before the single executive reassesses her financial plan, she must also take a good look at her money style. Some of the trickiest, most self-defeating behavior takes place when there is an undeclared war between two deeply rooted elements of a woman's money personality.

Consider Portia's dilemma. Still tan from her winter vacation in Aruba, she began collecting brochures outlining the wonders of Spain. One travel agent she'd used frequently in the past turned up a well-priced tour featuring comfortable lodgings, but far from the first-class accommodations she usually booked.

Months passed, and she still has yet to reserve a space. None of the accommodations seem good enough for a time when she wants to enjoy herself, yet Portia doesn't want to spend any more money to get them. She is longing to save.

Like many women, Portia can't decide what she wants to do. To some observers, her dilemma is simple: she wants to have her cake and eat it too. But beneath that crisp assessment lies a profoundly important issue of money management that often emerges as women approach their thirties: identifying what role your money style plays right now, and what role you want it to play.

What is different for single women is that no person will come along to change them. But in many cases, circumstances, and time, do the job instead. As they grow more conscious of the need for financial security, and more comfortable with their investment choices, both Reachers and Nesters often begin to consider the kinds of investments they rejected out-of-hand just a few years earlier.

What happened? For many, this is the time they first begin seriously to consider the fact that they may well remain single forever.

No matter how successful their careers or fat their bankrolls, many women reach a real turning point when it becomes clear they might not marry. It forces them to rethink just where they stand now and where they will end up. Conscientious savers, including many Nesters and some Drivers, will emerge from their introspection with a measure of confidence. Not so for most Reachers, who will come face to face with the reality of an empty bankbook.

There is nothing like panic to make a Reacher hustle. Her quest is single-minded: to make up for lost time. Now is the time for those who preferred escape to wake up and those who chose to enjoy to buckle down. To do so, they should go backward to the future and follow the up-and-comer's agenda.

A New Emphasis: Keeping More of What You Make

For the moment, it can look as though the Nester has broken from the pack. Faithfully socking away money as her friends toured Europe, she now boasts a comfortable cushion. To keep her edge, however, she must place new emphasis on the same concerns as her friends who are Drivers: avoiding taxes and growing capital.

For every woman whose blossoming salary is swelling her investment coffers, the most important shift is the role that taxes will play in her decisions. Steadily, salary increases are bumping her into ever-higher tax brackets. And the new tax laws are making it harder than ever for her to keep those earnings for herself.

To plot an effective tax strategy, you must mentally divide your income into two categories—income you earn from work, and income you earn from investments. Sorry to say, it is harder than ever to avoid paying taxes on the paychecks you bring home. Starting in 1987, Congress has curbed or cut many time-honored tax breaks. Your basic tack is to claim each and every one of the deductions you merit. Beyond that, you should aim to at least postpone taxes through retirement savings programs or salary deferral plans.

That leaves your income from investments. **Your real hope is to keep more of your total income by reviewing—and in some cases, revamping—your personal portfolio.**

The problem with your personal portfolio is simple: any earnings will be taxed the year you log them unless you take steps to prevent it. Under the new tax law, worse things can happen. After all, with marginal tax rates dropping steadily toward the 33 percent mark, you can hang on to at least 67 cents of every dollar earned. For many women, that will make income-producing investments such as CDs, Treasury securities, and dividend-yielding stocks just as attractive as they were in their low-paycheck years.

Even so, taxes remain an important issue for any woman earning more than $30,000 or so. For starters, you should give your income-producing assets a sharp-eyed review.

For women at or below the 28 percent bracket, U.S. Treasury securities make the most sense. They offer high yields exempt from state and local taxes. Those who are moving into the 33 percent bracket might value the tax-free payments afforded by municipal bonds. Although state and local taxes are due on the payouts, many governments waive the bill when holders buy local issues.

You can buy individual Treasury securities through a bank or broker for a fee, or purchase them directly from the Treasury. But opt for a municipal bond fund rather than individual issues unless you are investing at least $50,000 in order to be sure you are sufficiently diversified.

To calculate the precise point at which a tax-free return would equal or exceed that of a taxable investment, turn back to the table on page 40. **If the current rates on tax-free income produce more money for you now, you also may want to swing your cash reserve into a tax-free money market fund.** Such funds provide the same security of principal and easy access to money as conventional money market funds, but because they invest in tax-free securities, you pay no taxes on their earnings.

Another way to hold down your tax bill is to swing your savings into investments that pay little or no current income but aim instead for capital gains. Stocks and real estate are the two best examples.

To reach for growth, consider shifting out of any high-dividend-paying stocks into those whose sights are trained on long-term appreciation. These might include growth or aggressive growth stock mutual funds. If you have pulled together at least $10,000, you also can consider buying individual shares of stock, although you are better off waiting until you have $15,000 or more.

Because they have lost their favorable tax treatment, capital gains are no longer quite as lucrative from a tax point of view. Any profit you pocket on such sales will be taxed at your current rates. Even so, you don't owe tax until you sell the asset, so you will keep your current bills down. More important, **over the long haul stocks have earned far more for their owners than investments in cash or fixed-income securities.** And so long as time is on your side, you can afford to gamble that that trend will continue.

To diversify into real estate, consider **real estate investment trusts (REITs)** or all-cash real estate limited partnerships. REITs are much like mutual funds. They pool the investments of countless buyers to acquire a variety of real estate holdings and distribute the income and profits from them as dividends, a portion of which may be tax-free. Most are publicly held companies whose shares are traded in the stock market. Thus, they offer you the chance to benefit from real estate appreciation without losing access to your money.

All-cash real estate limited partnerships invest in income-producing properties only, and pass the rental income on to the investors. All-cash means the partnership owns the properties outright, so none of the rent is diverted to pay mortgage expenses.

Many women are good about adding new investments but fail to weed out sluggish ones. Passbook savings accounts that may have served a purpose when you first were building assets have no place in your holdings now. Instead, your portfolio might look like this:

UP AND RUNNING

Money fund or tax-free fund (Fallback fund)	5% - 50%
Municipal bond or other income fund	5% - 15%
Real estate	10% - 40%
Growth stocks or growth stock fund	15% - 25%
Aggressive growth stock fund	10% - 20%

Peering Down the Road

If you have not been making steady contributions to an IRA, by all means start to do so now. Even though you can no longer write off the deduction once your adjusted gross income tops $35,000, you still can sit back and smile as your earnings grow tax-deferred. Aim to set aside the full $2,000 each year.

The one shift you might consider making is in the kinds of investments you make with those funds. If the stock market is booming and you are making stock investments, think about using *some* of your IRA funds to do so. That way you can put off paying taxes on the expected increase in the value of those securities at your relatively high current rates.

Such a decision represents a gamble, however. If you *lose* money rather than make it, you cannot replace those funds. You can only continue adding $2,000 a year. But the gamble may be worth it, particularly if you hedge your bets through stock mutual funds rather than buy individual issues. Over the years, stocks tend to do better than fixed-income investments, and you still have the luxury of time to wait for losers to turn around.

Your growing career clout may also give you the chance to do some consulting or other freelance work on the side. Do it. That way you have the chance to open an account similar to an IRA known as a Keogh.

Keogh plans were designed as a way to let self-employed people set up the same type of pension benefit as corporations provide for their employees. But even if you are covered by a pension plan at your primary job, you still can funnel part of any independent income you earn into a Keogh. The rules are complex, but in effect you can contribute as much as 20% of your sideline or self-employment income, up to $30,000 a year (and in some cases more). You can deduct your contribution from your taxable income, and once it is invested, all earnings build up tax-free. As with an IRA, access to Keogh funds is limited; generally you cannot withdraw money from a Keogh until age 59½ without paying a 10 percent penalty.

Keoghs shine under the new tax law. **For one thing, Keoghs enable high wage earners to get around the IRA restrictions and make tax-deductible retirement savings. What's more, being self-employed becomes an excellent way to shelter income under the new tax laws.** Simply put, entrepreneurs can write off the costs of earning money. That means that as a self-employed worker, you can deduct the costs of items like professional dues, subscriptions to magazines in your field, and the like, as well as such miscellaneous expenses as mileage to and from your own business or a sideline business appointment, postage, and the like that you incur on your sideline job. (Salaried employees, by contrast, can only write off unreimbursed business expenses that exceed 2 percent of their adjusted gross incomes.) In addition, if you establish a home office, you can deduct the costs of maintaining that as well.

The rules here are tricky, and you should huddle with a tax pro to determine exactly what you can do. And you'll need to show a profit in three out of five tax years in order to prove to Uncle Sam that you *are* trying to earn money. But if you can launch a sideline business, by all means go for it. **The best benefit of all is the fact that as tax rates drop, you can keep more dollars than ever of the extra you make.**

Make no mistake, even IRAs and Keoghs will not be nearly enough for most workers to secure a comfortable old age. For one thing, IRA millionaires will face a world where life's necessities are equally pricey. If the cost of living rises at the same 8 percent a year that one's investments are appreciating, the groceries that cost $100 now will demand $1,006 in 30 years.

Prize the special savings perks your employers provide. Ask about any profit-sharing or stock purchase plans, 401(k) programs, or other vehicles that will let you use cheaper, pretax dollars to build your reserve.

The new tax law also makes **annuities** more attractive savings vehicles. An annuity is a contract with an insurance company. You hand over money, either in a lump sum or on a regular schedule; in turn, the insurance company invests those funds, then returns them to you in a series of payments that either begin immediately or at a future date (a deferred annuity). Under most annuity plans, you are guaranteed checks for as long as you live, if that is the way you choose to receive your payout. However, you negotiate the pay-out schedule with the company, and can if you like elect to cash out your investment sooner.

Annuities boast one feature that can make them highly desirable: you do not have to pay taxes on the earnings that accumulate in your account until you pull them out. As a result, they offer the sheltering arm of an IRA. Also like IRAs, you'll be hit with penalties if you take out the money too soon. If you hold an annuity less than 10 years, the IRS demands a 5 percent penalty on any funds you take out, plus, of course, all the income taxes you've postponed on the earnings. What's more, the insurance companies themselves will slap on penalties for backing out early.

If you have earmarked those funds for retirement, those drawbacks should not discourage you. But you should approach annuities cautiously nonetheless. The ultimate value of your nest egg depends on how wisely your contributions are invested. The safest annuity is a **fixed annuity,** which guarantees your principal back plus a preset, or fixed, rate of return. To play it safe, insurance firms usually invest such funds in conservative instruments such as bonds. The problem is, many annuities pay downright skimpy returns, and if interest rates surge up, even a number that looks good now will fall short of market levels. Before buying any fixed annuity, check to see how much it is paying, how long that rate is guaranteed and under what circumstances it would rise or fall.

A **variable annuity,** on the other hand, offers the chance of greater total return but also greater risk. Such programs allow you to invest your money in more speculative but potentially more rewarding investments such as stock or real estate. The total in your account at retirement depends on how well those investments perform. Neither principal nor interest is guaranteed. In the worst case, you won't even get all your money back.

Whether or not you buy an annuity depends on your age, the size of your bankroll, and your attitude toward risk. If you are older or can afford to set aside a great deal toward retirement, annuities should be among the options you consider. But because these are, after all, funds that you want to be there when you need them, you should steer clear of variable annuities unless you have the energy and skills to watch your investments closely and are comfortable with the possibility you might lose some of your cash. Be sure to deal with a solid, diversified insurer if you act. Unlike bank CDs or Treasury securities, which effectively are backed by the federal government, annuities are backed solely by the company that issued them. Check fees carefully. Sales commissions and annual administrative costs vary widely.

Now that your assets have swelled, chances are you have less need for life insurance. The exception: if you have gained responsibility for a parent or other relative. But be sure the coverage you do have still reflects your wishes about the proceeds. You may want to change the beneficiary named to inherit those funds.

While you're at it, check to be sure your **disability insurance** coverage has kept pace with your soaring salary. This may be a good time to increase your coverage. If you have accumulated a fair-sized emergency reserve, you might be able to keep the premiums down by increasing the waiting period until you would collect your first checks.

You can protect your bankbook as well as your earning power by adding an **umbrella liability policy** to your homeowner's coverage. The greater your assets, the more likely someone will sue you over even the smallest injury.

LIVING TOGETHER: BLENDING BUSINESS AND ROMANCE

A growing number of women are edging partway out of the single state by living with a man they love. Marriage it is not. But for better or worse, if not for richer or poorer, it is best to temper romantic liaisons with a businesslike understanding of the responsibilities each will take on. While you cannot guarantee the outcome of the relationship, you can take steps to make sure that money will not be the reason it ends.

If you are in love, it is easy to feel as though you already *have* an understanding—when what you really have is a set of unspoken but conflicting opinions. Assume nothing. What seems perfectly clear to you may never have occurred to your lover. Whether you are an independent woman trying out a relationship or a mature woman setting up housekeeping with a widower, talking through your attitudes can help you to understand one another's priorities and establish patterns that will let you achieve them.

One caution: no relationship is permanent. Marriages falter, spouses die. Endings are no less likely in live-in arrangements. **Be sure you establish your own personal values and goals.** If they differ from those of your partner, bend, if you wish, for the good of the relationship; but be sure you do nothing that threatens your own long-term security.

Carl, for instance, is a carefree spirit. To him, good financial planning meant getting the best deal on plane tickets to Hawaii for Thanksgiving break. Joanna was smitten with his laidback style and gladly shared the bills to sustain it. Before long, however, she found herself dipping into her savings to cover her charge bills each month. Soon her concern caused the two to bicker, then quarrel nightly. When the relationship ended, she had run her reserves down to $2,500.

The Immediate Concerns

Before you move in, or he shows up, draw up a list of the property each of you brought and its condition. To insure your combined holdings, you have two choices. If you moved in, your partner can take out a rider on his insurance adding your goods to his. Or you can take out a separate policy on your own. That might be best: any reimbursement for loss would be sent directly to you. Discuss the merits and costs with your insurance agent.

While you have pooled your furniture and shared the closets, you need to consider whether you also will combine your funds. By and large, unmarried couples follow one of three routes:

- all funds separate
- all funds pooled
- both separate and pooled funds

In the beginning, at least, the first course is best. That method leaves you free to do what you want with your funds and less likely to criticize what your partner does with his. But it postpones the real issue of how the couple will handle its hoard. **Most unmarried couples are wise to manage expenses the same way they handle income**—if partners maintain separate checking accounts for personal use, they should pay for personal bills—facials or cigars—individually.

That leaves the question of common bills. For small purchases such as a VCR or stereo, aim for one partner to buy it outright. That way, ownership is clear if the two part ways. **If a couple really wants or needs to share the costs, they should decide in advance how they will split the property if they separate.** One option is to sell it, although secondhand goods fetch far less than their replacement cost. You can promise to let one partner buy the other out. Or you can agree that it will belong outright to one of you. Whatever the case, write your agreement on the sales receipt, and sign and date it.

Sharing other expenses fifty-fifty is easiest if both partners have comparable income and assets. But if one individual earns much more, a strict division of expenses could prove limiting. **Over the long run, the less-monied partner can end up feeling at the short end of a permanent stick.** Many couples find that splitting joint bills such as rent and food proportionately works best in such instances.

The most ticklish situation arises when one partner's economic circumstances change dramatically. Say one loses a job or decides to go back to school, wins a bundle in the stock market or makes partner in a law firm. Discuss in advance how such situations would be handled and the rights of each partner to be supported by or share in the success of the other.

In any event, be very careful about co-signing loans. If your partner fails to repay for any reason, you are liable for the entire amount. That could cost you plenty. What's worse, if you have any trouble shouldering that debt, it could sandbag your own credit rating.

For the same reasons, it is wise to avoid joint credit cards and borrowing or lending funds. **If you must play banker, put it in writing.** The agreement should specify the rate of interest charged, if any, the size and frequency of payments, and what will happen if the borrower falls behind.

Long-Term Concerns: Do You Need a Contract?

The very fact that unmarried couples have chosen to leave the knot untied shows that they value their own independence. That frame of mind is squarely at odds with eliciting promises and writing them down. Yet **the only way to create legal rights that will outlast the relationship is by drawing up a contract.** Without one, unmarried couples have few if any of the legal privileges of married ones, no matter how long they have lived together or how much they have shared.

Contracts can be as detailed or general as you prefer. As a rule, you should aim to spell out each partner's rights to property acquired during the relationship and who gets what and pays what when it is over.

Technically, you can create an agreement on your own. But if there is much property involved or other issues to sort out, you can increase the chances your contract will stand up in court by consulting an attorney. Courts generally recognize such pacts so long as they violate no laws and are entered into freely. Any agreement, however, should be carefully drafted to avoid all mention of your sexual relationship lest a scrupulous judge void it.

As you consider your contract, give special thought to long-term issues. **While you may be willing to pool some or all of your income, putting your savings in one pot is tricky.** If you open joint accounts, you lose control over the money. While the relationship flourishes, that might not matter, but matters could change if the relationship goes sour.

As long as either one of you can withdraw the funds, your partner could raid joint savings without your knowledge or consent. If, on the other hand, both signatures are required for action, a recalcitrant lover could tie your hands simply by refusing his okay.

Homes and cars are often too costly for one partner to swing on his or her own. But owning such assets jointly can also prove troublesome. If you plan to buy a home together, draw up a written agreement outlining the terms of the deal. It should specify how the home is to be owned and how payments and tax breaks will be shared. The contract also should include arrangements for selling or otherwise disposing of the property in the event the relationship ends—how it will be valued and how any profits would be shared.

When taking title to a home, your choice has considerable importance. If you buy as joint tenants, you own the property equally and one will inherit if the other dies regardless of any provisions in his or her will. That is one way to ensure that you will pass property on to your partner if you die. If you are not splitting the cost fifty-fifty and want to formalize that division, say, a seventy-thirty split, you may take title as tenants in common. In the event one of you dies, his or her share will go to the next of kin unless other arrangements are made in a will. The purchase may require you to take out a mortgage. If both sign, each is fully responsible for repayment.

Aside from buying a house or holding other property jointly, if you want your partner to share in your wealth after you die, you must draw up a will. Otherwise, your estate will be divided according to state law, which will not recognize your partner's contribution. Because the law governing live-in relationships is changing, be sure to work with a lawyer.

If you prefer, you may name your partner as the beneficiary of your life insurance policies. While most employers will go along, you may run into a roadblock if you try to take out a policy on your own. **Some carriers have been reluctant to honor such requests for fear that your partner's interest in keeping you alive did not sufficiently exceed his interest in the proceeds.** One way to get around that stand is to name a family member when you buy the policy, then switch the beneficiary later.

You also can leave your partner the death benefits if you die before collecting your rightful claim to a pension or profit sharing program. Should you want your partner to receive an ongoing pension payout upon your death, you must explore your company's options; not all plans allow you to do so.

If you have children together, your offspring will share the same rights to inheritance and support as if you had married. To prove those rights, however, both parents should sign a statement acknowledging their relationship to the child.

SIX

ADDING MARRIAGE AND A FAMILY

The shift from ''me'' to ''we'' involves a single letter of the alphabet. But in one stroke of the pen, a woman's life changes. Once she marries, she is no longer an independent woman charting her own financial course. She must balance her needs with those of her husband—and those of the couple they now represent.

MONEY MANAGEMENT FOR NEWLYWEDS

While they were dating, Janet and Matt learned a great deal about each other, from favorite foods and favorite songs to where they grew up and how they were raised. But until a few days before the wedding, they knew virtually nothing about each other's finances: what assets each held, what debts, what money plans and dreams. Taking up such questions seemed akin to a violation of the other's privacy. In the end, the subject came up only because they planned to open a joint checking account. Like many newlyweds, the two instinctively decided to merge their finances. They saw the move as a symbol of their decision to make a long-term commitment to one another.

Laudable as such sentiments are, that decision could backfire. In today's marriages, each partner can easily have invested years developing a sense of independence. **A sudden loss of financial control can be unsettling. For many women who marry after years of solo living, a better move might be to keep separate accounts and either pay bills jointly or add a joint account for that purpose.**

Just as they should discuss their spending, couples should review their debts. **If you are about to marry, be sure your partner knows of any debts you bring to the marriage, such as student loans or outstanding department store bills, and that you know what he owes. Agree early on about who will be responsible for repaying what.** If one of you is deeply in debt, resist the temptation to pile up yet more as you furnish your new home. Not only do you want to be sure you will not incur more than you can comfortably repay, you want to make certain that credit will be available for more important purchases such as a car.

Hang on to your own credit identity as well. If you already hold credit cards, don't automatically drop yours if accounts overlap. If you have taken your husband's name, just change the *last* name on your account. **"Mrs. John Smith" can be any woman married to your husband and her credit record is nothing more than an extension of his. "Mary Smith" will build a file of her own.** If any of your new cards is sent under your husband's first name, return it promptly. New accounts you open with your spouse are automatically reported under both names.

As with credit cards, women who adopt their spouse's surname must spread the news to their financial contacts along with social friends. Notify your personnel office as well as every bank, mutual fund, insurance company, and other financial organization with which you deal. Don't overlook professional groups, your alma mater, and the local motor vehicle bureau.

Add the Social Security Administration to your list to be sure that credit for your continued work will go to your account. Expect a new card from the agency with your new name but same number.

For all the benefits of doubling up on salaries, two incomes catapult couples into a higher tax bracket. More tax planning advice follows on page 171. For now, be sure that a hefty bill does not catch you blind-sided. **Calculate roughly how much tax you will owe come April. Chances are, it is more than the two of you would have paid if filing separate returns. Begin now to set aside the funds.**

If you already have a will, you must revise and update it. If you don't have one already, it is time to acquire one. **While laws vary by state, in many instances your husband will end up with only a third to a half of your estate unless your will provides otherwise.** The rest might go to your parents or other relatives. Likewise, you could end up with just a fraction of his belongings if he dies without a will.

At the same time, review your choice of beneficiary for all assets. If you have life insurance, a savings or retirement program or stock-purchase plan from your employer, or personal holdings such as an IRA or Keogh, you likely will want to name your husband beneficiary.

Writing a Contract

Hard as it is to contemplate dying now, it's even more difficult to imagine divorce. But the chances that your marriage will end are great. Fully one out of every two marriages ends in divorce; the average union lasts only seven years. Fifty percent of remarriages also end in divorce.

That trend means that **two-career couples should give serious consideration to exchanging contracts before they exchange vows.** The longer each has been working and the greater the assets, the more there is at stake. Contracts can be especially valuable if either partner enters the marriage with personal business interests, real-estate holdings, earning power, or other substantial assets or has children or other concerns from a previous marriage.

Women who plan to work to support a spouse while he finishes school, whether college, law school, or other professional education, should be especially watchful. For some, the sacrifice has boomeranged. Degree in hand, their husbands have left them with no claim to his burgeoning earnings and no comparable skills of their own.

Simply put, a premarital agreement is a contract between parties spelling out specific arrangements for their forthcoming marriage. (Less frequently, couples draw up such an agreement after the marriage takes place.) Such contracts can cover just about anything, with provisions ranging from religious instruction for children to whether one partner will relocate if the other receives a promising job offer. Most often, however, the focus is strictly financial and expresses the couple's intentions for dividing the property if the marriage ends in divorce or, in the case of second marriages, what will happen after one or both partners die.

Contracts can seem cold and decidedly unromantic, especially in the first blush of courtship. Indeed, drawing up a contract is even harder than writing a will; all of us concede that we will die one day, but few enter a marriage believing it will fail.

Yet **writing a premarital agreement has its benefits; essentially, a couple anticipates potential problems and resolves them.** Each partner knows where he or she stands. In the broader sense, too, the exercise encourages both individuals to discuss what they want and expect from the union. By bringing those concerns out into the open, it can actually help prolong the marriage.

Couples who still are hesitant should realize that by marrying at all they are accepting the terms of contracts that the state already has drawn up. The most common are state laws which entitle each spouse to a certain percentage of the estate if one partner dies, stipulate how ownership is determined (regardless of who paid for the property or who holds title), and set down the rights of both to financial support and property in the event of divorce.

In your situation, however, you may want your spouse to waive his rights to the pediatric practice you built in the years before you met. Or your fiancee may prefer that you give up your rights to certain assets so they will go to children from his first marriage upon his death. In some cases, you may want to wait and see. Many contracts allow for changes as the marriage endures; for instance, you might gradually increase the share of the less-monied spouse to fifty-fifty over several years.

So powerful are these documents, the best way to write one is with the help of a lawyer well versed in matrimonial law. Each of you should retain your own counsel to represent your interests.

FOR RICHER, FOR POORER: MESHING TWO MONEY PERSONALITIES

For most couples, the most formidable task is not merging two sets of books but meshing two money personalities. Whether you are a newlywed or a veteran of many years, your marriage deals with money in two ways—what is said on the surface and what is meant underneath.

On the surface, every couple must blend two different sets of incomes and goals into one charter for the union. Just as important, a husband and wife must address what amounts to a hidden agenda. **In every marriage, money concerns are governed by an unwritten contract—a collection of hopes and dreams, assumptions and expectations just as real as the vows they take. And in most marriages, problems are far more likely to stem from the hidden contract than the surface issues.**

The first thing each couple must decide is whether they want to mesh at all. When Steve and Julia married, they kept all their finances separate. Nothing, not even a joint checking account, bound them together. Every time they went to spend a major sum, the effort would founder on one disagreement or another. They could not even settle on a car. Julia wanted a costly European model that would last many years; Steve preferred to spend as little as possible.

The two had trouble overcoming their fear of throwing in their lot together as a couple. That can prove tougher still when one spouse has more assets than the other. Ellen inherited $45,000 from her grandmother after she and Daniel had been married two years. At first, her thrill of being a woman of independent means led her to put all the money into Treasury securities in her own name. When the couple had to pay taxes on that interest on their joint return, however, Daniel erupted. ''Are we married or not?'' he demanded. By her actions Ellen was saying, yes, but I'll be the rich one.

Keeping money separate not only can paralyze the day-to-day functioning of a relationship, as it did with Julia and Steve, it can diminish the sense of common goals and a common future, as Ellen found out.

This is not to say that all money should be pooled. But **before any serious money issues can be settled, every couple must first determine whether they want their commitment to the relationship to include their respective fortunes.** That done, the real hard work begins.

Money is a prime cause of friction in marriage. At times, the reason is simple: there is not enough to go around. A growing number of women today work because their incomes are needed to make ends meet. But even the poshest of salaries do not free partners from fights.

Squabbles can arise over anything—how much he spent on a suit, you on the health club, both of you on gifts, or who bears the blame of buying 500 shares of a health care stock that cannot take care of itself and now is worth less than a third of its original value.

Nowhere is blending two money personalities more difficult and more critical than in a marriage. Women lack the unquestioned authority which steels their power when dealing with children and the independence which serves as a buffer with parents. Unlike unmarried couples, spouses tend to think long-term, a fact which immeasurably increases the number of questions at issue. Joint decisions by nature imply compromise. And "compromise" is all too often another term for "fighting."

George and Cynthia moved from a New York City co-op to a suburban colonial last fall. As the forsythia in the backyard began to bloom, he suggested they consider hiring a gardener to take care of the property.

Cynthia was outraged by the thought of paying anyone $100 a month to cut the grass. After arguing for half an hour, George left to take a ride in the new car they had bought to drive to the train station.

To resolve this issue, and any other fight, both partners need to determine the real agenda. George may be looking ahead to hiring a gardener just as he remembers his father doing when he was young. Or, worried about mounting pressures at the office, he could be unwilling to spend the little free time he foresees on lawn work.

Cynthia, for her part, could be anxious about how much the couple already has spent to set up their new life-style—including the new car. And she may be concerned that the burgeoning overhead puts far more pressure on her to succeed at her job. Or part of her dream of suburban living may have included a windowbox of tumbling geraniums, and she fears a gardener would deny her that pleasure.

A thorough discussion of the deeper issues behind a money spat can often reveal a way to solve the problem. After pressing George to explain again the reasons he wanted a gardener, Cynthia discovered that he was jammed up at work but foresaw an unexpected commission that would offset the lawn care bills.

Cynthia still wasn't convinced. Her position points up another pitfall in meshing money styles: even when you understand your spouse's reasoning, you will not always agree.

The task of getting along is easiest when similar personali-

ties marry. Two Drivers can happily pursue independent investing dreams, each with a separate portfolio if they like. Two Nesters can build their wealth together, content to see seven European capitals in as many days and spend their other vacations at her parents' home in Florida.

But in money styles as with other traits, it seems all too often that opposites attract—and spend the rest of their lives trying to change one another. At its simplest, one partner may be a Reacher and want to spend, and the other a Nester longing to save.

When a woman who is a Nester marries a Reacher or a Driver, she often gets what she wants, but at a fearsome cost. Such women can gravitate easily to the role of compromiser. They value domestic tranquility over decision-making power.

Alice knows that Jim has always wanted to own a sports car. His longing is very real to her, as is her desire to see him happy. But she also badly wants to put away more money than they have been saving. The only way she sees out of the dilemma is to take the task of saving on herself. Alice buys all her clothes in discount outlets and bargain-hunts compulsively for appliances. Jim has a Porsche parked in the garage.

Stephanie found herself in the opposite situation. Her husband was so bent on wielding control that he demanded she account for every penny spent and even scrutinized the grocery store receipts. She followed Matt's dictates for three years while their nest egg doubled. One day, a week before the first vacation they had shared in that time, she stopped at the local department store on her lunch hour and charged $2,200 worth of clothes.

Stephanie's behavior was clearly retaliatory and sabotaged her husband's cash-building program. She may even have hurt herself in the process, since their long-term savings were sharply depleted. But at least her actions put the real issue—who decides and what is decided—on the table. Alice's approach is more rational, but it also may be more self-defeating. So long as she gives in every time, the couple will never come to an abiding understanding of their joint priorities.

Friction between two styles isn't always bad. With genuine commitment to one another, partners can learn from their differences. Every marriage from time to time needs a Nester to look at a potential investment and say, "What could go wrong here?" And Drivers often can spur more cautious spouses to field sensible risks. "I've been thinking about what you said about taking more risks with our IRA funds," one man told his wife weeks after a long discussion about their retirement goals. "Why don't we take half the money in each account and move it into a good stock fund?"

In fact, matched pairs often falter in financial planning because they reinforce one another's weaknesses rather than their strengths. It is hard to rebel against your mirror image. Either you do not see your behavior for what it is or you do but cannot bring yourself to reject your own approach.

The worst case is the Reacher/Reacher marriage. Sue and Kevin have been to every island in the Caribbean. Because most of their dinner parties include clients, they entertain lavishly and tell themselves they can write it off. Both hold IRAs but have no idea what they are paying. Neither is likely to call a halt to their spend-now-pay-later life-style.

But even a pair of Nesters can be tripped up by their cautious bent. Joan spends evenings clipping coupons for laundry detergent instead of reading the professional journals that will keep her ahead in her field. Jeffrey's suits lack the polish of the executive suite, but he figures the money he's saving will make up for a slightly shabby image. Their best friends bought a house last year and are fixing it up weekends. Neither Joan nor Jeffrey would consider taking on that kind of debt until they had saved $50,000. Yet their friends stand to make up for all Joan and Jeffrey's years of scrimping with a profit on the sale.

Who Calls the Shots?

For all the problems a couple can face meshing two money styles, the most fundamental issues go beyond personalities to roles.

All discussion of roles boils down to just two elements:

- who provides
- who decides

Providing is fairly straightforward when both spouses work. Each one contributes a salary.

Deciding is what all the fuss is about. Unlike her mother, who may have gone along on her mate's say-so, today's career woman believes her fiscal contribution "entitles" her to a say in decision-making. She feels perfectly comfortable, far more comfortable than her mother ever was, in saying, "Not on your life. *I* want a new car." Or a fur. Or more money in the bank.

Once upon a time, life was much simpler. The husband worked, made the money, and doled out a portion to his wife. A woman kept house, entertained, and raised the kids. As women have poured into the work force, however, much of this neat arrangement has given way. **If money is power, our paychecks were bound to upset the old balance.** Where once there were roles, however restrictive, now there are not even patterns.

The extra money a second earner brings in is often part of the problem. When partners marry later, each may already hold deeply entrenched money styles and resent anyone who disagrees. If you are married to a man whose mother did not work, your husband may harbor secret doubts about his abilities as a provider. Other men are more than willing to share the burden of breadwinner but may fear that what they win in extra income they will lose in affection and moral support.

Yet because so much of our culture has bred women to behave in a certain way, and men in another, it's all too easy to unwittingly fall back into the traditional roles we are scrambling to escape. **To a busy working woman juggling demands of a career, social life, and often children as well, the sudden appearance of a husband willing to take over such time-consuming chores as investigating IRAs or dealing with the broker can seem nothing less than a windfall.** Trained by society to be the decision-maker, a great many men quickly seize that role when offered.

Other couples upend the old order entirely. Some women insist they call the shots because they are desperately, deeply afraid that any other pattern will make them the equivalent of a doormat.

Sorting out the provider/decider conundrum takes work, but it is time well spent. Here are the steps to follow:

• **Recognize who you are.** The insights you gain from assessing your money style are critical. How do you feel about debt, saving, investing? What do you fear most? Being bereft in your old age? Looking back and saying you bypassed too much? Share your feelings with your mate.

• **Urge your spouse to do the same.** Identifying his money style may be the most important task you undertake. Turn back to the money personality quiz on page 9 and take it together.

Whatever you see, don't be judgmental—no matter how convinced you are that your style is better. Blasting a spouse as a "spendthrift" or "Scrooge" won't give him a sudden flash of insight and can cause him to dig in his heels.

• **Listen when he talks, even if you do not like what you hear.** Roger had no interest in building a fortune. Life was too short to work too hard or worry too much. A competent engineer, he passed up an offer from a rival firm that would have meant more money but demanded longer hours.

That decision bothered Katie. Since her girlhood, she felt secure in the knowledge that she could always turn to her parents for money if need be. She hoped to start a family soon and wanted to be able to support her children in style and leave a large inheritance. To do both would require far more income than the two now bring in. Both Katie and Roger need to consider the next rule of meshing money personalities:

• **Accept the fact that you will have to compromise.** No practice, however long-standing, is inviolate. You may have always paid your charge bills the day they arrive, just as your mother did. Or you may lavish large tips at restaurants, just as your father did. There is no right and wrong way to handle money issues. There is only the way that works for the people involved.

In a good relationship, conflicting needs are negotiated. Sometimes both parties compromise. If you want to buy a fur and your husband wants a trip to Japan, you might both agree to cut down on long-distance phone calls and after-work drinks to help save for both goals. Sometimes, too, one wins and the other loses. The latter is part of a healthy marriage so long as the same person does not always concede.

Compromise means addressing your weak spots. The fact that you have any is not easy to admit, but no two people can find complementary strengths in each other unless each is willing to recognize his or her own weaknesses. It is all too easy for a Reacher to tell her mate she is taking needed risks to build their joint financial security, and lose $5,000, or for a Nester to ridicule a husband who loses money in the stock market even though he makes far more than he drops.

• **Know what you have to work with.** This is not as easy as it sounds. Couples who have trouble agreeing on how to spend money usually need to draw up a budget together. Couples who disagree on how to invest should write down where all their assets lie right now, and compute the percentage each element represents.

• **Set goals.** Before you can agree on a common agenda, you must know what you want it to contain. Don't assume you know what your partner wants, or that he knows what you do. Even so simple a decision as how much to spend on a vacation can spark widely diverging opinions.

Like the goals you listed in Chapter 1, group them by time frames. The first are short-term—money for Christmas shopping or next summer's vacation. Mid-range goals include targets for the next three to five years—a new car, or $10,000 saved. Long-range goals encompass your lifetime concerns—college bills, a vacation home, retirement security.

• **Set an agenda for reaching those goals.** Put price tags and deadlines on your targets.

• **Consider separating some or all of your investment funds.** If each partner is strongly opposed to the other's ideas, it might be better to divide the wealth for a while. Keeping all the family's assets in a money fund will never please a Driver, and too much in aggressive stock plays will only make a Nester uncomfortable. The alternative—putting everything into middle-of-the-road investments—might not satisfy either.

One benefit to calling your own shots: you will gain valuable investment experience. Forget about playing with a paper portfolio now. If you want to learn how to manage money, you need to know how it *feels* to do it.

If you do split your funds, make one promise: No second guessing or "I told you so's." The one who loses the money will feel bad enough without the other's carping. And a non-complainer makes it more likely that he or she will win the same consideration in return.

Some women are almost incapable of asserting themselves in financial discussions. Their conciliatory ways stem not from a desire to avoid friction so much as to avoid responsibility. These women concede to their husbands all the tasks of meshing personalities—setting goals, choosing priorities, picking investments.

When they married, Louise was delighted to let Mark handle the books. After a brief discussion, they agreed that she would use her salary for household expenses, and he would cover the remaining expenses. Over the years, however, Louise regularly spent well beyond the cash in her account, splurging on parties and new furniture and using credit when she ran out of cash.

When she had thrown the couple $4,500 into debt, however,

Mark insisted that she handle the bill-paying for six weeks. Seeing firsthand where the money went helped Louise temper her spending impulses. But the real boost to her resolve was Mark's notice that she could not lean on him indefinitely.

In some instances, any attempts to mesh money styles can dissolve in a burst of frustration. Pacts are made and broken or are never even reached. In these cases, time is needed to determine the best course.

A husband and wife who are consistently unable to agree on money issues or reach a compromise may decide to end the marriage. But in most instances, compromises emerge because one or both partners begin to adopt some of the spouse's characteristics. Some Nesters, for instance, can accumulate enough money that they begin to feel comfortable with their partner's risk-taking ways. In other instances, the husband's personality might change. Many male Reachers become far more conservative when they hit their thirties, succeed in careers, or have children.

DUAL-INCOME BANKBOOK(S)

Money is the tangible reflection of the power each person has in the relationship. **The goal is to strike a tender balance between each partner's salary-providing power and his or her decision-making clout.** Couples should support the notion of a team—shown by pooling resources—along with the independence and sense of personal control reflected in separate accounts.

How this is structured is extremely important in fledgling relationships. But the physical division of funds becomes less important as the couple's trust in one another grows. The more secure they are in the relationship, the less they need separate accounts to prove their individuality. Indeed, in later years many couples find that they can shift their bookkeeping arrangements radically without altering the power balance.

The choices include:

• **Pooled accounts.** All for one and one for all. Each partner deposits his or her pay into a joint account, and each one has equal access. Such even-handedness emphasizes that the couple functions as one economic unit.

This works best when the couple's incomes are roughly equal and money styles the same. Both can feel that they are getting back roughly what they are giving and neither will sabotage the system. It is especially important to agree on major purchases jointly. If one partner consistently raids the account for his or her needs, and the other is losing out, the loser will ultimately rebel.

• **Separate accounts, expenses split equally.** Each person keeps money separately and antes up for joint expenses. Contributions are divided fifty-fifty, with each partner paying the same share regardless of pay. This underlines the independence of each spouse, but also can exacerbate strains. It is especially tough to implement if the incomes are far from equal.

• **Separate accounts, expenses split equitably.** Each partner's contribution reflects the proportion his or her income represents of the whole. This is the ideal way for the lower-earning partner to assert a measure of independence.

• **Separate accounts, expenses allocated by type.** She pays some of the joint bills, he pays others. This is potentially the trickiest way to slice the pie. For starters, many couples split expenses on outright sexist lines, with his money going for items like car maintenance and hers for groceries. Such divisions tend to perpetuate myths that assign one partner or another responsibility for what should be shared roles. And problems arise when food costs shoot up more sharply than gasoline bills, or vice versa.

The basics/extras division that many couples follow is also fraught with dangers. In such arrangements, the man's salary covers basic living expenses while the wife's is either banked or put toward luxuries like vacations.

The problems here are twofold. Either the second earner hogs all the psychological bonus points for the comfortable life-style both salaries provide, or she gives herself a free ride. Many a working wife still sees her contribution as voluntary and therefore extra, no matter how important her income is to the family's well-being. This explains how many Nesters can deal with their own paychecks like Reachers, spending lavishly on themselves, even as they are fiercely determined to save their *spouse's* funds.

- **Pooled and separate accounts.** By most measures, the best way to go. Each spouse operates his or her account to fund day-to-day expenses. In addition, the couple maintains joint spending and perhaps one joint savings account. The common pool can be kept deliberately small or consist of a large fund from which each draws a separate allowance. This arrangement commits to paper both the autonomy of each partner and their commitment to one another and a joint future.

Even a token amount in a separate account can be a valuable buttress to self-esteem. A woman needs such accounts for practical reasons as well. Emergencies otherwise can leave her strapped for cash. Many banks freeze joint accounts immediately if one owner dies. While you can try to close the account before the bank hears the news, you are hardly likely to feel like doing so. And separate accounts also protect a woman whose irate spouse tries to grab all the family's cash just before he files for divorce.

On the surface, none of this should be any different for the one couple in five in which the woman outearns her husband. And many couples look at money as just a means to buy a high-flying life-style, no matter who's paying. But problems often do arise—and either spouse can feel them. **A high-earning woman can feel used when she sees her hard-earned dollars go for a husband's set of golf clubs. Her lesser-paid spouse may resent her success, or feel he is not fulfilling his role as provider.** More than in other marriages, an accounting system that keeps funds separate and allocates joint expenses in proportion to income works best in such cases. Each spouse makes a contribution and can consider the ante fair.

Who actually handles the paperwork is the least important issue. But never foist the task on a reluctant bookkeeper. In some cases, it might be better to delegate the work to the more compulsive of the two partners, perhaps a Nester or the Driver, so it is sure to get done. **The critical point of any accounting system is to make certain *someone* keeps track of what's going on.** If both partners are writing checks on the same account, for instance, they need to confer regularly. Whatever arrangement you adopt, be sure both partners are completely familiar with the family's accounts.

Saving: Easier or Harder?

For many two-income couples, earning money is the easy part. Keeping it is another matter entirely. **With greater incomes comes the tendency to buy more things.** Dual-paycheck couples look at the heady numbers on their paychecks and conclude they can easily afford the fancy cars, exotic vacations, and other perks that make their hard work bearable. And their long hours on the job mean many luxuries take on the trappings of necessities: housekeepers, dinners out, deliveries. Indeed, the more money there is, the more a couple is likely to spend and the harder they find keeping track of it.

In an insidious way, many career women find that taking a husband undermines what was once a fairly staunch savings program. Many highly motivated women, for instance, forsook vacations or took only the shortest of trips to advance in their jobs. But while they didn't mind working weekends when they were singles, those weekends take on great importance when a husband complains that he never gets to see his wife.

Discipline is the key to making the most of two incomes. **Couples should resist the temptation to act as rich as they are. The wisest live a life-style that one income will provide and use the other to build wealth and financial independence.**

Taming Taxes

Much of a working couple's second paycheck can seem more promise than provision. Before they even see the extra income, the U.S. Government skims off its share. And for married couples, the take is high. First off the top come twin Social Security assessments. Then the IRS takes its cut.

Despite efforts by Congress to balance the tax burden, unmarried couples still hold a tax advantage over those who wed. They can report separate incomes, thereby earning themselves two separate, relatively lower, tax brackets. **Dual-income married couples, by contrast, tend to pay a higher rate of tax than they would if each had remained single.** The IRS piles the second salary on top of the first, pushing the couple into a much higher tax bracket. With the exception of a standard amount automatically free of taxes to every wage-earner and a small percentage of the lower-paid worker's income, every dollar of the second salary is taxed at the first earner's highest rate—or more.

Uncle Sam is not entirely stingy, however. Some couples may wrest a better deal if they file separate returns. That is true if one partner has hefty medical expenses or deductible expenses. An individual can write off unreimbursed medical costs that exceed 7½ percent of income. While your bills might not meet that threshold if you file jointly, it might be possible if you file separately. While separate returns are taxed at a higher rate, the couple's combined bill might be lower.

Marrying also stands to restrict the benefits you can reap from the working woman's best tax shelter, her IRA. The good news first: as long as you are working, you still can have an IRA, and the earnings in that account will compound tax-free. And if neither spouse is covered by a pension plan, then both partners of a working couple also can claim a deduction for up to $2,000 each year, no questions asked.

After that, the new rules are tricky. If *either* spouse is covered by a pension plan, the IRS looks at how much you pull in together to determine whether you can have the write-off and how much you can take.

A couple with adjusted gross incomes under $40,000 can still deduct the full $2,000 for each working individual. Under the new rules, however, married couples filing jointly with adjusted gross income over $50,000 are out of luck. *Neither* spouse can deduct an IRA contribution so long as either spouse qualifies for pension coverage. For the purposes of this law, you can't deduct the IRA contribution to reckon your adjusted gross income. A pension plan would include a Keogh, if one or the other spouse is self-employed, or any employer-sponsored plans such as a 401(k), profit-sharing, or stock bonus program as well as a conventional pension program. And even if you or your spouse are not yet vested, but only eligible to build benefits, the strict terms would apply.

Couples reporting between $40,000 and $50,000 may salvage a partial deduction. The new rules reduce the maximum $2,000 deduction by 20 percent of any income in that range. For instance, if a couple's income comes to $44,000, then each could deduct up to $1,200 for an IRA (20 percent of $4,000 is $800, which when subtracted from $2,000 leaves $1,200).

Assets: Pooling Portfolios

Two-career couples are often so busy working that they do not take time to make their money work for them. Others are willing to do so but cannot agree on the next steps. Essentially, they must update the plans each partner held as a single to reflect their joint needs and money styles.

To mesh two portfolios:

- Take a good look at what each partner already owns and **find the common denominators.** Both may hold CDs, for instance, and feel comfortable having part of their money tucked securely away. That represents one area of agreement.

• **Decide which investments you cannot live without** and which you could part with. Explain your feelings clearly to yourself and your partner, and hear the same from him. One woman believed strongly that true wealth was made through real estate, and wanted to buy her own home. Another valued her $10,000 Treasury bill because it represented the safest investment she could make—one backed by the full faith and authority of the U.S. Government. Such feelings should be respected in joint holdings.

• **Look at the final lists** and see how they fit together. If you have invested all of your IRA contributions in mutual stock funds, perhaps your spouse should channel his deposits into a money market fund or long-term CD. For safety's sake, be sure that no more than 20 percent to 25 percent of your combined lode is invested in any one investment, whether a stock or bank CD. The only exception is real estate, which often represents a disproportionate share of a young couple's assets.

• **Figure out what you need to add,** and split the responsibility for researching, buying, and monitoring the new investments.

• **Make sure the additions reflect your personalities.** It may be clear that your joint portfolios are lopsided in one direction or another, whether loaded with risky ventures or top-heavy in income-producing assets. In striking a new balance, make sure the new purchases suit both spouses' styles. The suggestions in Chapter 3 can help you choose.

Before she married John, Elizabeth balanced her holdings between super-safe and daredevil investments:

ELIZABETH'S ASSETS

Money market fund	30%
Bank CDs	10%
Aggressive growth mutual fund	50%
IRA	10%

Because she was single, she felt comfortable putting fully half her holdings at risk. And at her relatively low salary, she had little concern about the tax bills on the income from her safety-conscious bank assets.

Compare her portfolio with John's:

JOHN'S ASSETS

Money market fund	20%
High-yielding bond fund	30%
Growth stock mutual fund	50%

With the couple's growing tax bracket, John's income-producing investments are less appealing. Too much of the return will be siphoned off by Uncle Sam. At the same time, his portfolio is too heavily skewed to the short-term. He has not yet opened an IRA.

In reviewing their assets, both Elizabeth and John realized that their higher combined earnings were spinning them into a far higher tax bracket than either faced as singles. To cut their tax bills, they first considered a tax shelter. But like many couples, they found they needed to wait. Despite their six-figure income, they did not have the net worth needed to buy them.

To be sure that buyers can withstand the potential loss of dollars in such deals, shelter sponsors usually require a minimum net worth to participate—often $30,000 to $100,000, not including the value of personal belongings or home equity.

Even so, Elizabeth and John can take advantage of other vehicles. **One of the wisest moves for tax-pressed two-income couples is to shift money out of conventional income-producing assets, whose yield is taxed at ordinary income levels, and into investments such as stocks that offer little or no current income or tax-free deals such as municipal bonds that let them keep all of the return they pocket.**

Thus the couple sold John's high-yielding bond fund and did not renew either CD when they expired. They switched their cash holdings to a tax-free money fund and pumped some of their dollars into a REIT. And John got an additional tax shelter by opening an IRA.

Even though it paid no current income, John was uncomfortable with Elizabeth's investment in an aggressive stock fund. Many couples share his preference to adopt a somewhat more conservative investment stance after marriage. They replaced Elizabeth's fund with a pair of somewhat less speculative but still risk-oriented growth funds. To be sure, they must pay taxes on any profits they reap at ordinary income rates. But stocks offer them the chance to win a greater total return on long-term investments.

The redesigned portfolio:

THE COUPLE'S PORTFOLIO

Tax-free money fund	20%–30%
Growth stock fund	10%–20%
Second growth stock fund	10%–20%
REIT	10%–20%
Company retirement plans	10%–20%

Often, a couple must allocate assets while they save for a larger investment, such as their first home. That goal calls for a somewhat different approach. Since they must preserve capital for this venture, they should not be willing to take on much risk in the stock market. And depending on how quickly they plan to act, they may be well advised to keep the bulk of their assets in safe, high-paying investments they can easily convert to cash. In addition to a money market fund, they can beef up their yield with short-term Treasury securities, Ginnie Maes, or CDs.

A wise married woman also must make her investment decisions with one eye on the divorce courts. Although happily married now, it is not certain she still will be a few years hence. Her basic protections should include a separate checking account, assets in her own name, and a solid credit rating.

Without credit in your own name, you may find yourself scrambling to replace that granted to your husband if you become divorced or widowed or are suddenly faced with illness or another emergency and your spouse's rating is shaky.

If you and your husband now share accounts, check to be sure that payment activity is reported in your own first name, not "Mrs. John Smith." As you open new accounts, take out at least one on your own merits. A creditor cannot legally require your spouse to co-sign your application.

Should your husband die or the marriage dissolve, a creditor cannot close the account for that reason alone. But you can legally be asked to reapply on your own merits if credit was based on your husband's income. If lenders doubt your ability to repay, they then can refuse to extend the account.

Getting More from Insurance

One financial planning bonus two-career couples enjoy is twin sets of fringe benefits. By astutely comparing both employer's offerings, they often can put together an insurance package that outshines their coverage as singles.

If either partner receives free group medical coverage, for instance, he or she may be able to add the other as a dependent. **As long as you do not pocket more than you actually paid, that may enable you to collect up to 100 percent of the cost of medical bills.** Submit the bills first to the company that covers the patient through his or her job, known as the primary carrier. Then send a copy of the application and the insurer's statement to the second spouse's carrier to see if any shortfall is covered.

If it costs money to double-up coverage, compare the provisions of both policies carefully. Weigh the size of the deductibles ($100 is common) as well as the premium itself and the percentage that is reimbursed. See whether or not dental and vision care is included. Your efforts may show that both policies are roughly comparable and you can save money by dropping one. Or it may make sense to add the spouse with less generous coverage to the package carried by the other.

To make the most of your fringes, keep duplicate coverage at a minimum. Many employers are making it easy to do so by offering employees so-called flexible benefit, or cafeteria, plans. That means you can choose a package of benefits from among several options. Use that freedom to balance your spouse's fringes. If he has excellent medical coverage that automatically includes you, trade in your health plan for another fringe of more value to you, such as extra life or disability insurance.

If you name your spouse as a dependent on your health insurance policy and he waives his coverage at his job, or vice versa, check to see that the dependent spouse is still included under the disability policies carried by his or her employer.

If either spouse's paycheck is essential to pay the bills, that person needs life insurance. As long as each partner can survive financially without the other, however, you are likely to be better off using those funds for another purpose. The exception: homeowners. If one spouse would not be able to cover the mortgage alone, consider taking out additional term insurance to provide the funds to pay those bills if need be.

A New Look at Retirement and Estate Planning

Two-income couples also can have a real advantage over other families when it comes to retirement planning. Not only do their dual salaries offer money to put aside, but they may have twice as many opportunities to shelter their savings.

For starters, each spouse can open an IRA and contribute up to $2,000. Couples earning less than $50,000 can trim their tax bill and build for the future to boot. Up to that level of joint adjusted gross income, each of you can write off the full amount you contribute. **But even if a high combined income means you can't write off your pay-ins, most couples should still rank IRAs as important asset builders.** Such accounts still enjoy a significant financial advantage: earnings on the investment aren't taxed until you start withdrawals. That allows your nest egg to grow steadily because you are putting the full before-tax, rather than after-tax, value of your investment income to work. In addition, separate jobs commonly provide two corporate pension packages as well as deferred compensation, stock purchase, or profit-sharing plans and 401(k) programs. If you can take advantage of all of them, do so.

If your finances force you to choose, couples should first plow the maximum into the one that matches the greatest percentage of contributions. If one plan matches 100 percent of an employee's ante and another matches only 50 percent, as a general rule the more generous package should get the nod.

But that is not the whole story. Couples should compare the terms that govern when corporate contributions are given irrevocably to employees and the circumstances under which workers can borrow against their lode. At the same time, couples should take note of how any contributions are invested. Some plans limit investments to company stock. That might not be nearly as wise a choice as a program that allows holders to choose among stock, bond, and money market options and to switch among them as economic circumstances change.

Perhaps the sharpest departure from the concerns of the single-paycheck family occurs in the area of estate planning.

It should go without saying that you need a will. But an astonishing number of couples never get around to making one. Don't be among them. You need one, if only for your own protection.

If your husband dies without a will, you have no control over what you will receive or how much in taxes you will pay. The same is true if you die first. The surviving spouse automatically inherits all jointly held property and other assets such as life insurance in which he or she is named beneficiary. As for what's left, the laws differ in every state. Your children, children from his first marriage, or even his parents might get a cut—perhaps as much as two-thirds. That could be costly indeed, particularly if your spouse dies in a plane crash, for instance, and is awarded a large personal injury settlement. Even the relatively modest assets accumulated over a lifetime—life insurance, IRAs, pension payouts, a home—can swell into a tidy sum that would be taxed far more stiffly than you might think.

The most basic estate planning decisions involve how you hold property—in your name, his name, or jointly. Each form of ownership has different rules governing what happens to the property when one owner dies and how ownership can be transferred. **Each method has advantages and drawbacks.** Which is best for any one couple depends largely on how wealthy they are and what they would prefer happen to that wealth when they die.

The most common form of ownership among married couples goes by the formidable name of **joint tenancy with right of survivorship.** Under this structure, each owner, known as a tenant, holds an equal share of the property. When one dies, the other automatically inherits the remainder. If there are more than two owners, the share of the one who dies is divided equally among the remaining owners.

Tenancy in common is more flexible. The property is not divided equally among the owners but can be split in any way they choose. When a co-owner dies, her share does not automatically slip to her other partners but rather passes to whomever she names in her will, whether her Aunt Millie or best friend. If the co-owner dies without a will, the property passes according to state law. If you are happily married, you probably do not need such flexibility unless you and your spouse are buying property with outsiders such as family members, friends, or business associates.

The third way to hold property is available only to married couples in certain states: Arizona, California, Idaho, Louisiana,

Nevada, New Mexico, Texas and Washington. Known as **tenancy by the entirety,** it gives each owner an equal share in the asset and automatic inheritance of the other's share, with one important string attached: one owner cannot sell or give away his or her share without the permission of the other. This type of ownership offers the greatest degree of protection to each partner.

These neat divisions can be upended in community property states. If you live in one of them—Arizona, California, Idaho, Louisiana, Nevada, New Mexico, Texas and Washington—you will need legal help before making any specific plans.

Joint ownership is reassuring and convenient. By its very nature, it is an enduring symbol of a marital partnership in which resources are shared. Over the short term, joint ownership of assets like checking accounts allows both spouses to get at the money easily. Over the long term, jointly owned property will pass automatically to the other partner at death. That cuts the time and expenses entailed in settling a will.

But there are disadvantages of joint property that couples should weigh carefully. For one thing, sharing ownership with another erodes the control of each. That could become nettlesome if the marriage sours or if both partners disagree strongly on a particular course of action.

The older you get, and the greater your assets, the better off you are likely to be with separate as well as joint ownership.

Your strategy flows from an understanding of federal estate tax laws. Estate taxes are nothing more than a tax on the transfer of property. Under current law, you can give your husband your entire estate or he can give his to you free of any federal estate tax. That feature is known as the unlimited marital deduction. Every estate also can leave $600,000 to others tax free by virtue of a feature called the unified credit. It is that benefit that many well-heeled couples frequently waste.

To be sure, the idea of a quick, tax-free transfer of wealth is alluring. **But leaving all the family assets to one another in your wills could make for problems. Wise planning takes**

couples one step farther, to the time when the second spouse dies.

While the assets of the first partner can be handed over tax-free, the tax bite on the estate when the second spouse dies—typically, the wife, since women tend to outlive men—could be sharp. She has no sure-fire shelter equivalent to the marital deduction. Her estate could be saddled with a hefty tax bill, and her heirs settle for less. What's more, if there are no children, the family of the first spouse can lose out as well. When the second spouse dies, that person's family will ordinarily split the inheritance, leaving the kin of the first spouse empty-handed.

In deference to women's longevity, consider the problem from a man's point of view. A husband boasting a million-dollar estate might feel proud to enrich his wife at his death by willing all her assets to her. When she dies, however, she can only give a fraction of her holdings—$600,000—to their children and other loved ones tax-free. As a result, her estate would face a bill for more than $200,000 in federal taxes alone.

To prune the bill on the second estate, couples should consider setting up trusts. The idea is for each spouse to will to someone else—not one another—as much as possible in order to take full advantage of the unified credit. That amount ($600,000 in 1986 and thereafter) would be spirited into a trust for another beneficiary, and only the balance of the estate would go to the surviving spouse. That way, the first $600,000 is not taxed in either the first or the second spouse's estate.

This need not leave the survivor at a loss for money. Typically, all the earnings on the assets in the trust are given to the wife (or husband, should he outlive her) in her lifetime. Only when she dies would the principal pass to the beneficiary named in the first spouse's will. What's more, **several estate planning techniques can be put in place that allow the wife to raid the principal itself if she wishes.** While the details are complex, they broadly include the right to:

- withdraw the greater of $5,000 or 5 percent of principal each year;
- ask the trustee to give out more money;
- collect additional principal for any reason at the trustee's discretion, and
- serve as sole trustee.

As they pile up assets in their estates, couples should also keep an eye on which ones they hold jointly. It's best to limit them to those with little or no capital gains potential, such as CDs or money market funds, and own appreciating assets separately.

That is because of the way the zip in value is taxed. Say a stock you bought for $20,000 is worth $60,000 at your death. Holding the stock in joint name could prove costly. Regardless of who paid for it, the law would assume that you and your spouse each own half. That means that if your husband died, only half the property would be eligible for the special treatment accorded assets on the death of the owner—the figure used to calculate any profit on the sale of the asset is stepped up from the original purchase price to the value at death.

As a result, the IRS would deem the jointly held shares you now own in full to be worth $30,000 for tax reckoning purposes—or half the market value. If you sold those shares tomorrow, you would owe taxes on $30,000—the difference between the stepped-up cost and the market value. Had your spouse owned those shares outright, the value assigned for tax purposes would have been $60,000, and no tax would be due on the sale.

But taxes aren't everything. A couple might want to keep their home in joint name. For one thing, it's likely that the widow or widower would want to remain there for the short run at least. And the tax laws have a special provision covering capital gains taxes on houses that could help keep the tax tab low. Up to $125,000 in capital gains from the sale of your primary home is exempt from income taxes if you are over 55.

Aside from drawing up a carefully crafted will, perhaps

the single biggest step couples can take to cut their estate tax bills is to get each life insurance policy out of the owner's estate. Ordinarily, the value of life insurance payouts are lumped into the owner's taxable estate even though she never saw the money in her lifetime. (The beneficiary does not have to pay taxes on them, however.)

A trust can cut taxes in this instance, too. Couples can set up an irrevocable trust to own the policies and collect the proceeds. Properly done, that step takes the cash out of the owner's estate. Just as with the first trust discussed, the surviving partner can receive income from the proceeds during her lifetime and pass the principal to another heir at her death, keeping the value out of her taxable holdings as well.

This and other estate planning techniques are complicated. State laws play a major role in determining the most effective tax-fighting strategy. Be sure to work closely with an estate lawyer when you devise your plan.

RAISING CHILDREN—THE $232,000 FAMILY ADDITION

Parents of a squawling newborn dream of the time their child will sleep through the night. But long after 2:00 A.M. feedings are nothing but memories, bringing up baby can make for troubled sleep. Bankrolling the trek from diapers to diplomas grows more costly every year.

The new arithmetic of parenthood is giving many couples pause. By some estimates, it will cost as much as $232,000 to raise a child born in the early 1980s to age 17. That does not include college bills that threaten to exceed many couples' lifetime savings. Faced with such figures, a second income can be a necessity. These costs can loom just at the time when the couple takes a cut in income, if mothers take off time to be home or opt for part-time work. Even full-time working mothers face a heavy load.

Like newlyweds, new parents must rethink each element of their financial plan. Having someone totally dependent cuts the risks they can take, and the consequences turn up at every step: saving, investing, insurance, and retirement and estate planning. The need to retool is especially acute for women who put off having children into their thirties. These mothers are faced with the prospect of squeezing the formidable expenses of child rearing, college, and retirement planning into a few short years.

Saving

The pressures to spend more are enormous. Pampers alone are a major budget entry. Bills for toys, clothes, music lessons, and gym classes follow in short order.

Working parents need to fight their tendency to overindulge their children. Many women vow that they will keep the costs in line. But Nesters, Reachers, and Drivers alike tend to change their tune when baby makes three. Nothing, they find, is good enough for their child.

That yardstick should include their cash reserve. Unexpected expenses have a way of cropping up with toddlers and teenagers around. If three months' expenses was a safe cushion before Barbara, or Adam, or Kurt, then six months' is a safer bet now.

Taxes: Your Children Can Be Shelters

Fortunately, the children themselves can help parents get through all this. For one thing, the IRS offers working mothers a helping hand in paying their child-care costs. It allows a credit—a dollar-for-dollar reduction in your taxes—for child care expenses of up to $4,800. As long as you pay someone to watch a child under age 15 while you work, look for work, or attend school full-time, you are eligible for this break.

The credit is allotted on a sliding scale. Families with an income of $10,000 or less may claim a 30 percent credit on expenses of up to $2,400 for one child and up to $4,800 for two or more children. As income jumps to $28,000 or more, the credit declines steadily until it hits 20 percent of expenses. The maximum tax credit for one child at that level is $480 and $960 for two or more.

Help is not limited to formal day care, babysitters, and housekeepers. In many cases the cost of summer camp or after-hours school programs may qualify. You also can include money paid to a relative as long as that person is not your dependent. One caveat: you must do this on the books. You may be required to provide the Social Security number of the person caring for your child, and the IRS will make an effort to track down her return to make sure she is reporting the income.

This benefit pales in comparison to the breaks that await parents who make the best use of **a child's most priceless assets: a low marginal tax bracket and the time to take advantage of it.** By shifting money from their name to their child's, couples can shelter part of their highly taxed income.

The last dollars earned by every parent are taxed at the highest level. But a child owes no taxes at all on unearned income up to $500, and can pocket another $500 at her relatively low rate. The more a couple earns, and the higher their tax bracket, the greater the benefit from shifting funds to their offspring.

Two successful lawyers, Donna and Paul, are in the 35 percent tax bracket. Last year they gave their daughter a $10,000 CD that yields 10 percent a year. Ordinarily, the couple would have paid $350 in federal income taxes on those earnings. But their child, who can take advantage of this tax break, pays $55. That leaves almost $300 for the family.

Shifting income is useful no matter the age of your youngsters. But **the best time to begin building a college fund is as early as possible. That way, the funds can grow at the child's favored rate as your youngster does.** Whether couples do so or not, however, often depends on their money styles. Nesters are more than willing to add another goal to their list, while

Reachers and Drivers are more inclined to think they'll work it out later.

The easiest way to shift income to a child is under the **Uniform Gift to Minors Act.** As its name implies, this device allows parents to give funds to their offspring while keeping control until they come of age. Such accounts are opened in the child's name, with a trusted adult as custodian. The necessary forms are readily available at most banks, brokerage firms, and mutual funds. Parents need do little more than supply the child's Social Security number and a check. Each parent can give a child up to $10,000 a year without incurring any federal gift tax.

A custodian tends the kitty until the child comes of age—18, in most states. Parents should avoid this role; were they to die before the youngster received the money, it would be returned to and taxed in their estates.

The problem with gifts is that they are just that, and cannot be retrieved. That means the child will one day take control no matter what happens in the interim. For Nesters, that prospect can be threatening. They often fret that they will give away money they themselves might need one day. Drivers may hold no such qualms. Outright gifts satisfy their needs to be good providers and to see that their loved ones face a secure future. Even so, many fear losing control over the money lest their child lack the maturity to handle such funds.

There's another, equally serious problem with giving money to your child. **After the first $1,000 in low-tax income, any unearned income of a child under age 14 is taxed at *your* rate.** That means that you not only lose control over the money you gave, you lose some of the tax benefit of shifting income in the first place.

This can happen fairly quickly. Take the example above. In the first year, the child can pocket $1,000 in interest tax-free. But in the second year those earnings will themselves throw off income. If they also yield 10 percent, the child will pick up an extra $100 in interest that is taxable at her parents' bracket. And that interest will yield interest. Until she turns 14, all earnings over $1,000 would be taxed at her parent's rate.

That makes shifting income to a very young child a far from perfect option. Even so, to wait until age 14 to begin a college cache is to wait too long. **Most parents with small tots should aim to set aside at least $10,000 in each child's name—or whatever amount when invested conservatively would throw off roughly $1,000 in income. That way they can take advantage of the tax break on such savings without giving away so much that they jeopardize their own future.**

The older the child, the more sensible this strategy. For one thing, by the time your daughter is 10 or so, you have a fairly good idea of how responsible she will be when she comes into her kitty. For another, once she turns 14 all the income again will be taxed at her own bracket. And by putting the money in her name, you won't be tempted to raid the account for another purpose.

If your youngster is already at or near college age, your best bet might be to look into a **home equity loan.** Under the new tax law, you can write off all interest on home equity borrowing used for college bills, as long as the loan does not exceed the current value of your home. In addition, you might be able to borrow money tucked away in a **401(k)** program at an attractive rate.

To be taxed at the child's rates, none of these funds can be used to pay food, clothing, and other expenses parents legally are obligated to provide. In rare instances, that might even preclude using the money for college. Check the law in your state before taking any action.

Assets: On to College

As a rule, parents should invest their first college dollars conservatively. With these funds, as with all investments, too risky a stance could leave a child with nothing. That brings them to the fifth point in the chart on page 47. Until the youngster's earnings top $1,000, one wise course is to steer deposits into steady income-producing vehicles such as money market funds, bond funds, Treasury securities, and CDs.

Because they are available for small sums, zero coupon bonds are a popular investment for college-bound cash. These securities pay no interest; the return is the difference between the heavily discounted issuing price and the value at maturity. That means parents are spared the task of reinvesting the income as it is earned. The IRS knows this, but taxes the child each year anyway on how much she should have received. But unless a lot of money is involved, most children owe little or no tax at their low marginal rates. Zeroes, of course, lock in current rates for long periods of time. The lower interest rates dip, the less attractive they are to buy. Holders risk losing out if rates rebound.

Once the child becomes a full-fledged taxpayer, another consideration emerges. **As long as ample time remains before the bills arrive, parents with ambitious goals but limited means should consider swinging part of the child's assets into growth-oriented investments such as stock funds.** While this can be hard for security-conscious investors, they should consider whether they will ever reach their goal unless they make a shift.

While such moves are risky, they hold out a lucrative promise: growth stocks and mutual funds tend to pay out relatively little taxable income when your youngster is small, so you give up less in the short run to Uncle Sam. And they stand to have grown considerably by the time college bills arrive and an older child can pocket those profits at her own tax bracket.

Another investment that offers postponed payoffs is the trusty **U.S. savings bond.** Series EE bonds perform much like zero coupon bonds: they pay no current interest. Instead, you pay 50 percent of the face value and pocket the interest in a lump sum when you redeem the bond. There's no state and local tax due on those earnings, and investors can defer the federal income tax on the bond interest until they cash it in. Parents eyeing college bills can put these features to good use. Buy one or several for your child, deferring the tax on the interest until she turns 14. When she redeems the bond, she'll owe tax at her low bracket (perhaps no higher than 15 percent) instead of your higher one.

Simplest of all, parents can also build a college fund and cut taxes by keeping money in their own names in tax-advantaged investments. In addition to savings bonds and **municipal bonds,** insurance-based products can also fill the bill. As discussed below, most parents need to pump up their insurance coverage. If you have the extra cash to invest, you can look into buying **universal or variable life insurance** for this purpose. Part of the premium you pay for such policies, discussed in greater detail in Chapter 2, goes to build a sideline fund that is invested. The benefit: those earnings accumulate tax-free, hence grow faster than monies placed in taxable investments. While your child is young, you have the benefit of the life insurance coverage your premium dollar buys. When she nears college age, you can borrow against the burgeoning sideline fund at favorable terms. Alternatively, if you no longer need the coverage, you can cash in the policy.

The problem with both savings bonds and universal and variable life policies is the return they pay. Savings bonds offered a minimum of 7.5 percent in 1986 if held for at least five years. But that rate was liable to change. And universal and variable life policies in many cases offer low or no guaranteed returns. Helpful as their tax benefits are, the total return on these investments depends on the amount you clear. Be sure to compare their yields with other investments before you sign on.

As bills pile up for diapers and dartboards, many parents will find precious little cash left over to invest at all. That should prompt them to consider for their own portfolio the same steady-yielding securities they prize for their daughter's. **Even parents with substantial assets might well adopt a more**

conservative investing stance than in their childless years. With a long-term responsibility in tow, they should be loath to jeopardize their financial security.

New parents might even consider swapping some or all of their individual stock holdings for shares in mutual funds. Trying to balance the demands of two jobs with the incessant demands of toddlers often leaves little time to manage their personal affairs.

Insurance: Needed to Replace You

Insurance plays a special role for parents: it serves as a stand-in for themselves. **Most new parents should upgrade life insurance coverage.** Chances are, a surviving partner would not be able to manage on one salary.

In planning your life insurance needs, take into account the relative salaries of the parents. If one vastly outearns the other, the lower-paid spouse needs a great deal more insurance to guard against the loss of that income.

Children, by contrast, do not need life insurance at all. Many agents argue that buying a whole life policy for your daughter while she is young will lock in a low lifetime rate. While that may be true, she likely will have no need of insurance until she has children of her own, and all the premium dollars over the intervening years will be wasted. The same goes for the notion of buying a whole life policy for a child as a way to finance her college bills. The interest she will earn on the investment slice of the premiums is not as high as she might garner on other deals.

Retirement and Estates: Planning for Three

The birth of a child underscores the need to move swiftly to shore up your own security. The urgency of this task depends on your age when you become a mother. **Women who have children in their twenties get the costs of child rearing out of the way early in life.** When the last college bill is paid, they may be in their mid-forties, with another 20 years to save for a comfortable retirement.

Women who have children in their thirties or later, by contrast, will face staggering tuition bills just as they should be stepping up their old age savings. Older parents may not twist free from college costs until their mid-fifties, or later, with barely a decade left to save for retirement.

To avoid having to choose between their children's education and their own security, every couple should carefully rethink its retirement planning program. **With all the extra bills that children bring, it's tempting to slack off on far-away savings goals in favor of music or gymnastic lessons for the kids—or just a well-deserved vacation away from them. Don't do it.** Even if you can only channel a few thousand dollars a year into your retirement kitty, you will be grateful for those dollars later.

One of the best ways to pile up cash is through a 401(k) program, if either you or your spouse can join one at work. Because your contributions are subtracted from your pay, you don't even see the money. That means you're less likely to miss it, and certainly less likely to fritter it away. Try also to keep funding your IRAs steadily. Even if you do not get a write-off for your ante, the money still grows tax-free.

At the same time, mothers must make key changes in estate planning. Every mother hopes her child will enjoy a rich and full life. Ironically, as she contemplates her daughter's future she must contemplate her own, and take steps to provide for her child if she is gone. The most important task is to name a **guardian.**

If one parent dies, the other will automatically keep custody of the child. The problem arises when both die together, driving back from a dinner with clients or a vacation in the mountains. Unless you appoint a guardian, the courts will decide where and how your children will live.

In choosing a guardian, your first aim is simple: look for

someone who will raise your child as you would prefer. Women who started families later in life are more likely to turn to brothers or sisters or trusted friends than parents who might not be around. If you choose a couple so that your child will have both mother and father stand-ins, name just one of the two guardian in case their marriage falters. If you are not in regular touch with the person you selected, be sure to keep her informed of your child's development. Tell her where to find records of important information, such as allergies and medical treatment. Some parents also put together a memo discussing their preferences on such personal issues as drinking, dating, and sex roles.

If you have provided well, your offspring stand to inherit a substantial sum when you die. To manage those funds, parents should look for a candidate comfortable with money decisions and record-keeping. The person who oversees your child's fiscal welfare must know how far the legacy will stretch and how far it won't and how to make the most of the assets at hand. To protect the child's interests, courts often require guardians to submit detailed records and ask permission for major expenses. To avoid such red tape, consider setting up a trust to hold the property in the estate.

In some cases, the child's guardian may be well suited to serve as **trustee.** If not, a well-drawn agreement will leave her free to hire investment advisors. Or, parents may appoint a second individual to serve separately as trustee or as co-trustee with the guardian. If your sister is a banker, or if your lawyer or accountant is close to the family, they might be tapped to serve. Banks and trust companies also are traditional curators in such instances. Their talents lie more in preserving than growing wealth, however. And any professional trustee will charge a fee for such services, generally a percentage of the funds overseen.

Another benefit of establishing a trust is to ensure timely distribution of the funds. Should a child inherit money outright, she can take control of the assets when guardianship ends, usually at age 18, and use them as she wishes. A trust can delay that event or see that assets are transferred gradually over several years. To tend a large brood, a so-called sprinkling trust can give a trustee broad discretion to give each child what she needs. The eldest might pocket less, since most of her needs were paid for while her parents were alive. But a younger child could receive the bulk of the inheritance to pay her college bills.

SECOND MARRIAGES: FINANCING THE PAST, PRESENT, AND FUTURE

Women who are planning to marry a second time must look out for themselves. Nothing, not even the prospect of life with a man they love who will solve all their problems, should obscure that goal.

Not all of a woman's concerns are financial, of course. But a great many should be. **A second wife-to-be must find out precisely what she is getting into. One thing she is not getting is a clean slate.**

In second marriages, more so than in first unions, each partner has a past, and each past entails financial consequences. In some cases, for instance, so much of the prospective husband's income could already be earmarked for his first wife and family that little is left for his new bride. Put quite bluntly, she could end up supporting him, springing him from a one-room studio into a four-bedroom house. And all she'd get in return is another set of birthdays to track.

Among the key questions to be asked before any second marriage are those that pertain to the couple's joint financial future. What are each partner's income, assets, and debts? What resources will be shared? What will remain separate property? Who will be the beneficiary of his life insurance and medical coverage? What about retirement and pension rights? Will the couple retain separate bank accounts and credit cards? What are the terms for the purchase and sale of homes? If she stops working to have their child, how will she be compensated if there is a divorce?

If her prospective husband has also been divorced, add other questions to the list. What are his financial obligations to his ex-wife and children? How long will they continue? What about the routine expenses of visiting a child by a former marriage?

You'll need to decide how you want to manage your income and expenses. How you want to *own* property is another issue entirely, with far-reaching implications. For advice tailored to your individual circumstances, consult a local accountant or attorney.

If children are involved, the concerns are broader still. **No matter how fond your new husband might be of your children from a previous marriage, if you die they will not inherit any of his money—or the funds you build together in your new life—unless they are named in his will.**

If your new husband dies without a will, you might suffer as well. In some states, property he holds separately might be passed to his children, including any from a first marriage, regardless of your own needs. In other instances, his own offspring might be cut off.

The answers to these and other related questions should be committed to paper, and the couple in turn should discuss drawing up a prenuptial agreement along the lines discussed earlier in this chapter. In many cases, that is not necessary, so long as roles and expectations are clearly drawn. If they do decide to formalize their agreement, both partners should be sure to hire lawyers to represent their interests.

SEVEN

'TIL DIVORCE DO YOU PART

For better or worse, a working woman may be more likely to divorce precisely because of her career. Independent women can take care of themselves and they know it; they have the money and confidence that in past years came only through a spouse.

At the same time, the stress of managing two careers is enormous. All too many women end up juggling the roles of social secretary, interior decorator, general contractor, and housekeeper in addition to shouldering the demands of their career. Add to this children, shopping lists for sand toys or soccer uniforms, and bouts of flu, and the stress may be more than the marriage can bear.

But working women facing the end of their marriages can find themselves in a paradoxical situation. While their changing roles may have made it more likely that they will divorce, changes in family law that reflect those roles have made it less likely that they will profit financially—or even come out whole—from a split. In the past, for instance, the breadwinning husband continued to support a dependent wife if the couple parted ways. Today, working women who can support themselves often are simply left to do so.

That seems only fair. Yet the assets the couple built up together may not be dealt with in an equally even-handed fashion. **By and large, women walk away with less than half the family's pot. They are most likely to end up short-handed if they cannot agree on a settlement with their mates and end up in court.**

To come out even if not ahead, managing the financial terms of the split must be high among a divorcing woman's prime concerns. Yet divorce exerts almost unparalleled pressure on a person's life. Many experts peg it second in stress only to losing a husband to death. Natural as they are, when unrecognized and unchecked, emotions can do you in.

Sally doesn't see what all the fuss over divorce is about. It is quite clear to her that she would be better off without Rick, financially as well as emotionally. In his shuffle from job to job, he has barely matched her contribution to the marital till and last year spent the little they had managed to save on stereo equipment. Now that her divorce is imminent, she looks back at their six years together in anger, and she wants to get even. To her, the divorce is a way to right two wrongs—the marriage and the wasting.

Although she does not realize it, Sally's feelings are common among divorcing women. There is a strong pull at such times to reduce complex, tangled issues into simplicities and paint one another into roles. Even when the divorce is your idea, the temptation is to call your spouse the "bad guy."

The problem with blaming your partner is the logical consequence Sally feels: to want revenge. People in divorce are rarely generous, either emotionally or financially. Many are angry for what they see as wasting the best years of their lives, or failing to save the money that would be so handy now. If her husband is seeing another woman, the hurt and betrayal a wife feels can intensify such thoughts.

In many such cases, many women let their emotions rule their common sense. If husbands are remiss, the thinking goes, then they should pay. A woman who is angry with her spouse for initiating the split can fight to the end to keep his favorite reading chair. Or shares of stock. Or more. But that kind of thinking can backfire. Women who have held out for settlements more generous than their husbands could handle have been left with nothing in the end when courts awarded lower sums or recalcitrant ex-spouses never got around to paying.

Because of their ability to put money issues above all others, Reachers can often be among the best divorcing women: they want to maintain a comfortable life-style and see all too clearly how much money will be needed to do so.

By contrast, the very independence most Drivers demonstrate can keep them from demanding their rightful share of marital property. Confident in their ability to make their own way, they would rather settle matters and move on. They may forget to consider the consequences if their present positions disappear in an unexpected takeover or inflation suddenly jumps to double-digit levels.

Nesters are not likely to give up too much too soon. But they need to pay close watch lest they fail to put the proper value on the financial and emotional terms of the settlement. Such women can come to care more deeply about the armoire the two of them discovered in a back country shop than how they would be taxed if awarded the 1,000 shares of stock they bought together the same year. Given their deep need for financial security, promises of future income are especially tricky for Nesters to assess. The prospect of so many thousand dollars a year in pension benefits to commence in 20 or 30 years is in no way equal now to the sum of those payments, since they will not have the use of the money in the meantime, yet many women fail to make this critical calculation.

To Whom Can You Turn?

The best way to avoid these and other strategic mistakes is to hire a good lawyer. While it is possible to obtain a divorce without one, it is not recommended. Only if you and your husband both work and pull in similar salaries, and there are no assets, substantial debts, property, pension rights, or children and your marriage has been short and you never worked to help your spouse through school should you consider divorcing on your own.

As with any other candidate search, the wise manager shops around before she settles on a lawyer. Ask friends and relatives who have been through a divorce for nominees. Make appointments with at least three before you sign one on.

You are looking, first and foremost, for someone with whom you can talk. **Your lawyer is the pivot around which your settlement will be constructed. You will need to tell her everything of importance, and to feel comfortable doing so.** While personal recommendations and the attorney's reputation play an important role, so do your feelings. Trust your intuition in making your choice.

Beyond her attitude toward you, assess each lawyer's approach to the job. You need a person willing and able to go to court for you if she must. But that is not your first choice of tactics. **Steer clear of anyone who seems to be preparing for war conditions rather than peace talks.** A lawyer who broadcasts the "get him good and nail him to the wall" philosophy will find it hard to settle out of court.

An attorney's style includes her availability. Check how much time she will give your case and share with you if you call. A member of a large law firm, for instance, will have help from a paralegal as well as a less experienced associate. By delegating routine matters, she can help keep your fees down. But you should know what her role will be and whom you will deal with when.

As befits a business deal, one of your chief concerns is cost. **Get an estimate of what your case might entail.** Most lawyers charge by the hour. This can approach $250, or higher, depending on whom you talk to, how she practices, and where you live. Even a simple divorce can easily cost more than $1,000. In an acrimonious divorce, the tab can run well into five figures.

Before she begins to work on your case, many attorneys who bill by the hour charge a retainer, or up-front, fee. This can range from $2,500 to $10,000 or more, depending on your case. In this arrangement, your initial fees are deducted from that sum. Once your costs begin to exceed that level, you will be billed for expenses as they occur.

The retainer agreement should specify how charges will be determined and when and how they will be paid. It should note under what circumstances, if any, the fee would be raised or a refund issued. It also should note which additional expenses, such as photocopying and phone bills, you will be expected to pay.

The total can seem shockingly high. **However you arrange for billing, try to pay the tab yourself, even if you must borrow to do so.** The fact is that your spouse will offer a less generous settlement if he knows he must pay your legal bills, too. And you will hold greater clout with your own counsel if you control the purse strings.

If you cannot afford the fee that is quoted, ask if the lawyer will discount her rate or allow you to spread out payments over time. Tap the women's section of the local bar association for the names of attorneys who might be sympathetic.

If such tactics do not work and if borrowing would prove a severe burden, there are alternatives. Most states offer a federal or state-run legal aid program. Other services routinely provide discounted legal advice. Such operations will refer a client to a lawyer in her area who will handle the case for half the going rate or less.

In an effort to cut fees or friction, many couples consult divorce mediators before they turn to lawyers. These professionals are usually trained in social work, psychology, or law. Their goal is to bring about a negotiated settlement that forestalls an expensive, often emotionally divisive court battle.

Yet mediation is often a costly solution in its own right. Regardless of the agreement reached, each party must hire a lawyer to put it into legal language. And a woman is well advised to work with an attorney along the way.

Nesters and Drivers are often drawn to mediation in hopes that it will lessen tension or end the whole business more quickly. But **divorcing women should be aware of the difference in philosophy between mediators and lawyers. Mediators are paid to arrive at a compromise that reflects the interests of both parties. Lawyers are paid to advocate the solution that is best for their client.**

While mediation may in fact cut both trauma and costs, such savings are of little value if you compromise too much in order to arrive at an agreement. Keep your lawyer informed about the progress of negotiations, and be sure she reviews the final agreement thoroughly. If you have reservations about the outcome of any mediation, consider renegotiating the compact with an attorney.

By the sheer force of its impact on your life, an impending divorce often unleashes a basic change in a woman's money style. In many cases, the lack of knowledge about what lies ahead can make even a competent, self-sufficient manager reluctant to strike out and deal with the future. Women who confidently oversee a staff of sixteen or who have long played an equal role in their marriages may find themselves suddenly looking for someone to lean on. In some cases, they are not even aware of their impulses.

Rachel was determined to handle her divorce in a calm, businesslike fashion. Before settling on a lawyer, she canvassed all her friends and colleagues for advice and interviewed a total of eight.

That was the last of her take-charge moments. For months, she was unable to make a move without consulting her lawyer. When her apartment lease came up, she called to discuss whether she should renew. When she laid plans for her annual vacation, she called to ask whether she should treat herself to a bash or save her pennies. When her attorney asked her opinion on any aspect of the settlement, Rachel would say, "Do whatever you think best. That's why I hired you."

Angela went one step further. She wanted someone on her side at last, to refight her old battles with her spouse and produce a settlement that would right old wrongs. When her attorney counseled a more objective approach, Angela blew up at her as well. No matter the compromise offered, Angela nixed each one. In the end she refused to follow sound legal advice, and began looking for another attorney.

Both women fell into the yawning trap that awaits every divorcing woman, no matter how successful or self-confident. Rachel, normally a Driver, saw the strain weaken her resolve to keep charge over her life. Angela remained true to her nesting instincts, but became so extremely dependent she came to want more than any lawyer could ever give her. Neither woman ended up with the best settlement for her needs.

The best way to deal with the lawyer you hire is to respect her but also respect yourself. That means to get, and stay, involved but to keep matters on a professional plane. Keep a daily log of all conversations. Time the length of phone calls and visits. Hold social chitchat to a minimum and write down your questions before your conferences if that helps you conserve your time. Read all documents that she gives you. And never give away originals of your own.

Finding Out What's At Stake

If you have been actively involved in the money side of your marriage or if you have long been planning to leave, you may already be familiar with the financial underpinnings of your relationship. Otherwise, you must become so now.

To win the best settlement you can, you must know what is at stake. **Do not wait until the divorce is well under way to begin your search. Once bitterness sets in, it is not always easy to obtain any records, let alone honest ones.** Even the most upright of husbands can attempt to hide wealth so you will not take your share.

Your first task is to create a master list of the family's **assets.**

Begin with the value of your home if you have one. Ask a realtor for a written update of what it might fetch in today's market. Then catalogue its contents. Start by taking color pictures of every room, closet, and drawer to establish your life-style as well as the extent of your assets. **If you fear a bruising fight, consider removing personal property such as jewelry from your home or from a joint safe deposit box so your husband does not seize it.**

Turn next to your financial assets. Photocopy or take down pertinent details of all financial documents, from bankbooks, brokerage statements, IRAs and pension and stock option plans to life insurance policies. Get copies of your tax returns for the past five years and your husband's W-2 forms. Put all this in a safe place. If need be, rent your own safe deposit box.

Some of the most significant assets a family holds are intangible. Divorce settlements are increasingly coming to reflect that fact. The pension of a working spouse, for instance, can now be put on the table just like a bank account. So long as the divorce decree meets certain requirements, a woman can wrest a claim against her former husband's future pension. Consider retaining an accountant to size up its value. Even though you might not collect for years, such payments can nail down a valuable source of future income.

A woman's right to a share in the benefits from her husband's education is less well established. But one who worked to help put her spouse through school may win reimbursement for part of those costs or a cut of his future earnings.

Next tally the family's **debts.** These include any mortgage on your home as well as other loans, charge account bills, tax liabilities, and the like. If you helped your spouse pay off any debts he incurred prior to the marriage, be sure to alert your lawyer.

Your last task is to construct a record of **how much you spend.** Your settlement will reflect in part how much it costs you to live as you are living now. Make separate notes on any child care expenses to backstop any request you make for child support.

The Settlement

Once each has hired a lawyer, a couple draws up a separation agreement. By and large, it can contain whatever division of property and other assets the couple deems appropriate. At least 80 percent of all divorces are settled in this fashion. The remainder are thrashed out in court.

Avoid that route if you possibly can. For one thing, the cost of a full-fledged court battle could easily be triple that of a negotiated settlement. For another, you may go through it and still not get what you were looking for. Going to court makes the most sense when your husband and his lawyer are so obstinate you need a third party to bring an element of reason to the proceedings.

When couples cannot agree, a judge will impose an agreement. The danger there is that you have lost control. You may get what you conclude is a good deal. Or you may find a judge who says that because you can work you are entitled to very little.

If you are pressing for trial for emotional reasons, it is all but impossible that you will be satisfied. Marcia, for one, was furious with her husband for leaving. She rejected the settlement he proposed out-of-hand. In her eyes, Peter was not giving enough. ''When I think of how much money he's making, I could spit,'' she frets.

After wrangling for six months, her case ended up in court. The judge awarded her a more generous settlement, but her legal fees ate up much of the additional funds. And she is no less angry about Peter's past injustices. In her plans, Marcia overlooked a critical element in divorce proceedings: **when you go to court, you get more or less property than in the proposed settlement. You don't get the chance to prove you were right and he is wrong.**

In dividing the pot, the judge will follow practices set by state law.

A handful of states—California, Louisiana, and New Mexico—

go by rules that are known as **community property.** That means that all property is split fifty-fifty, regardless of who owns it legally.

The remaining states have adopted some version of a relatively new system known as **equitable distribution.** As its name implies, the theory behind this standard is that marital property—all family assets acquired during the marriage—is to be shared equitably, regardless of who holds title to it. (Inheritances and other property a spouse received as gifts before or during the marriage remain the property of that spouse.) In addition, Arizona, Idaho, Nevada, Texas, and Washington are community property states that allow their divorce courts to consider each spouse's contribution and need.

But **equitable does not necessarily mean equal.** Assets are rarely split fifty-fifty. The division is largely based on the length of the marriage, the relative incomes, and other contributions of both spouses and age and earning power of each.

Indeed, under a system of equitable distribution, a working woman's earning power assumes the status of a major asset in the marriage and a major liability to her settlement prospects. **The better a woman can support herself, and the less property accumulated over the marriage, the less she will end up with.**

For most women, in fact, support is becoming a thing of the past. Traditionally, a woman could count on collecting alimony until she remarried or her ex-husband died. But now, the very word alimony has given way to the term maintenance.

Payments, such as they are, generally are given only to help a woman get back on her feet financially. Such sums tend to be earmarked for further schooling or other training that will enable her to work and support herself. **In the vast majority of cases, maintenance checks are for a small amount and a short time, perhaps as little as two to three years. If you already hold a good job, you likely will collect nothing. If you make more than your spouse, you stand to pay out alimony.**

To divorce successfully in equitable distribution states, therefore, strategy is crucial. Since maintenance is rare, a working woman should concentrate on walking away with the greatest amount of property she can claim. A woman whose earning power is weak, however, might try for a cash settlement so she can go back to school.

Before agreeing to any settlement, women should be sure it guarantees the greatest protections possible. The specific provisions, of course, will reflect your individual circumstances. And by and large, your lawyer will offer the wisest counsel here. But discuss your concerns thoroughly. The following questions should serve as a starting point:

• **What are the tax consequences of the settlement?** The time to plan for tax savings is during negotiations. Be sure to go over the tax impact of any agreement with an accountant or other tax pro.

A key consideration in any settlement is who is taxed as a result. To decide, the IRS focuses on the purpose of any payments you receive from your former spouse (or pay to him, if that is the case).

The tax law pits separating spouses against one another. **Alimony payments can be deducted from the taxable income of the payer; child support payments cannot.** Not surprisingly, the paying partner prefers to hand over alimony. Recipients, however, have just the opposite stake. They must report any alimony as income on their 1040, but child support comes tax-free.

New provisions of the tax law tighten the definition of what qualifies for the alimony tax break. If the amount in question is more than $10,000 a year, payments must be in cash (not property) in consistent amounts over at least six years. That makes it less likely that your spouse can disguise child support payments, which tend to decrease as a child becomes self-supporting, as alimony to win the tax benefit. It may also encourage him to try to negotiate smaller child support payments at the outset.

At bottom, a divorcing woman's interest is in pocketing the largest after-tax income possible. To see what either party will get, the couple should look at each spouse's future marginal tax rates. If your spouse has smaller income or has sheltered much of it, you may be in a higher tax bracket than he. In that case, you might prefer to collect payments that are not considered alimony in order to avoid paying tax on those sums. If your husband can give you more if he labels the check alimony, you might be better off structuring the settlement along those lines.

In many ways, however, you are better off receiving a lump sum than continuing payments, no matter what they are called. Promises of support often evaporate—and with them, all signs of your ex. With a lump sum, however, you need not rely on your former husband's integrity. But as with alimony, there can be a tax pitfall in accepting certain payouts now.

Either spouse can give the other any amount of property with no immediate tax consequences. But if an asset transferred to you has appreciated, you will be responsible for paying the capital gains tax when you sell. Say you received stock worth $50,000 that was bought for $10,000. You will owe tax on the gain—in this case, $40,000—when it is sold. If you are in the 28 percent tax bracket, you would owe fully $11,200 on the sale. That means the real value of any appreciated property to you is much less than might at first appear.

While the legal fees for a divorce are not deductible, funds spent for tax advice on these and other issues may prove to be valuable write-offs. So long as you itemize, you can deduct any expenses for tax advice, financial advice, and miscellaneous expenses that exceed 2 percent of your adjusted gross income. Turn back to Chapter 4 for a complete listing of those that qualify. To play it safe, ask your lawyer to break out any tax-related services as a separate item on her bill.

- **Who is responsible for debts?** If you hold any joint credit cards with your husband, you are legally responsible along with him for repayment of the full amount of those debts. That also is true for any loans you may have co-signed as well as any income taxes owed for the last year of your marriage if you file a joint return.

• **What happens if inflation resurges?** The settlement may seem comfortable now, but inflation will diminish its value. Will that money be enough to see you through the years ahead? One protection is to link any maintenance checks to the cost-of-living index or to include a flat yearly increase. The longer you will be receiving payments, the more important this feature is.

• **What happens if your ex-husband's salary rises sharply?** Unless there is a preset agreement, you would not share in his good fortune if he wins a major promotion. An escalation clause tied to his income would increase your payments as his earning power rises.

• **Who pays for extraordinary items?** Many successful women are content to give up any claim to a former husband's support. But they give no thought to the consequences if they become unemployed or are disabled. If they do not hold or are not given substantial assets at the time of divorce, such women should consider a clause mandating support if they are out of work in the future.

Children can also run up enormous bills. Some are impossible to foresee. What if your daughter needs braces or special education? Others, like college expenses, are predictable but far off. Some couples agree to pay according to their ability when the time comes; others include specific arrangements as part of the settlement.

• **What happens if your former spouse does not pay?** Your agreement should provide for a penalty if payments fall more than a certain number of days behind. And it should stipulate that he will be liable for all legal costs if he breaches the agreement and you are forced to take him to court.

• **What happens if he dies?** As long as you are depending on your former spouse for income, whether for yourself or your children, you must be protected against the loss of that sum. Be sure that the settlement includes adequate insurance on his life, with you named as beneficiary and your children, if any, named to collect if you have died. And check to see that he is carrying enough disability insurance that he can continue to provide income even if he cannot earn it. The agreement also should provide that you are given copies of any pertinent policies so you can verify that payments are maintained.

Once the agreement is signed, get a copy and keep it in a safe place.

SINGLE AGAIN

A woman rebuilding her financial plan after a divorce may find that few of her needs have changed—or that most of her old concerns have been supplanted by far different, and more pressing, issues. The impact depends on the terms under which the marriage ended.

A young woman who divorced early in the game may find her money concerns much the same as they were when she was single. A woman whose marriage lasted longer and who built up many of her assets together with her spouse needs to look closely at how many of those assets she retained.

As long as they take measured steps to hold on to their new riches, those who pocketed a juicy settlement stand to see out their lives in good financial form. They are the rare ones. **Most working women divorcing now will find that they have lost a fair chunk of the property and other holdings they worked so hard to accumulate, and may well find themselves falling behind compared with their single friends.**

But that shortfall can be more than made up by what they have gained in experience. Singed by her settlement and chastened by the sight of a marriage shattered, the luckiest will live her lifetime braced by the knowledge that she can rely on only herself.

Saving: Playing It Safe

On your own again, the best approach is conservative. **Until you have a firm grip on how much it costs you to live alone and on what you plan to do next, aim to spend as little as possible.**

Some women don't have to be told to save. For Nesters, a divorce can represent the ultimate calamity—the prospect of losing the financial security they thought was in the bag. Washed over with fear, they may in fact overreact. The outlook need not be dire. As long as they are working and independent, most women stand to make their way just fine, if not on quite as grand a scale as their former situation afforded.

Any threat to their standard of living, however, can sorely strain Reachers. Many blindly refuse to concede that life has changed and that they must scale back their expectations. Although her husband's position as a corporate lawyer paid three times her salary as a market researcher, and her settlement was small, Debbie insisted on living just as she always had before Bill left, taking cabs and buying only the most expensive cuts of meat. To spruce up her image at the office now that she is single again, she scooped up four new outfits at the town's poshest boutique.

She, like many other born-again singles, justifies her spending as needed expenses or harmless ways to pick up her spirits. Of course, one new dress is no threat in most cases. But unless you are bringing in a handsome salary and already have salted a nest egg away, draw the line at a new wardrobe.

Taken together, the loss of a husband and a life-style can undermine any woman's equilibrium. A few are so shattered by the prospect that nothing is good enough any more. Such women complain bitterly about every aspect of the divorce. They lambaste their spouse, his lawyer, their lawyer. So overwhelmed are they by the changes they face, they cannot decide how to deal with any them. They put off decisions, even important ones, like whether to take out more life insurance. Their most intense feelings concern money and the beautiful things they will have to give up.

Katharine lived well. Her husband inherited a large sum of money when he turned 25 and earned a six-figure salary in his own right at a prestigious investment banking firm. Over the years, she came to feel entitled to the luxuries his money provided. Indeed, she soft-pedaled her own career ambitions because the extra income never seemed to amount to much.

Facing divorce, Katharine does not know what to do. She is reluctant to consider stepping up her commitment to her job. And there's no way she is willing to scale down her expectations. She also cannot walk through a department store without buying a present for herself.

Any woman who fools herself into thinking that nothing has changed after divorce will regret it later. Unless your divorce has left your bankroll precisely where it would have been had you remained single, *and* you are comfortable in that spot, you need to examine your spending patterns to be sure that they are in line with your situation now.

Closely tied to your ability to spend is your credit rating. **For starters, be sure to sever all ties to your spouse.** If you held any joint accounts, notify each lender that you are divorcing and will not be responsible for purchases made after a certain date.

It is illegal for lenders to close your account simply because your marriage has ended. As long as you are working, in fact, your income should entitle you to credit in your own right. Ask the lender to transfer any jointly held cards to your name alone. The lender may do so willingly or ask you to reapply.

If you file again, you are not required to list as income any alimony or child-support payments you receive. But if you need them to qualify, be prepared to show a steady payment record. If you are turned down, look for a bank that will extend credit provided you open a collateral or sideline account backing the credit line. In such cases, the bank can seize the money in the account if you default on the charge payments.

Taxes: Time to Recalculate

Because no tax is withheld on maintenance, although maintenance is taxable income, check with your accountant to see if you must pay estimated taxes. If so, payments are due in April, June, September, and January. Be sure to take into account all monies from your former husband. His outlays for life insurance to benefit you or payments made directly to doctors, landlords, and others can be considered taxable income.

While your tax status ultimately will change, you must keep an eye on the calendar. Unless a decree of divorce was issued by December 31, a couple is considered married for the entire year, even though they may have been separated and living apart. As such they can file either joint or separate returns. Both parties should compute their tax bills under both filing methods, and negotiate the best arrangement. If there is no agreement, file using the single tables. You can always amend your return to file jointly later.

Once your divorce is final, you will return to the ''single'' slot in the tax tables. That may result in a somewhat lower tab than you paid as a member of a high-powered two-income couple or it may boost your bill. Calculate your potential liability now so that you are not dealt a surprise come April.

Assets: Wait Before You Act

Your first months reeling from the shock of a divorce are no time to make serious investment decisions. **A new single's first concern is to preserve her assets without making long-term commitments.** Over the short run, the best place for all her funds, whether maintenance checks or a lump sum settlement, is a money market fund.

Some divorcing women will need to supplement their salaries

with income from their investments. Yet if they have a relatively small nest egg which must tide them over into retirement, their task now is delicate. They must strike a careful balance between squeezing income from their funds and ensuring a measure of future growth. Throwing all their assets into income-producing ventures would mean that their principal would cease to grow, and over the long run would stand to lose value.

Your first step is to boost the size of your emergency fund. **Without a husband's salary as safety net, you need to move swiftly to create your own. Aim to stash three to six months' expenses in easy-access investments.** To boost the yield you collect, put just one to two months' worth in a money market fund and the rest in CDs coming due within six months.

One good way to deploy your remaining income-oriented assets is to buy CDs in staggered yields. Resist the temptation to tie up a large chunk in one asset. While a given rate might seem sky-high today, it could prove meager if inflation—and interest rates—heat up.

Some part of your assets should be channeled into holdings that aim for capital growth. In addition to stocks, real estate has long proved an asset whose value paces inflation. If you do not have a home of your own or would like to participate more in this market, you might consider buying shares in a REIT, or real estate investment trust.

With the trauma of divorce still fresh, many women find they do not want to have to spend a lot of time on their investments. Mutual funds are good solutions in such cases. If you are not yet fifty and can support yourself, select one or two funds that seek solid capital appreciation. If you are older, push more into growth-and-income or income funds, and steer clear of aggressive or highly speculative offerings.

A newly divorced woman's portfolio might take on this look:

TENDING TO $100,000 OR LESS

Money market funds	10%–25%
Bank CDs or other income-producing investments	10%–40%
Stock mutual fund	5%–15%
Second stock mutual fund	5%–15%
REIT or real estate	5%–20%

Women who have pocketed a settlement worth more than $100,000 have greater opportunities as well as greater challenges. They should consider those funds the bedrock of their retirement security. However lush their settlement appears, it should be tended carefully. Few women can expect a similar windfall to replace it if squandered.

Just as with a smaller nest egg, women must weigh the income they might garner against the profit they could gain through wise investments. In this case, **a larger lode gives divorcing women the leeway to put somewhat more emphasis on capital growth.** For a woman whose earning power also is high, taxes may play a pivotal role in allocating assets. Pumping too much taxable income from her portfolio would only increase her bill to Uncle Sam.

A $100,000-plus portfolio should be widely diversified among investments. For growth, tap a range of growth, in aggressive growth mutual funds as well as individual common stocks. Give thought to forays into both real estate and gold as inflation hedges. If tax-sheltered income seems appropriate, consider tax-free money funds or municipal bonds.

One mix might include:

MANAGING A $100,000-PLUS NEST EGG

Money market funds (tax-free if warranted)	10%–20%
Growth stock mutual fund	10%–20%
Aggressive growth fund	0%–10%
Quality common stocks	0%–10%
Municipal bond trusts	10%–20%
Real estate (home, REITs, limited partnerships)	10%–40%
Gold	0%–5%
Speculative plays (options, margin)	0%–5%

Insurance: Putting Yourself First

For most two-income couples, a second salary serves as an insurance policy of sorts. Without that backstop, a newly single woman should rethink every phase of her insurance coverage.

Many women often are awarded the house as part of a divorce settlement. A fire or other loss to the property might threaten to wipe out a single woman's bankbook. Most women should consider adding a rider to their homeowner's policy that would pay the full costs of repairing or replacing the home and its contents.

Then, new singles must protect themselves. **Disability insurance is now the most important policy you can hold.** Depending on the size of your cash reserve, you may want to slice the waiting period on any policy you now own (that is, shorten the period between the onset of disability and the initiation of payments) or pile on more coverage. If you have no children, you likely will not need life insurance. But be sure to remove your husband as beneficiary on any policies at work, as well as on IRAs or corporate benefits such as deferred compensation or profit-sharing.

Take care of the health of your health insurance, too. As long as you are working, your employer's policy should be enough. But if part of your settlement includes a return to school, you will need to pick up coverage elsewhere.

The first place to look is to your ex-husband. Although many corporate plans say a spouse's coverage ends when the marriage does, he may be able to negotiate another arrangement. Most policies, for instance, allow workers to "convert" a spouse's coverage to an independent policy and a new law requires many companies to extend such coverage for up to three years at the employee's expense if asked. In such instances, the policy will cover pre-existing conditions—a boon if you have a chronic illness. Don't delay. Usually this must be done within six months after the divorce.

Your ex may suggest that he simply keep news of the divorce and submit your bills as usual. While that practice is widespread, it is not wise. If the insurer finds out, it could refuse to pay.

Retirement and Estate Planning: On Your Own Again

If you do not remarry, you will once again be solely responsible for your old-age security. Be sure to take full advantage of IRAs and any corporate benefit programs that allow you to salt away retirement funds.

Working women qualify for Social Security benefits by virtue of their own careers, of course. In some cases, however, they may pocket bigger checks by opting for the benefits they can claim as a wife. Even if you divorce, you often retain the right to your wifely benefit. Because the rules governing such situations are complex, you should review your choices with your local Social Security office.

As long as you do not remarry while your former spouse is living, you are eligible to collect Social Security benefits as a divorced spouse when you retire. What's more, once you turn 62, you can collect based on your husband's earning record, even if he is still working, as long as you were married for at least 10 years and have been divorced for two. If your former spouse dies, you are entitled to a widow's benefit as early as age 60.

You may decide to marry again. In that case, your benefits as a spouse would end. The exception: if your ex-husband has died, your payments likely would continue.

If you have not yet done so, revise your will.

A GAME PLAN FOR SINGLE MOTHERS

Single mothers ought to have more of everything—more emergency reserves, more insurance, more investments, a bigger house. In fact, the only things most have "more" of are more bills and more worries. In many cases, single mothers have become the nation's new poor.

Saving: Better Than Buying New Toys

Most divorcing women win custody of their children, and with that a daunting burden of support. A few also win promises of a husband's help in paying those bills. All too often, however, the father skips out. In 1981, only 47 percent of women awarded child support were paid the full amount by their former partners. Many women chasing down errant husbands found they had moved out of state, spurned court-ordered appearances, or simply disappeared. While efforts are under way to enlist state governments in the battle to force payment of child support dollars, the outlook for such tactics remains hazy.

That leaves most mothers on their own. **While children can be a tremendous source of joy and solace in the months and years following a divorce, they can also be the pressure behind a mother's biggest money mistake—failing to save money.**

When Veronica's marriage ended, she won custody of her two sons, aged four and seven. Determined that their lives should be as much like their friends' as possible, she sees that the boys take music lessons and attend a local camp each summer. Says she, "They don't have a father. I don't want them to miss out on the rest of life, too."

Veronica and countless single mothers are letting guilt over ending their marriages spawn unwise financial decisions. Worried that their children will suffer because they messed up, such women try to provide more for their offspring than is realistic or necessary. **Overly generous mothers may be giving children advantages now, but they threaten to hand over a far greater disadvantage later—a mother who cannot support herself in her old age.**

For most of the 5.9 million women raising children under age 18 alone, saving will never be easy. They must choose priorities ruthlessly and cut spending to the bone. Much of the advice for Reachers in Chapter 3 can prove valuable to them now. Make a budget, stick to it, and include some amount for savings every month, no matter how small. The important thing to realize: money in the bank is just as real a way of showing love as tickets to a local ball game.

Taxes: Help from Uncle Sam

As long as you are supporting your children, Uncle Sam will give you a hand. If you pay more than half the costs of support, you can calculate your federal income tax using the special head-of-household tax tables. These rates fall somewhat between the more costly single tabs and those reserved for married couples.

What's more, the tax law has been changed to give a tax break to any parent who makes a home for a child. Since 1985, if your child lives with you for more than six months out of the year, you can claim an exemption—in 1987, $1,900—for each child on your federal tax return, even if your former spouse provides most of her financial support. And even if you do not claim the dependency, you can write off any medical bills you pay.

After providing a home, the single biggest expense of a working mother probably is child care. Tax benefits can offset some of these costs, too. As long as you pay someone to take care of your youngster so you can work, you are entitled to the child care credit outlined in Chapter 5. Hard-pressed working women who hold down two jobs in order to make ends meet are entitled to yet another break. You can deduct the costs of travel between the first and second job.

Assets: Play It Safe

If you are lucky enough to have a good job, good home help, and a good divorce settlement, you may well have a lot of money to position. In that case, take your cue from the portfolios outlined above or in the chapter devoted to a single woman's concerns. **If you are like most single mothers, however, the question of how to allocate your assets might more aptly be phrased: "What assets?"** Women who barely manage to pay the bills simply don't have much in the bank.

With less money in hand, the most important assets a single mother can harness are time and her child's low tax bracket. Any dollar you set aside now is more valuable than one saved next year, for the interest it earns will earn interest as well in the years ahead.

As they do build up assets, single mothers should follow the basic portfolio-building steps outlined in Chapter 4. But there is one important exception. **Once a cash reserve is logged, independent singles usually are wise to take some fairly risky moves to try to build capital. By and large, single mothers cannot afford to do so.** Their money is simply too precious to risk chancing on speculative investments. They should funnel most of their holdings into safety-first investments. Any risks they do take should be prudent. Because they offer wide diversification, mutual funds can present an appealing option.

Insurance, Retirement, and Estate Planning

Single mothers tend to slight themselves when it comes to looking ahead. But **harsh as it sounds, it is a mistake to let your children take priority over providing for your own security.** Whatever it takes, strive to salt away at least $1,000 in an IRA each year. Notch the full $2,000 if you can. Should your employer offer a 401(k) or other benefit program that matches money you save, take advantage of it. Such efforts are especially important for older mothers who lack the cushion of time. If they had children in their thirties, they will be in their fifties when college bills hit, precisely the time when it is most important to pump up their own retirement kitty.

To protect your children in case you do not get that far, make sure you hold enough life insurance to pay for their support and much of their college expenses without you. A term policy is your best bet. Be sure it is renewable. Check, too, whether your employer's disability coverage is generous enough to support your children as well as yourself if you cannot work. If not, buy more.

A will is essential. In essence, you are planning not for your death but for your child's life. If you have offspring under age 18, it is vital to name a guardian to care for them if you are not around. If their father is still alive and sees them regularly, he often is the best choice. If that arrangement troubles you, you can name whomever you wish to serve as guardian. That preference would not necessarily be respected, however. If he wanted custody, your ex-husband could challenge the will in court. Many judges are reluctant to deny a father his parental rights, even if you have remarried and your child is now much closer to her stepfather.

EIGHT

GROWING OLDER: YOUR BEST YEARS

"I'm growing old."

She may be turning 40, 50, or 60. Whatever her age, every woman one day wakes to the realization that she is fast becoming closer to 70 than 20.

While it may be emotionally healthier not to think of yourself as an "age" at all, that approach won't do much for your bankroll. Women whose years are piling up find a new set of financial dictates springing from their place at midlife.

THE MIDDLE YEARS

Critical choices loom. Many of a woman's lifelong goals—educating her children, buying a second home—are close at hand and her abiding concern, retirement, is not that far behind. Yet even if she has not put in place the measures to meet those goals, time is still on her side. Provided she moves swiftly now, prudent steps can mean the difference between getting along and just getting by.

For many women in their 40's and 50's, their peak earning years lie just ahead. They have survived the hectic, demanding 30's and 40's—and prospered. Countless others find themselves free for the first time from the demands of child-rearing and are launching satisfying careers. With a woman's life expectancy growing, she can look ahead to many fruitful decades.

Beating the Retirement Clock

Married or single, laying plans for a comfortable retirement takes on overriding importance. The name of the game: beat the clock. You need to pin down old-age security before you stop working and can no longer take meaningful steps.

Few of us want our life-style to change upon retirement, except perhaps for the better. **When you chart how much you would like to have when you no longer are working, guess high.** Once you retire, certain expenses, such as commuting costs and pantyhose, will decline. But increased medical bills stand to more than make up for such savings.

As a rule, a working woman should aim to replace a minimum of 65 percent to 75 percent of her salary when she packs up her desk. If you have modest interests, you might settle for a smaller sum. But don't sell yourself short. Your post-retirement years may hold out your first chance to travel extensively, for instance, or to pursue interests long shunted aside in favor of building a career. More important, **your cache will likely have to last a long time. Our lives are stretching out. If she makes it to age 65 in the year 2000, a woman will have a 40 percent chance of living into her nineties. If she turns 65 in 2010, her odds of living that long are fifty-fifty.**

To make any sensible attempt to direct your retirement planning efforts, **you need to put numbers on two goals—what you want to live on and how much you must have saved to produce it.** Both calculations involve guesswork, for you must also try to calculate how inflation will balloon your income needs and how swiftly your own savings can grow to keep pace.

As you pencil down figures, be sure that your assumptions for inflation and appreciation are in sync. If you assume the cost of living will skip ahead by about 5 percent a year in the next decades, it is unrealistic to expect that your own assets will mushroom by 12 percent annually. That would require a nearly flawless hand at picking fairly risky investments year after year. It is more realistic to expect to garner returns roughly 2 percent to 3 percent over the rate of inflation over the long run.

The table on the next page will help you calculate the amounts you need. Brace yourself. The numbers will be staggering. Even if inflation continues to amble along at a relatively docile rate, the sum you seek mounts steadily. Assuming the cost of living rises just 5 percent a year, any target you set doubles in fourteen years. A woman who is 45 now might seek an annual income of $40,000 in twenty years. If inflation runs at 5 percent a year over those years, she would need 2.653 times that sum to enjoy the same income at that time. That comes to $106,120.

To get this money, you will tap three sources. Take time now to size up what each might provide:

• **Social Security.** No matter what your age, Social Security is designed to replace a part, but only a part, of the income you earn. Your precise benefit depends on how long you have worked, your age at retirement, and whether you can boost your take by trading on a spouse's earnings record. At age 65, a working wife can collect either the benefit she has earned or half that of her husband's, whichever is greater. The chart on page 225 shows the maximum payouts now envisioned.

To safeguard your check, be sure to oversee what the Social Security Administration is recording for you. Errors creep in regularly, and the agency may refuse to fix them after more than three years have passed.

Keeping tabs is simple. Your local Social Security office can provide a form (SSA-7004) to request a report of the earnings

TABLE 8.1

Sizing Up Inflation

To figure how much a dollar will be worth down the road, find the number of years until you need a given sum in the left-hand column. Then locate the rate of inflation you expect across the top. Multiply the sum you seek by the number in the column where the two points intersect. The result is how much you will need at that date to equal your goal in today's prices.

Number of years	Average Annual Rate of Inflation											
	3%	4%	5%	6%	7%	8%	9%	10%	12%	14%	16%	18%
1	1.030	1.040	1.050	1.060	1.070	1.080	1.090	1.100	1.120	1.140	1.160	1.180
3	1.093	1.125	1.158	1.191	1.225	1.260	1.295	1.331	1.405	1.482	1.561	1.643
5	1.159	1.217	1.276	1.338	1.403	1.469	1.539	1.611	1.762	1.925	2.100	2.288
7	1.230	1.316	1.407	1.504	1.606	1.714	1.828	1.949	2.211	2.502	2.826	3.186
8	1.267	1.369	1.478	1.594	1.718	1.851	1.993	2.144	2.476	2.853	3.278	3.759
10	1.344	1.480	1.629	1.791	1.967	2.159	2.367	2.594	3.106	3.707	4.441	5.234
15	1.558	1.801	2.079	2.397	2.759	3.172	3.643	4.177	5.474	7.138	9.266	11.974
20	1.806	2.191	2.653	3.207	3.870	4.661	5.604	6.728	9.646	13.743	19.461	27.393
25	2.094	2.666	3.386	4.292	5.427	6.849	8.623	10.835	17.000	26.462	40.874	62.669
30	2.427	3.243	4.322	5.744	7.612	10.063	13.268	17.449	29.960	50.950	85.850	143.370

TABLE 8.2

What Social Security Might Pay

If you reach retirement age in...	Your Annual Benefit (in 1986 dollars) Average earner (earning $17,493 in 1986)*	Maximum earner (earning $42,000 in 1986)*
1987	$ 6,994	$ 9,295
1990	7,298	9,867
1995	7,725	10,708
2000	8,295	11,923
2005	8,913	13,257
2010	9,574	14,645
2015	10,284	16,014
2020	11,049	17,261
2025	11,870	18,550

*Social Security benefits are based on your earnings over your working lifetime, not just your last year's pay. This chart assumes that you retire at age 65 having earned at either the average or maximum level over your entire career.

SOURCE: Social Security Administration

credited to your account. Don't be alarmed if the figures seem low. The numbers do not indicate how much you earned but rather the base on which Social Security tax was levied.

In looking ahead, keep in mind that some of your Social Security benefits may be taxable. Whether that would be true for you and if so precisely how much you would owe is a complicated formula now, and may well change many times before you retire. But the trend is clearly toward taxing part of the take of well-heeled retirees. Under current rules, tax will apply if your taxable income plus any tax-free income you earn plus half your Social Security benefit together come to $25,000 or more. For married couples filing jointly, the figure is $32,000. Half the amount over those ceilings or half your Social Security benefit—whichever is less—then is subject to tax at your regular rates.

• **Pension Plans.** If you are now or someday will be vested in your company's retirement plan, your benefit will be tied to your pay over the years and how long you have worked. Your personnel office can tell you whether you are guaranteed a pension now or how long you have to work to win one. It also can give you a rough idea of what your checks might come to, although a fat raise or enviable promotion could change matters. A working wife should ask her spouse to size up his own plan and find out what would happen to her if he were to die.

The problem, of course, is that many working women have jumped from job to job to further their careers. In the process, they have set back, if not eliminated, their chances of collecting any pension at all from their employers.

• **Your Assets.** That means that your own savings are likely to provide a great deal of your post-retirement income. **While you are working you *must* use your paychecks to acquire assets that will form the base of your future financial security.** At retirement you will take back those assets and convert them to income again.

To see how well your current pool of savings can support you, turn again to the table on page 224. It will help you to guess how much your funds on hand will total when you go to use them. Say you have put $50,000 aside. If you assumed a 5 percent rate of inflation earlier, you might figure that with skillful but fairly cautious steps you could earn 8 percent on those funds in the decades ahead. In twenty years, your hoard would swell to $233,050.

Then, consider how much income you could squeeze from your coffers. Since you likely will be leery of putting that money at risk in your retirement years, you might plan on finding investments that also yield 8 percent. That means your holdings would throw off $18,644 a year.

To supplement your private savings, of course, you also will be cashing in on any other retirement savings programs you hold. The table on page 90 will show what you might expect your IRA to be worth. Add to that any funds you've managed to salt away in Keogh, 401(k), profit-sharing, or other corporate programs for a clearer picture of what your assets might total. Convert those sums to annual income figures as well. Be sure to allow for taxes. Many people automatically assume their tax brackets will be significantly lower at retirement. But if you have done a good job saving, that will not necessarily be the case.

Add the income your own funds would generate to what you expect from Social Security and a pension program. Then take a hard look. How does that figure compare with the $106,120 you seek?

Chances are, you will fall short. After all, to be able to spend more than $100,000 a year when your salary is zip is an audacious goal. And you've not yet had the benefit of the many years of paychecks ahead to work toward achieving it. Even so, to bridge that shortfall, you must begin to act now.

Unavoidably, you need to save more money. The older you grow, the greater the percentage of your income you can afford to—and should—salt away. Press to channel at least 15 percent of gross income toward savings now.

Older women often can free up more cash to save by trimming back on their life insurance. If your children are grown, or you already have set aside enough to pay for their schooling if you die, you can feel free to drop some coverage.

Just as important as saving more money is the need to make the most of the opportunities you have. Calculations you have made underscore the critical role a pension—any pension—can play in securing your retirement years. If you are considering a job change, your pension prospects take on greater importance. On one hand, a fatter paycheck could free you to save more money. Even so, it may make sense to hold off another year or two if by doing so you can nail down a payout from your current employer.

Consider the situation carefully. If you do decide to make a move, look closely at your new employer's pension offerings. It often is possible to cut a deal that makes up for some or all of the benefits you were on the brink of winning at your old job.

Burgeoning salaries also free a woman to take better advantage of the perks that accompany them. To make your savings work as hard as possible, make the maximum use of any program, such as a **401(k)**, that allows you to salt away pre-tax dollars. Like many highly valued employees, Roxanne was awarded a $12,000 bonus by her boss last year. If she doesn't need the cash to live on and her company offers a deferred compensation plan, she should give top priority to shuttling her windfall there. The move would not only cut her taxes, but will build her retirement stash.

The second broad way to boost your assets is to pump more income from the cash you have. The 2 percent to 3 percent margin over the rate of inflation you calculated earlier is certainly doable. **You can also take more risks with some or all of your savings to try to squeeze out yet more capital. Whether or how much to do so is a highly individual decision. By taking on risks you also take on the possibility that you will blow—not billow—the nest egg you have built.**

Yet for most women, the middle years are precisely the time to take this chance. A thousand dollars now represents a much smaller slice of your income and assets than when you were younger, and any losses are far easier to recoup. **In the seven stages of an investor's life, you are likely approaching the time when your portfolio balance can swing furthest to the right, and reflect the greatest assumption of risk you ever will shoulder. In fact, for most working women, these years represent their last chance to take big risks for big gains.** As they approach retirement, all women will gradually edge their portfolios back into a more cautious configuration.

Most working women in their prime earning years can feel comfortable steering at least half their assets into risky investments. The younger, wealthier, and gutsier you are, the greater this percentage can be. Yet even the most gun-shy of Nesters needs to carefully weigh her own situation here. Make no mistake, shrinking from any risk at all will mean that she settles for less.

At the same time, highly paid professionals need to be particularly watchful lest their efforts are undermined by the IRS. As your salary balloons, dodging the tax man likewise takes on growing importance in your plans.

With a greater net worth and income to their names, many women may find themselves seeking out **tax shelters** for the first time. To be on the safe side, move into such deals only if you hold CDs, stocks, and other investments worth at least $50,000 over and above the value of your home and car. And plan to do without any funds from your investment for a long time, perhaps forever. Many tax shelters run for ten years or more. Cashing out in the interim can be costly. And the risk is that you will not get any of your money back at all.

Tax shelters come in two varieties. So-called **private placements** are the more aggressive strain. Best suited for investors in the highest brackets, they offer the lushest write-offs on your investment. The ante can be sizeable. As private deals, the pools are small, and members often must kick in at least $20,000 or more.

Public partnerships, as the name implies, are open to many more investors. The crowds mean that your initial contribution can be as little as $2,000 to $5,000 a unit. Such deals tend to be structured more conservatively, and offer smaller write-offs than private plans.

As a result, they offer plusses for investors on two fronts: by and large they are safer, and they are viewed with a more beneficent eye by the IRS. In recent years, the tax agency has singled out tax shelters for sharp scrutiny. It aims to disallow any where the tax benefits far outweigh the economic benefits. The relatively less venturesome public placements are more likely to pass muster.

Even so, potential tax shelter investors must be wary. Be sure to run any scheme by a tax professional. As a limited partner, you will be allowed a share in the economic and tax benefits of the business you invest in—whether real estate, oil and gas drilling, research and development, or the like. That may allow you to deduct a measure of its real or paper losses, as well as other tax breaks.

Still, **tax shelters are not the panaceas they once were. The new tax law has rewritten shelter rules so that it is more difficult to benefit from them.**

For starters, many existing shelters cut your taxes by throwing off losses in the early years which investors used to shelter their regular income such as wages, salary, or dividends. No more. **The new law aims to limit deductions for losses from investments in which you do not take an active management role, called "passive" losses, to the amount of income you collect from similar investments.** To protect existing shelter investments, the restrictions are being phased in over five years, beginning in 1987. In addition, by eliminating the lower tax rate for capital gains, investors now must pay taxes at ordinary rates on any profit they ultimately pocket when they sell the shelter investment.

But the news is not all bad. You can take advantage of those losses over the short run if you also invest in shelters that throw off current income. That would include all-cash real estate limited partnerships. And any paper losses you do not take right away needn't go to waste. You can stockpile them indefinitely until you can use them against any profit you make when you sell out.

Now more than ever, tax shelters are not for everyone. **If you are in the market for a shelter, examine it first for its before-tax yield and make the opportunity for tax savings a secondary consideration.** Shelters whose principal values were to generate tax losses are no longer viable, but those with underlying economic value can still prove useful financial planning tools.

Since you are delegating all management powers to the shelter's sponsor, investigate that person's track record before making any shelter investment. Be sure that person has experience in similar ventures. In the best deals, the sponsor has an interest in the project as well. Also check into the fees and sales commissions you will be charged.

In some programs, investors are required to put up funds over a series of years. Be sure you can afford to make the payments you promise now that deductible losses are harder to come by. And in some instances, tax shelters can spark unexpected costs in other ways as well. Certain tax shelter deductions must be taken into account when computing your taxes. If they are great enough, you may have to pay a penalty tax of sorts under the so-called alternative minimum tax rules. That could knock out some of the benefits you were counting on. Check with your tax pro to make sure.

Owning your own home remains one of the most accessible shelters of all. If part of your financial plan includes buying a larger one, consider taking out one of the increasingly popular fifteen-year mortgages. Not only will you pony up less overall, you will have paid off your home by the time you retire. Parents who are looking to bankroll a child's college education also can use the income-shifting techniques outlined in Chapter 5 to whittle down their tax bills.

A woman who is taking on heavy risk now might distribute her holdings in this fashion:

AN AGGRESSIVE PORTFOLIO

Money market fund (tax-free, if appropriate)	5%–10%
Growth stock fund	20%–40%
Aggressive growth stock fund	10%–20%
Real estate	20%–30%
Limited partnership, muncipal bonds, or other tax shelter program	0%–20%
Bond or income fund	10%–20%

Of course, there are caveats. If you are in sight of reaching your long-term goals without taking on excessive risk, think twice before taking on highly risky moves or making long-term commitments of the sort that shelters entail. After all, high-powered portfolios can be hit with heavy losses, and if you do not need to run that risk, you might not wish to do so.

But most women aren't in this position. And it is the latter conundrum that Reachers often must confront now. Years of carefree living may have left them with precious little in the bank to take risks with. **If you are eyeing your retirement prospects with a faint edge of panic, sit tight.** While you must take steps to improve the prognosis, they do not include a free-wheeling risk-taking program that is just as likely to lose your capital as grow it.

Your first emphasis, in fact, should be on the other end of the ledger: saving. **If you lack the capital to work with now, then you must run flat out to accumulate it. Cut back on spending, hard. Be ruthless in your priorities.** Aim to save between 20 percent and 25 percent of your pretax income. Consider moonlighting or launching a sideline business to supplement your earnings, or bargain aggressively for salary and other perks in the years ahead. Look carefully at the corporate benefits you merit at your job. Any opportunity you have to tuck away tax-free funds must be prized. And consider the fact that you may end up working longer than you might prefer to build your holdings.

When you go to take risks, by all means hedge your bets. Buy mutual funds, not individual stocks, to reduce the chance that one bad pick will blow out your base. Consider dividing your assets among several funds to further guard against a crippling loss.

If you have not done so yet, be sure to draw up a will. The discussions in Chapters 5 and 6 should help you focus your thoughts. Women who dutifully discharged this task years ago should be sure the document still reflects their needs. Even as simple a change as moving to another state may mean that revisions are in order.

Parenting Your Parents

For many women, duty includes the role of daughter. As older Americans are living longer than they ever imagined, and inflation and illness have eaten away at the value of their savings, many women find themselves planning not just for themselves but for their parents.

Figuring out how much help is needed is a matter of paper and pencil. **Just as you projected your future retirement budget, you must evaluate your parents' present one.** Expenses and aspirations are very individual, of course. But depending on their life-style and expectations, many families face a shortfall.

It is in covering this gap that planning techniques can prove useful. For purposes of strategy, parents are no different than children now. Both can be dependents, and both are likely to be in lower tax brackets than you. This means that one of the most effective ways to package your aid is by giving money away outright, so that the interest on the money it earns is taxed at their relatively low bracket. If you can afford to give a larger sum, so that your parents can live off the income it throws off and save the principal, you need not lose the money altogether. You can give the money to your parents in a trust with the understanding that it will come back to your children upon your parents' death. While you may have to pay gift tax on part of the transfer, this arrangement makes sure the funds stay in your family.

Many women don't have the extra cash to give away, even if only temporarily. In that case they can consider borrowing it. If they borrow against their homes, interest on the loan, of course, is tax-deductible. And if your bracket is high, it may well cost you less to borrow to help than to give away after-tax money outright.

The vast majority of the elderly still live in independent homes. Often they are house-rich but cash-poor. Parents can take out second mortgages or home equity loans (discussed in

Chapter 9) but may not be able to pay the interest on those loans.

There is another choice. A growing number of programs known as **reverse mortgages** allow persons over age 62 to tap the equity built up in their homes. As the name implies, the owners are not borrowing money to buy the house but rather in effect to sell it. The lender agrees to extend a loan based on the property's value. It will pay out that money in a lump sum or, more likely, in monthly checks over the owner's life, depending on her life expectancy. Not a penny must be repaid unless she sells the home. When she dies, title goes to the lender, who sells the house and uses the proceeds to repay the loan. Payments are guaranteed for the owner's lifetime, and if she dies before receiving all the money due from the loan, her heirs will receive the difference.

The tricky part concerns who is entitled to the profit if, as is likely, the home appreciates after the deal is signed. In most cases, the lender is. If the owner wishes to pass on some of the appreciation to her heirs, she can put up only a percentage of the house for the loan, but she will receive less overall.

Women who take over the bulk of a parent's support find their efforts blessed by Uncle Sam. Any child who provides more than half of a parent's support may claim each as a dependent so long as his or her annual income (not counting Social Security payments and municipal bond interest) is less than the exemption allowance ($1,900 in 1987). If you are sharing this burden with brothers and sisters, and none of you contributes more than half, you may take turns claiming the dependency exemption provided you contributed more than 10 percent of the cost of support during the year in question.

Even if her parents are hale and financially secure, a daughter is well advised to grow familiar with their financial affairs. Many parents, of course, are reluctant to reveal such matters. But a frank discussion can ease the stress of handling their estate at their death and, more important, can ensure that their own wishes will be carried out. **If your parents simply do not**

want to talk about money, they can help immensely merely by committing the outline to paper. No dollar amounts are necessary.

The highlights include:

- **Their will.** If they do not have one, of course, you should encourage them to write one. If they do, note its location and the names, addresses, and phone numbers of the lawyer who wrote it and the executor it names. Where to find any special funeral instructions or other last wishes.
- **Safe deposit box.** Location, owners, contents.
- **Key records.** Social Security numbers of both parents. Location of birth and marriage certificates, divorce papers, military records.
- **Money advisors.** Names, addresses, and phone numbers of their insurance agent, banker, stockbroker, accountant, real estate agent, attorney, financial planner, and benefits officer with current or previous employers.
- **Assets.** Bank accounts, stocks, bonds, annuities, and the like as well as the names, addresses, and phone numbers of the institutions involved. Include all major items of property, as well as the location of title, deed, and loan or mortgage papers for homes, cars, cemetery lots. Note in whose name property is held.
- **Debts.** All credit cards held. Any sums owed on or borrowed against your parents' home, car, life insurance policies, and such. Names and addresses of those who owe them money.
- **Insurance.** Name of issuer, policy number, date and amount of coverage. Don't overlook policies that might pay off the debt on such big-ticket items as homes and cars upon the death of the borrower.
- **Other benefits.** Any pension, profit-sharing, insurance or other proceeds from a parent's current or previous employers or professional, fraternal, or military service organization or union. Health insurance may pay some bills if death was the result of illness or accident.

• **Taxes.** Where to find tax records for at least the previous five years. If one of your parents owns a business, note partners, if any, and names, addresses, and phone numbers of its attorneys and accountants. Location of business records.

If nothing threatens now, your parents might consider ways to protect themselves in the event they cannot care for themselves. One way is to grant you the **power of attorney,** or the ability to act on their behalf. A more elaborate but often useful tack is to draw up a trust, generally called a **living trust.** Depending on your concerns, there are many variations. The common aim is to transfer income, property, or other assets to a child or trusted other. That ensures that their wishes will be respected even if they are incapacitated. And it can also help keep assets in the family if a serious illness or need for extensive nursing care threatens to deplete their savings.

POST-55 PLANNING

Women who are facing retirement in a decade or less must begin their final swing toward that goal. To position yourself, you must undertake a broad, long-term program to whittle down your exposure to risk and put in place the income stream that will finance your way.

The reason to start now is to retain control. Timing this effort is as important as any other step you have taken thus far.

When you hit 65, or retirement age, you will in all likelihood want the bulk of your assets redeployed into income-producing investments. If you have adopted a relatively aggressive investing stance at midlife, that move will represent the single biggest shift in your portfolio in your lifetime.

To make this shift without undoing all the benefits of your planning thus far means that you will need to cash in your holdings judiciously as opportunities unfold. No woman can count on the Dow to set a record on the day of her retirement bash. Since most business cycles last several years, a wise woman sets aside several years to implement her shift.

If you will need all of your money on a specific date, consider liquidating your investments in equal segments over the four years or so before retirement. That approach would tend to even out your luck. Chances are that you will garner top dollar on at least some of your investments.

On the other hand, you might try to manage the process more actively. In that case, look for chances to cash out winning positions when the stock market is healthy. If you sense that it is about to spiral down, and your own retirement years lie just ahead, consider stepping up your redeployment program. View any money that you keep in growth investments as cash that you will not want to touch right away.

If you have put off starting an IRA or have just returned to the work force, don't automatically rule out opening one now. Even women who stand to pocket a solid pension when they retire should hedge their bets. If you are laid off, fired, or grow ill and are forced to retire before you reach age 65, you may end up with far less than you expected. The only way to be absolutely certain of retirement security is to build it yourself.

Even at this late date, your own efforts can still pay off handsomely. If you put away $2,000 a year in an IRA earning 12 percent, you'll have $30,309 waiting for you at the end of ten years, almost double your investment. Table 8.3 shows just how quickly your savings might grow.

Just as with your non-IRA portfolio, plan to invest these funds defensively. Any woman within five or six years of her target retirement date should begin shifting her IRA assets out of stocks and other volatile investments when the market is strong and put new cash into low-risk ventures.

In the process, you can take advantage of a little-known quirk in the law to boost your yield while retaining flexibility. Most bank CDs pay higher rates on longer-term issues. Even if you are on the brink of retiring, feel free to seek out the highest yields offered, regardless of the term. While you might want to

TABLE 8.3

Late-Blooming IRAs

Years in plan	Total Contribution	Annual interest rate 8%	10%	12%
1	$2,000	$2,160	$2,200	$2,240
2	4,000	4,492	4,620	4,748
3	6,000	7,012	7,282	7,558
4	8,000	9,732	10,210	10,704
5	10,000	12,670	13,430	14,230
6	12,000	15,844	16,974	18,178
7	14,000	19,272	20,870	22,598
8	16,000	22,974	25,158	27,550
9	18,000	26,972	29,874	33,096
10	20,000	31,290	35,062	39,309
11	22,000	35,954	40,768	46,266
12	24,000	40,990	47,044	54,058
13	26,000	46,428	53,948	62,748
14	28,000	52,304	61,544	72,558
15	30,000	58,648	69,898	83,506

cash in some of those securities before they come due, most banks do not levy the standard penalty on early withdrawals of certificates held in an IRA account once the owner turns 59½.

For any woman this age, a will is a must. Keep a separate list of assets in the same place you keep your will. The list on page 235 highlights key areas to cover. And if you have not yet done so, draw up a letter of instruction listing any preferences you have for your final arrangements.

In addition to the considerations discussed in Chapters 4 and 5, well-heeled women might want to consider reducing their estate by giving some of it away. Many Nesters and Reachers find this strategy difficult to consider. They are reluctant to part with any funds that they might need themselves down the road.

In most instances, their hesitation is wise. **Your most important goal is remaining financially independent throughout your lifetime. While you may feel certain that anyone on whom you showered such largesse would help you if you needed aid, you cannot count on generosity. What's more, you don't want to be in the position of having to ask.**

But for those successful women who stand to retire with more than enough income and assets to meet their present and foreseeable needs, occasional or regular gifts to loved ones can sharply cut the taxes otherwise owed on such funds if they were handed over after your death. Under the law, you (and your spouse, if you are married) each can give $10,000 a year to an unlimited number of recipients without paying any federal gift tax.

Sometimes, a woman might consider a gift of some size, perhaps her whole estate, to a public charity or other worthy group upon her death. In such instances, you have every right to make sure your bounty is used in accordance with your wishes. If you plan a major gift, meet with members of that institution together with your lawyer or another advisor to discuss your expectations. Should you wish to endow a professorship at your alma mater, for instance, you normally would be expected to offer a minimum gift. If your bequest might fall short, the school can work with you to accumulate the needed funds, perhaps by investing your donation to throw off income over a period of years until the target is reached.

Just as important as supervising what happens to your assets when you die is figuring out what would happen if you lived but were unable to care for things yourself. Just as she may have laid plans for her parents' infirmity, a wise manager considers how her own affairs would be handled if she grew ill.

The simplest step for married women, of course, is to maintain joint investments. If she is not well, her husband can continue to manage them. But owning property jointly can have undesirable consequences, as discussed in Chapter 5. There are other options, some of which may prove particularly valuable to single women.

One is to give someone you trust a **durable power of attorney** that allows that person to act for you in the event you cannot act for yourself. While an ordinary power of attorney is invalid once a person is incapacitated, a durable power, as its name suggests, would continue. The person named would be able to collect and spend your money as needed.

Some states do not recognize such powers. In that instance, another possibility is a living trust. In such a case, you serve as co-trustee with someone you would want to handle your affairs. As long as you are well, you retain full control of your holdings. But if and when you are not able to function, your co-trustee can step in.

The Lure of Early Retirement

No matter how committed you are to your career, the idea of retiring early can often prove beguiling. And depending on where you work and how successful you've been, it may prove easier to do than you think.

The first question, of course, is whether you can afford to quit. Because you are stepping down and likely to live long, set your sights on matching at least 75 percent of your exit income. Your aim, after all, is to enjoy yourself. Do so. Later, that will be less important as you slow down.

To see how close you come, check first with your personnel benefits office. It can calculate precisely how much pension and other retirement income you would receive when you leave.

Look next at what Social Security might offer. If you have been working at least nine years, you can begin to draw your benefit as early as age 62. The number of years you must log on the job rises to ten years in 1991.

If you make an early getaway, however, your check is cut—permanently—by 20 percent a year; it does not bounce back up to the full level when you hit 65. While that sounds like a painful sacrifice, remember that you are pocketing three extra years' pay in the process. As a result, you will likely still be ahead of the game until a dozen or so years pass.

Then, check back to the retirement income you targeted earlier to see if your own holdings can add enough to help you swing it.

Even if it looks as though you'll have enough to get by, look closely at what you will be giving up by doing so. As with Social Security benefits, freedom comes at a price. In many instances, your retirement package is cut drastically—anywhere from a third to a half—if you opt out early. What's more, you are forgoing potential salary increases that otherwise would be considered in computing your benefit.

Under a typical pension formula, a 62-year-old woman earning an average of $56,000 in her last five years of service might pocket a pension of $30,000 or so if she hangs on to age 65, and logs in three raises and a total of 30 years of service, compared with just $20,000 or so if she leaves at age 62.

Be sure to size up your insurance coverage before you exit. Even if your employer pays for all your health coverage now and automatically extends your health plan until you die, for instance, you may be charged to maintain the coverage in the period between early retirement and when you turn 65.

Your chief concern, however, should be inflation. **Even a moderate rise in the cost of living might put acute pressure on your holdings.** Some companies periodically sweeten pension payouts, but few are required to do so. And while Social Security payments are pegged to inflation, you may not see the extra dollars provided by the cost-of-living increases, because many corporate plans are designed so that their payouts are cut by part of any Social Security increases.

The Financial Realities of Retirement

Suddenly you are no longer a working woman. Years of lunch at your desk can now give way to lunch on the veranda. But you still have work to do to ensure your old-age comfort and to cash in on the many years devoted to your career.

A retiree's greatest challenge is to coordinate her newfound income. If she is eligible to receive her pension in a lump sum, or if she is considering a program of IRA withdrawals, she may be eyeing one of the single largest checks she will receive in her lifetime.

What to do with that money is tops on her list of concerns. A key factor in your decision should be the tax consequences. Before setting any course, compare your options carefully. In many cases it is wise to discuss your options with a tax pro. In general, they include:

- **Lump sum.** If you take all the money at once, the IRS offers an unusually generous pat on the back for all your hard work for those who turned 50 before January 1, 1986. Such distributions generally qualify for a special tax break known as 10-year forward averaging that can sharply cut your tax bills. So great are its benefits that the IRS considers it a once-in-a-lifetime option.

The rates start as low as 5.5 percent and apply regardless of any other income you earned that year. That means that you might pay a levy in the teens or 20's on your windfall even though your other income was taxed in the 33 percent bracket. To qualify, you must pocket the entire amount at once from a plan to which you've belonged for at least five years.

Persons who turn 50 after January 1, 1986, don't lose out entirely. Once you reach age 59½, you still can choose to calculate your tax on one lump sum payout using a similar formula called 5-year forward averaging. In essence, it lets you compute your tax as if you received your windfall in equal installments over 5 years, rather than in one fat check. As a result you'll still pay less tax than you would reporting your payout as ordinary income.

If you prefer, you can skip taxes now by **rolling over** part or all of a lump sum distribution into an IRA. To do so, you must act within 60 days of receiving the cash. The benefit of such moves is that the entire sum would continue to grow tax-free. But when you retrieve the money, withdrawals will be taxed at ordinary income rates.

• **Monthly payouts.** Not all pensions even give you the option to cash out at once. Instead, they dole out a monthly check as long as you live. In most cases, you also can opt for a guaranteed lifetime payout in lieu of a lump sum settlement. If you do so, and you are married, one choice remains about how you handle your take.

• **Survivor benefits.** All pension plans allow retirees to take what is called the ''joint and survivor option.'' That choice cuts the retiree's checks during his or her lifetime in return for continued payouts to the surviving spouse when the retiree dies. **Whether it makes sense to hedge your bets with a lower payout now depends on your overall financial situation.** Will you or your spouse have enough to live on when the other dies, or will the pension still be important? How much lower will the pension be if you opt for the lower payout? How likely is each of you to live? How long did your parents survive?

The most conservative option is to cut a deal guaranteeing lifetime income to both partners. But retirees should also consider other ways of providing the same security. They can use their cash on hand or a lump sum settlement to buy an annuity that will serve the same function or can carry life insurance on both spouses that likewise would represent security for the survivor if the retiree died. Both options have flaws, however. Annuities must be reviewed carefully to make certain that the income they pay is in line with market rates. And life insurance premiums can be prohibitively high for persons over 65.

By most measures, you are wise to take a lump sum payout at retirement if you can. Holders can win enviable tax treatment either through use of either 10-year or 5-year averaging or an IRA rollover. Once taxes are paid, the principal is theirs to keep. They can raid it for emergencies or pass it on to their heirs. Monthly payouts guarantee a check as long as you live (and your spouse if you so choose) but in most cases nothing remains for your estate.

If you take a lump sum settlement, your choice between 5-year or 10-year averaging and an IRA rollover should be influenced by how soon you need the money. If you must draw on that capital to live immediately, chances are the reduced forward averaging rates will prove to be the most beneficial option. If you do not need to tap those funds for a while, however, and the amount involved approaches six figures or more, you might do better to roll the money over into an IRA.

All workers must begin to wind down their IRAs no later than age 70½. The minimum withdrawal each year is determined by a complex formula that takes into account your life expectancy and, if you like, the beneficiary you designate.

Many women consider working at least part-time after retirement. But that may not prove financially worthwhile. In 1986, women 65 and over could earn up to $7,800 a year and still collect full Social Security benefits. But for every $2 you earn above that sum, you will forfeit $1 in benefits. Once you turn 70, there's no limit on how much you can earn and still collect. In any event, the costs of working—clothes, commuting, and the like—nibble further at your profits.

While some women find it hard to stop working, others find it equally difficult to start spending. Many Nesters who have done a marvelous job of piling up assets for later use hit a roadblock when later comes. Their savings patterns have become so entrenched they find it difficult to shift gears.

Eric and Marcia had long talked about the great vacation they would take when they retired. The first stop was San Francisco, with a side trip to the California wine country. Then on to Hawaii for a month of sea and sky. Neither could remember the last time they'd had a whole month off.

When the spate of retirement parties and dinners ended, Eric began pulling out travel brochures and making calls. Marcia hung back. Soon the reason for her reluctance became clear. "I don't know if this trip is such a good idea after all," she remarked. "What if we need the money later?"

Marcia's nesting instincts have taken hold so strongly that she is clutching at her assets. Such women cling desperately to their cash on hand, even if diligent efforts have built a nest egg fat enough to meet their identifiable needs.

If they are ever to enjoy the results of those efforts, however, such women must learn how to break away and spend. **But to them, spending now represents an even greater risk than investing ever did: they *know* that once they have signed the check, the money is gone, period.**

Marcia might be more comfortable postponing the trip while she tries a variation on the techniques Nesters learned in Chapter 3 about dealing with risk. Women who clutch will never feel free to spend unless they are convinced they can afford to do so. They must review their retirement outlook again.

They know firsthand what it costs them to live, and what they will be collecting in Social Security and pension payouts. They know what they have saved. If there's enough, together, to provide comfort and a cushion, they should let themselves savor the fruits of their accumulating years.

In fact, the biggest mistake such women and all retirees can make lies not with their spending decisions but with their savings. Their concern with preserving capital can lead them to place all their funds in secure, fixed-income investments. But that step, of course, has risks of its own: it overlooks inflation.

Just as diversification is a vital part of your portfolio while you are working, it plays an essential role when you retire. Steady payouts that leave you standing still are not good enough when the cost of living is marching upward. **Even the most conservative women with the smallest nest eggs need to put some of their funds into investments whose value will keep pace with inflation. The single greatest mistake any retiree can make is to grow dependent on a steadily eroding fixed-income payout in her later years.**

The more capital you have, the greater the percentage of your portfolio you can put at risk. Even so, you may want to prune out all investments aiming for aggressive growth. With your earning years behind you, you would find it next to impossible to recoup from a staggering loss. One relatively less risky way to do so is to invest in real estate, whether through direct investments of your own or by buying shares in property management firms such as REITs. Such investments often can provide tax benefits. If your bountiful savings have kept you in a high tax bracket, seek out tax-free income.

A typical retiree might consider this sort of mix:

POST-65 PORTFOLIO

Fixed-income investments (money market funds, Government securities, bonds)	50%–80%
Growth stocks	5%–20%
Real estate	5%–30%

Although many women are reluctant to spend any of their accumulated capital in their retirement years, you can plan to withdraw both principal and interest annually if you choose. That is an especially useful option for women who have managed to cobble together large hoards. But it also can serve as an escape hatch of sorts for those whose holdings are more modest. **By drawing down your capital, you can supplement the income it throws off.** Of course, such steps must be taken judiciously. The table on the opposite page shows how long your funds might last.

A woman over age 65 may also trim back her tax bill by taking advantage of several other special features of the tax code. At their age, single women who do not itemize may claim an extra $750 standard deduction; taxpayers who are married may take extra $600 standard deductions instead.

One of the most lucrative tax benefits is reserved for those who move from a large home to smaller quarters as part of their new life. You may exclude from taxes up to $125,000 in profit from the sale of your home if you were 55 or older on the date

TABLE 8.4

How Long Will Your Money Last?

Number of years	6%	7%	8%	10%	12%
1	0.9434	0.9346	0.9259	0.9091	0.8929
3	2.6730	2.6243	2.5771	2.4869	2.4018
5	4.2124	4.1002	3.9927	3.7908	3.6048
7	5.5824	5.3893	5.2064	4.8684	4.5638
10	7.3601	7.0236	6.7101	6.1446	5.6502
12	8.3838	7.9427	7.5361	6.8137	6.1944
14	9.2950	8.7455	8.2442	7.3667	6.6282
16	10.1059	9.4466	8.8514	7.8237	6.9740
18	10.8276	10.0591	9.3719	8.2014	7.2497
20	11.4699	10.5940	9.8181	8.5136	7.4694
25	12.7834	11.6536	10.6748	9.0770	7.8431
28	13.4062	12.1371	11.0511	9.3066	7.9844
30	13.7648	12.4090	11.2578	9.4269	8.0552

None of us, of course, knows quite how long we'll live. But this chart can help you pinpoint exactly how long your funds will last. To use it, decide how many years you think you will be withdrawing cash. Find that number in the column on the left. Then read across to the annual interest rate you are earning on your assets. At the point where the two intersect, divide the number you see into the sum you have saved. The result is the amount you can withdraw each year before you run out of money.

Say you have put aside $250,000 earning 8% a year. If you want the money to last 20 years, divide $250,000 by 9.8181 (the number where the 20 years column intersects the 8% column). The result, $25,463, is the amount you can pull out each year before you exhaust your original nest egg.

of the sale and the house had been owned and lived in as your principal residence for at least three of the previous five years. This benefit must be managed carefully, for you can only do it once before you die.

The older you grow, the more likely you are to tap your **health insurance** coverage. Most companies continue to provide some sort of insurance for their employees at little or no cost. But depending on your employer's plan, that policy may not meet all your needs. Don't assume that Medicare is enough. That program simply does not cover the costs of high-priced doctors, prescription drugs, health exams, and extended hospital stays. In fact, Medicare on average covers less than half the costs of retirees' bills. Your aim is to seek out a lifetime, noncancellable policy with unlimited or high coverage for individual items not eligible for Medicare payouts. If your employer's group plan is not available or not broad, take out a supplemental policy on your own.

Some women go to their retirement party without a will, or are married to men who do. For most hard-core procrastinators, the reason is not so much fear of dying the instant pen meets paper as the conviction, no matter how illogical, that they will not die so the effort involved is wasted.

Often these are the same women who thought they somehow would never stop working. Now that retirement is imminent, however, such persons can see that even the most unimaginable prospects indeed come to pass. The flurry of activity in lining up Social Security, pensions, and other payouts has set the stage for how they will operate when they stop working. A will should be seen as nothing more than a contract setting the rules for how things will go when they stop living.

IF YOU OUTLIVE YOUR HUSBAND

No woman is ever quite prepared for her husband's death. No matter how long the illness or how blessed the release that death represents, the loss is always stunning. And it hurts. Yet widowhood is an achingly familiar stage in a woman's life. Seventy percent of women outlive their husbands.

If there is any time in life when her emotions will overwhelm her thinking, it is now. Women who have put off learning how to take care of themselves, including many Nesters, are most bereft. But even those who have long played an equal role in family affairs can be shattered by this change.

Procrastination and indecision mark such widows' lives. Andrea was well prepared on paper for her new life. She long ago had insisted on checking and savings accounts of her own, and she was closely involved in the family's finances. She made all her own decisions about an IRA and a small inheritance she had received from her father.

But after Joe's death, she could not bring herself to deal with many things. Married to a doctor, she had always hated the "MD" plates on their car. They symbolized that fact that his patients always seemed to have more claim on his time than she did. Even so, it took her a year to have them switched. And she has yet to make any changes in the stock portfolio she inherited.

Some women feel a rush of anger at their husbands for leaving them alone. Even survivors of a good marriage often resent their husbands for dumping the welter of money decisions and financial red tape that follows a death in their lap. And if, as is often the case, the final tally shows less money there than envisioned, many women grow afraid as well.

Many times now, the focus on the past is stronger than that on the present. There is much that remains to be sifted through, mulled over, and resolved in a widow's mind. Nonetheless, a new widow must begin to pull herself, however gently, into the present. There is also much that must be done to settle her spouse's affairs.

When to Act, When to Wait

Over the short run, painful as the notion sounds, you must draw on your skills as a manager and delegate as many tasks as possible. **The first and only rule to follow now is to make no decision that cannot be undone.**

Your initial concern is to track down a series of pieces of paper that will form the bedrock of your financial security. Foremost is your husband's will. It will determine much of what happens next. One clause will name an executor to supervise the work involved in settling the estate. If you are named executrix, consider hiring a lawyer to help you out. If your husband dies without a will, recruit an attorney to outline your options.

If your husband prepared a list of the family holdings, or you know where such papers are, your next tasks are immeasurably easier. Otherwise you must conduct a thorough search for assets and the documents, such as veteran's discharge papers, that can prove your claim to them. Begin the paper chase by looking through any formal money records or files. Search your husband's desks and cabinets at home and at work and go through the safe deposit box.

Even the tiniest snippets of paper might provide clues. Check registers, for instance, might show payments to a brokerage firm that in turn might hold stocks or other securities. Last year's income tax return could list income from money market or other mutual funds, bank accounts, securities, or other assets. **If you find an insurance policy, call the agent;** often they handle more than one type of coverage and could lead you to other holdings. Even seemingly out-of-date policies might prove valuable; many remain valid although you no longer pay premiums. If you suspect your husband owned life insurance but cannot find the policy, the American Council of Life Insurance, based in New York City, can search for you.

Your husband's service at work and war may have value to you now. **Contact his present and previous employers.** One or more may come through with payouts based on life insurance coverage, pension benefits, an IRA, 401(k) or other savings plan, unused vacation and sick pay, and final medical bills. Similar benefits may be on tap from fraternal or professional organizations and the Veterans Administration Office, if he served in the armed forces. Some professional organizations carry insurance policies on their members. Others may refund the unused portion of dues or premiums on health insurance coverage.

Another source of benefits may be **Social Security.** Call your local office to discuss how to apply; you will not get checks automatically. You'll need records of your spouse's Social Security number and most recent salary as well as copies of the death certificate and military discharge papers. To establish your tie, bring along a copy of your marriage certificate as well as birth certificates of any children you might seek aid for.

The last paper you need will be the death certificate. Get at least ten copies.

Savings: Start Small

A new widow's first concern is the cash to pay immediate bills. In some states, you may find your access to joint accounts partly or totally blocked until the bank is convinced the contents will not be needed to pay taxes. Although the practice is not officially encouraged, women with little funds in their own names may want to raid a high-balance account before news of her husband's death spreads.

Later on, you must draw up a budget to see how much it is going to cost you to live now and how easily you can meet these needs. Depending on how well you had planned as a couple, you may have to scale back spending in some areas. Even so, be sure to save at least a small amount regularly.

Any woman who held joint credit cards with her spouse should see that they are transferred to her name. Just as if you were divorced, you could be asked to reapply. But most working women's earning power should provide sufficient to merit credit in their own rights.

Taxes: The Last Tallies

Taxes, it seems, can never be escaped, even after death. You will have to file a federal estate tax return within nine months of your husband's death; state requirements vary. In addition, your husband's last federal income tax return is due by April 15 of the year following his death. Because tax laws in these instances are complicated, be sure to consult a lawyer and tax pro for help.

You can file a joint federal tax return for the year of your husband's death and you probably should: the rates are lower. Be sure you understand how much of your holdings now are taxable. In some cases, for instance, you may owe tax on part of the income earned by your husband's estate, even though you have not as yet received it. At the same time, other income, including life insurance and certain pension payouts, may be tax-free.

In the years ahead, you may be entitled to further tax breaks. One possibility: using joint rates to calculate your federal income tax bill for two years after your husband's death. As a rule, you can do so as long as you do not remarry and have at least one dependent child. In later years, you still may be able to cut your taxes by using so-called head of household rates. These fall roughly between the low joint rates and higher tabs paid by single persons. That would be the case if you do not remarry but continue to maintain a house for a parent, child, or other dependent.

Assets: Steady, Now

The size of the sums you now are dealing with and the emotions you feel conspire to make these money decisions among the most difficult a woman can face. Nesters who long ago decided to swing part of their assets into stocks may find themselves suddenly worrying about their portfolio's safety. Normally prudent Drivers can make reckless moves to brandish control over just one aspect of their lives. Before you make any long-term plans, be sure to recruit a good money advisor to help.

Your first big decisions concern how to take control of any life insurance or pension benefit payouts. Pensions were explored earlier in this chapter. **Life insurance proceeds** offer similar options. Until you are certain of your choice, leave the money on deposit with the insurer. Most offer a type of money fund that pays market interest rates and will honor checks written against the balance.

As a permanent measure, you generally can choose among:

- **pocketing interest only.** You may continue to keep your funds with the insurer and receive regular payments of the interest it earns.
- **arranging for a lifetime income.** You use the proceeds to buy an annuity that guarantees a specific payment each month for as long as you live. The money never runs out, but the checks never get any bigger either, and there's nothing left over when you die.
- **taking cash in installments.** You can choose to collect the proceeds in installments along any schedule you wish. You may, for instance, want to reduce gradually the size of the payouts as your children grow older or you become eligible for Social Security benefits.

• **collecting all the money now.** In many cases, taking a lump sum may be best. With cash in hand, you can choose how to invest the money. Funds left on deposit with the insurer are invested by its money managers, who tend to be highly conservative. In your case, you might prefer more venturesome deals or to funnel some cash into tax-free investments.

Nesters and Reachers still may think twice about annuities. Such programs do promise a secure, dependable flow of checks to spend. But as discussed earlier in this chapter, annuities can tie you into a fixed rate of interest that might seem woefully small just a few years hence. If you value the security of an annuity, the real reason is because you are concerned you will live a very long time. If you still are relatively young, put some of that living under your belt, and hold off until you are nearer 65 to buy one. At that point you will be offered a higher annual payout because your life expectancy is shorter.

Whether you have received a comfortable settlement or are concerned about your situation, stay loose for a few months. Ask your banker and broker to transfer any jointly owned securities to your name, but don't make any commitments yet. **Put new money into no-bind assets like money market funds, short-term CDs, or Treasury securities. If you fear you may be tempted to blow some or all of your funds, lock them up.** Many Reachers are well advised to buy a fistful of one-year CDs. If they do need some cash, they can crack into one and incur only a small penalty.

Later on will come time to redeploy your assets—and those assets should be reviewed carefully. Many widows are reluctant to change the choices their husbands made. But that is probably unwise. After all, those decisions were aimed at providing for the two of you. Some holdings could be far too speculative for your interests now. Or too much could be salted away in tax-free investments that no longer make sense.

The same goes for your husband's financial advisors, if you have relied on his choices. During the highly emotional days when you were settling affairs, one may have made a thoughtless remark that bothers you still. Another may simply rub you the wrong way. **Feel free to make any changes you wish now, regardless of how hard someone may have worked or how well your husband may have liked that person. You are your own woman now.** Tips on how to choose money advisors follow in Chapter 12.

As you rework your holdings, bear in mind that the smaller your nest egg, the greater the percentage that should be kept in cash, CDs, and other less risky ventures. Unless you are quite young, you cannot afford to lose much of your stake. And the more you depend on your portfolio for income, the greater the share you might allocate to income-producing assets such as bonds.

At the same time, you share the inflation-fighting concerns of all women. The sooner you are likely to retire and stop building your capital base, the more you must pay attention to the threat that a rising cost of living will erode your future life-style. The advice for retirees is equally apt here: put part of your holdings into investments that stand to grow in value, whether high-dividend paying stocks, REITs, or an all-cash real estate limited partnership.

The following portfolio might work for an older woman with a limited nest egg bent on conserving most of her cash. Suggestions for a widow pocketing a large windfall appear in the next chapter.

CONSERVING CASH

Money fund, CDs, Treasury Securities	30%–60%
High-yielding stock or bond fund	10%–20%
Real estate	10%–20%
Growth-and-income stock fund	10%–20%

Insurance: Time to Rethink

If you are the sole source of your own support, your earning power is critical. Double check the disability coverage provided by your employer. Your husband's estate may well have left you far more secure. But if you could not live off your employer's out-of-work package and the income from your holdings, pick up an additional disability policy to see yourself through.

Collecting on your husband's life insurance may eliminate the need for your own. If your coffers are bulging, you may be wise to drop any term policies you hold. But if parents or children still rely on you for support, the old rules hold. Carry enough insurance so that their needs will be covered if you die.

Retirement and Estate Planning: You Have a Lot of Living to Do

Even if you no longer need the income, give serious thought to remaining at work. Distracted as your thoughts may be, your job stands to fill the void your loss has created. The money will come in handy, too. For one thing, you can continue to pile up funds in your IRA. More than that, you have the chance to contribute the maximum to any other retirement savings programs.

For women whose financial circumstances are less steady, the need to rethink retirement is even greater. Your husband may have died before working long enough to merit a solid pension. Or he may have chosen to collect those checks in a way that cuts you off now. The retirement sections earlier in this chapter give you pointers on how to size up your lot and make the most of the remaining time.

Although the last thing she wants to think about is death, a widow must take time out to rewrite her will. If you have children, it is vital that you name a guardian who would care for them if you died soon. Even if you are childless or yours have grown, many estate planning issues can be determined with new certainty. While your first instincts may have been to provide for one another, now that you are alone you have a freer hand in apportioning your assets.

NINE

MONEY CHANGES: HOW TO HANDLE THE BAD FALLS AND THE WINDFALLS

At every stage in our lifeline, money plays a potent role. But when our financial circumstances suddenly change, for better or for worse, money's power over our lives intensifies.

A sudden shift in how much money we have—or haven't—calls for an equally dramatic change in our money plans. More important, when financial change knocks out part of our reality, it also chips away at the sense of self the old circumstances helped create. **The patterns we developed to manage our finances—our money personalities—can be swept away as we struggle to cope with the powerful feelings unleashed by our new fortunes.**

Profound life changes often spark equally profound transformations in our money personalities. Some money changes, like being without a job, can be temporary, and the shifts in money style they bring short-lived as well. But others, like coming into a large inheritance, can permanently alter our money habits.

WHEN THE PAYCHECKS STOP

Nearly every woman faces the loss of income at some point in her life. One of the most painful circumstances is losing a job, whether you were fired outright or your position disappeared in a cost-cutting drive. When the economy is tottering, many women can also be saddled with cuts in pay to boost their employer's flagging profits. Even the birth of a child or a husband's promotion can bring tight times if a woman chooses to take unpaid maternity leave or quit her job to relocate with her spouse.

On the list of sources of executive stress, losing a job is tops. No matter what job she held or how much she earned, the change in roles can spark a questioning of identity. **For many working women, their identities are bound up in their work, more so, perhaps, than they realized.** "All of a sudden I felt at a loss," said Sheila. "I went to a party and someone asked what I did. I used to be a banker. Now I think of myself as a blank."

Such feelings are often accompanied by very real financial concerns. "My biggest question," she confides, "is how long I can live without a job."

No such worries plague Melissa. The day after her job was eliminated along with her department, she treated herself to $1,000 worth of new clothes. "I owe it to myself now," she reasoned. "I need to look good at my interviews."

Melissa's reaction was typical of many Reachers and Drivers. Neither can quite believe she has been shown the door and both feel certain that good times lie just around the corner. Of the two, though, the Reacher faces the greater difficulty surviving between paychecks. She may find it all too easy to deny what is going on to herself. As a result, she will fail to take the proper steps soon enough in the game. To the extent that she equates spending money with self-esteem, she may, like Melissa, try to build back the good feelings she lost with a shopping spree. At the same time, she is the most vulnerable of women. Her cash cushion often is thinner, and likely can only see her through a matter of weeks before drastic action is necessary.

While Drivers may know full well what is going on, they run the risk that they will not be able to share that knowledge with others. Their salaries and positions shaped an identity that flourishes on responsibility and power. When they lose their jobs, they lose face. A few women react by pretending that nothing has changed, and set out for work each day only to wander about. They shield the news from friends and contacts who could prove to be invaluable sources of emotional help and job leads.

To make ends meet until they return to work, Drivers must press to keep their managerial instincts. Their ability to take control of a situation will prove invaluable as they negotiate a severance package and retool their budget.

Nesters may be in the best position of all to weather a job loss. Like Sheila, their first concerns are often financial. Yet their overall fiscal stance is suited to hunkering down. Their cash reserves already are full, their budgets lean. The Nester's biggest problem, in fact, may be her frame of mind when she returns to work. By confirming the Nester's view of the world as a harsh and hostile place, losing a job often reinforces her tendency to avoid risk and keep assets super-safe.

Weathering a financial crisis often has hidden benefits. We may find out we are a lot toughter than we think, always a good thing to know. For all of us, too, it offers the chance to review financial patterns and improve. Many Reachers, in fact, can find in the problem the chance to impose a measure of fiscal discipline.

How to Get Your Due

If you've lost your job, you are not likely to feel you hold the upper hand in any dealings with your employer. But you probably have more clout than you imagine. One of your most important tasks now is to use it.

Certain extremely valuable benefits probably are yours as a result of company policy. More important, you often can win others if you ask. Corporations are becoming increasingly generous with workers, especially valued ones who were eased out for reasons other than poor performance. Many view former employees as potential customers and business contacts. Others try to wind up matters graciously to maintain goodwill among those who remain. In some cases, they would rather sweeten a deal and part on good terms than risk a lawsuit from a disgruntled former employee.

Your best settlement will come if you keep matters on businesslike terms. The best way to make any requests is in writing. The same goes for the answers you receive. Press beyond vague promises of ''We'll take care of that'' for written confirmation of any deal you cut.

Among the options to explore:

- **Unused sick and vacation time.** This may well be part of your company's standard departure package. Check that the personnel department's records are consistent with your own.
- **Severance pay.** If you are part of a mass lay-off, you may not have much leeway here. Employers are reluctant to grant special privileges to one worker for fear all will demand the sweetened terms. But if your case is an individual one, you may be able to negotiate a handsome package.

Always seek some severance pay. Even if this is not a common practice at your company, your boss may be willing to make arrangements. At minimum, ask for a week's pay for each year of service. The typical benefit is two. If you are offered a severance package, counter with a more generous proposal of your own. If your boss offers one month's pay, for instance, ask for three.

Make it clear that you are looking for income to tide you over, not for a free ride. But try to keep any arrangement open-ended. If you have not found a job by the time your pay package expires, you want to be in a position to go back and ask for more.

• **Fringe benefits.** Some of your most valuable compensation never showed up in your paycheck. This includes health and life insurance coverage and other fringe benefits. Such perks are relatively easy to extend. Many employers routinely maintain insurance on former employees for up to several months.

Do not overlook benefits that can help you replace the job you lost. You will have a better chance of finding a new position if it looks as though you have not left your old one. Hold out for the use of an office, telephone, secretary, and even continued use of your title if you can.

• **Cover stories.** Go over the story your boss will give to any prospective employer calling for references, and find out precisely how the job termination is listed in your personnel records. Try to get a letter from your employer summarizing the reasons you lost your job.

That will prove valuable when you seek out your next source of income, unemployment benefits. Brace yourself. As a rule, Washington would be only too happy to have you conclude it is too much trouble to file a claim. ''I have had to wait on line for hours,'' one woman complains. ''You're not treated graciously. It's a demeaning experience.''

But advisable. So long as you left your old job involuntarily, you are legally entitled to unemployment checks, and it is a sign of shrewdness, not inadequacy, to claim them. **If you find yourself thinking of them as something akin to welfare, think again: both you and your employer contributed to the funds you now are seeking.**

Consider too the fact that the money may come in handy. The better your old job, the longer you may have to wait to replace it. As a rule of thumb, expect to look one month for every $10,000 in salary you earned. That means if you were pulling in $40,000, you should prepare to spend four months hunting for your next position. Even if you are receiving severance checks, you still may be entitled to collect.

Your first step is a phone call to your local unemployment office (listed in the phone book under "State Government"). They will outline the application procedure and can give you an idea of how long it will be until you receive your first check. The sooner you apply, of course, the quicker it will arrive. Be prepared to wait a week or two, possibly longer.

The amount you'll receive is linked to how long you've been working and the salary you commanded. Usually you must have earned money in two quarters of the previous year to qualify. In 1986 you could expect a check for anywhere from $100 to $300 a week. In most instances, you can draw benefits for up to 26 weeks or until you find a new job.

Savings: Build a Budget

If you are like most working women, chances are you never worried much about a budget. Even steady savers are more likely to have a budget in their heads than on paper. While that method can work well in ordinary times, a sudden loss of income calls for a more organized approach. **To get by, you will have to cut your spending. The best way to see where is on paper.**

Whatever your deepest concerns, bring them out in the open now. What do you fear? That your money won't last? That you will have to settle for an unsatisfying job because nothing better will come along? That there won't be another job? That your spouse or lover resents your loss of income? That you will get sick and be unable to afford a doctor?

Unfocused anxiety will rob you of your ability to concentrate on the job at hand; putting a label on your fears can help banish them. As you focus on your concerns, draw up a budget. The exercise can be reassuring. **Women who are frightened to see their paychecks falling away often relax when they write down exactly what they must spend and see how small that figure can be.**

One of the most important entries is for your creditors. A loss of income is a short-term proposition. But failing to pay off your bills and damaging your credit rating in the process is a long-term problem you want to avoid at all costs.

If your debts are moderate, the way out is clear. Pay the minimum on each account until you begin working again. If you have a pile of bills, the situation is more complex. Take time first to write down each debt you owe and the amount.

Say the list is formidable, and you find you cannot make even the minimum payment. Get in touch with each lender. Think of the task as reporting in on the status of a project. No boss likes to be hit blind-sided by last-minute news that the report will be a month late. Taking the initiative with your creditors can go a long way to defusing a potential crisis.

All lenders want nothing more than to get their money back. They want you to be able to repay, and they bend deeply to allow you to do so. Depending on the situation, they can cut your monthly bills, stretch out the time you have to repay, or let you hold off payments entirely for a while.

Mortgage lenders are a special case. The worst move you can make is to ignore the problem. They too have no interest in foreclosing on your home. But the sums involved are so large that they will take heed at once if you miss a payment.

Make an appointment with your banker to discuss the situation. Be prepared to indicate how soon you expect to find work, and how much you can afford to pay each month in the interim. If you are in dire straits, the lender might be willing to forgo all payments for a few months. More likely, you can negotiate smaller payments for the short run with the understanding that you will make up the shortfall once you are back at work.

At the same time, your banker might suggest you take out what is commonly called a **consolidation loan.** Such deals provide the money needed to pay off all your debts in full. That promises an end to juggling accounts and due dates and will see that you do not lose any credit cards. But you may lose money on the deal. Such sums often are only available at stingingly high rates. Take out a consolidation loan only if the interest you will pay is lower than that on your oustanding charges.

If your particular set of lenders proves uncooperative, you may have to make some tough calls. **As a rule, it is better to pay each one a little than to stiff some and pay others off in full. If you cannot even do that, pay necessities first.** Cover your rent or mortgage payments and utility bills. Also aim to keep up the minimums with lenders that report most quickly to credit agencies. These include major national charge cards such as Visa and MasterCard, and department store chains like Sears, Roebuck & Co.

Next most likely to flag late payments are airlines and auto lenders. If you simply must put off someone, there is less risk with American Express, and most department stores and oil companies, which generally do not report unless you are at least 60 days late. While you must bear the consequences of short-changing them, your actions are less likely to harm your credit rating. The same goes for most dental and doctor bills, although a growing number are turning over unpaid accounts to collection agencies.

The second most important line item in your budget is for job search expenses. Be sure to allow funds for printing a resume, making calls, going to interviews. Bear in mind that if your plans include relocating, you may incur hefty travel expenses for interviews in neighboring cities.

No matter how strapped you are, you must hang on to your emotional health. Set aside some funds for relaxation and entertainment. As your job search wears on, you will need to get out, if only to a movie.

Tote up your bare-bones budget and compare it with the cash you expect from severance and savings. This is precisely the sort of emergency that your reserve is there for. You may find that your income from all sources is enough to let you live much as you have been for a while. If you cannot get by by spending less, however, you'll have to take steps to raise cash.

As long as you have pruned your expenses sharply, you

want to borrow money before you sell off assets. It is always harder to rebuild a nest egg than to pay back a loan. The exception, of course, is when you doubt you can repay borrowed funds.

Consider these tide-me-over tactics:

- **Bank lines of credit.** You may already have overdraft privileges on your bank checking account or a line of credit. That means you can in effect write yourself a loan for immediate cash. The drawback to this approach is that banks tend to charge their highest rates on such funds, and the interest on those and other consumer loans is only partially deductible.
- **Credit card lines.** National credit firms such as MasterCard and Visa offer the same privilege. You can get a cash advance for the difference between any purchases you have made and the amount you are authorized to charge. These lenders also tend to charge steep fees. What's more, the tab will begin running the day you pocket the cash, even if you are not charged interest on conventional purchases until a later time.
- **CDs and other bank accounts.** To cut your out-of-pocket borrowing costs, you can use bank assets as collateral for a loan. Most banks will lend you a sum nearly equal to any deposits you hold at a rate that is two or three percentage points higher than the interest you earn. The same goes for passbook savings accounts. But you are better off putting those funds into a CD and borrowing against that. If the balance is too small to open a CD, cash it in.
- **Stocks and other securities.** Your broker also will lend you money at relatively low rates if you put up securities as collateral. You can borrow up to half the value of the assets you pledge as part of a margin account. This option is discussed in greater detail in Chapter 11.
- **Life insurance.** Most universal and whole life insurance policies build up equity known as cash value. Typically, the owner of a $50,000 policy that is five years old can borrow about $2,250. The oldest policies offer the best rates, and they

can be very low indeed: most policies taken out in the 1970s charge between 5 percent and 8 percent.

To apply, ask your agent or the insurer for a form. But do not borrow the maximum; you'll want to leave at least enough to pay the next premium so you will not lose your coverage if you still are strapped. If you die before the loan is repaid, of course, the insurance payment will be reduced by any outstanding loans and interest owed.

• **Your home.** As a rule, you can borrow up to 80 percent of the equity in your home—its market value less any mortgage you still owe—from a bank as well as from many brokers, finance companies, and credit unions. On a $100,000 home with a $30,000 mortgage, for instance, a lender might extend a loan of up to $56,000.

Some programs are set up as revolving lines of credit at rates that vary with market conditions. That means that you can take down a loan and repay it at your convenience so long as you make the minimum payment that is set. While some programs let you borrow as little as a few hundred dollars, arranging them can be costly. Most make sense only for large sums. Homeowners also can take out second mortgages on their property, but these loans tend to run for at least five years.

Borrowing against the equity in your house is a tricky issue. You must be very, very careful that you can afford to repay the loan in timely fashion; otherwise, you risk losing your home, which would be a disaster. On the other hand, when entered into cautiously, home equity loans *can* make more sense than other kinds of consumer loans. That is because you can deduct the interest you pay on any amount equal to the original purchase price plus the cost of improvements you have made, up to the fair market value of your home. That sharply cuts your after-tax cost of raising cash.

• **IRA.** Contrary to popular thinking, money socked away for retirement in an IRA is not locked away forever. You can withdraw some or all of your funds once a year so long as you replace the money within 60 days. The catch: if you don't get it back in time, you must pay ordinary income tax on the earnings you withdraw plus any deductible contributions you have made *plus* a 10 percent penalty if you are under age 59½. Unless you are absolutely sure you can repay the funds, you probably are wise to hold off. You likely will need the money even more later than you do now.

• **Retirement savings.** Other retirement plans may also allow you to borrow or even withdraw some of the money you have set aside. The rules vary according to the type of account and the employer. In general, you can easily borrow up to $10,000 or half the value of your stake in many corporate savings plans. Some 401(k), thrift, and profit-sharing programs also allow you to withdraw funds under hardship conditions. You'll have to pay a 10 percent penalty on any cash you pocket. But as with IRAs, you should reserve such raids for the most dire of circumstances.

Taxes: Keep Records

The good news about unemployment checks is that the sums start off tax-free. No taxes—federal, state, local, or Social Security—are deducted from the amounts you receive.

The bad news is that you will pay taxes later. The new tax law ended a long-standing break on such income.

Your accountant can help you get an extension on tax payments if need be. If you do not have a history of late payments, you'll find the IRS can be surprisingly flexible. Whatever you do, don't fail to file because you lack the cash to pay. Not only can that get you into trouble, you'll incur hefty penalties at a time when you least need more bills. Interest on late payments can easily run 5 percent a month on the amount you owe.

Another reason to seek tax help is if you stand to receive either your severance pay or pension benefits in a lump sum when you leave. Your tax situation can influence how you choose to pocket those sums. In the case of severance benefits, for instance, you might be better off scheduling a series of payments in order to spread your income out over more than one calendar year. Your pension choices are discussed below.

One of the few benefits of losing your job may well show up on your tax form. If your search drags out beyond your severance pay, you may not earn as much money this year as you had anticipated. With less in income, you will owe less in taxes.

If you itemize deductions, you may win another tax break. As long as you look for a position in your current field, chances are you can write off some or all of the money you spend to do so. Under the new tax laws, you can deduct certain unreimbursed business and miscellaneous expenses that come to more than 2 percent of your adjusted gross income. And with a lower income, it will be relatively easy to reach that point. There's a complete list of the items that qualify as write-offs in Chapter 4. To be sure you don't lose the potential deduction, keep a written record of all your **job search** bills, including the costs of printing and mailing resumes, transportation to interviews, long-distance phone calls, employment agency fees, and the like. And if you move to accept a new post, unreimbursed **relocation costs** can also trim your tab. Check with your accountant.

Assets: Shift the Mix

One of the best ways to squeeze out more cash on which to live is by shifting the mix of assets in your portfolio. But easy does it. No matter how acute your needs may seem, avoid taking steps that *cost* you money over the long term in order to pump out cash in the short run.

Dierdre was a geologist in a major oil firm. When her employer was taken over by a much larger company in a bruising takeover battle, she and scores of others lost their jobs. Panicked at the prospect of fighting dozens of rivals for new work, she decided to prepare for a long siege. To see herself through, she cashed out all her stock holdings in a single afternoon at an average loss of 25 percent.

Dierdre had the right idea but the wrong timing. **Women who need income can wring more from their portfolios, but they should be careful not to garrote their value in the process.** Before selling any stock at a loss, consider whether you might be able to hold on for a while and squeak by. Dierdre, for instance, found another job in three weeks, and could have made it through without liquidating any of her funds.

Because much of her holdings may be tied up in less liquid assets, a Driver often faces the hardest retooling task. Often, her best course is to borrow against those funds instead of cashing them in. A broker can help her lay plans. If she can sell off some shares at a profit, she might shift out of stocks that pay little or no dividends into higher yielding securities such as utility firms.

Any woman facing the loss of income should take her new tax picture into account. With sharply lower income in sight, she no longer needs to search for tax breaks. Cash that was wisely committed to a tax-free money fund, for instance, should likely be switched to a conventional money fund that pays higher rates.

A Nester's portfolio is the easiest to rework, since many of her holdings may already concentrate on throwing off cash. Even so, she should watch to keep her options open. If a CD is set to mature, for instance, she should whisk those funds into a money market or other easy-access account rather than renew it for even the shortest of terms. If she has not already done so, she can boost yields by pruning out any emotionally reassuring but laggard investments such as passbook savings accounts.

Insurance: Get a Backup

Insurance is the one area where cutting expenses does not make sense. Much of your coverage may well have been provided by your employer. Unless you will be covered under your spouse's plan, one of your most important goals is to replace your insurance. With no paycheck as backstop, you need such protection more than ever.

As a rule, health and life insurance coverage expires one to two months after you leave. But a recent law allows many employees who are fired or laid off to ask to keep their health coverage for 18 months at their own expense. That is especially valuable if you have a medical condition that required a doctor's consultation within the preceding year.

If that tack fails, give some thought to how long you think you might be out of work. If you feel your prospects for finding a new job are good, plan accordingly. Because you will pick up new coverage with your new job, look for a short-term policy that will cover you for three months or so. On the other hand, if judgment suggests you may be out of work for a while, line up longer-term coverage. **To avoid paying the steep fees commanded by individual policies, look for a group policy.** Professional associations and many credit unions often offer relatively inexpensive programs.

The same goes for life insurance. Your employer may be able to extend your group coverage at a low rate, or you might pick up a low-cost policy from a professional organization. But before you act, give some thought to whether you need any at all. If you have no dependents who rely on your income, or your spouse can support himself, consider dropping your coverage for now.

Retirement Planning: An Unexpected Bonus?

This retirement is only temporary. But one aspect you must touch on now has a great deal to do with your more permanent departure from the job—sorting out what you are entitled to from your pension and other retirement or savings programs.

Even if you have not been working for your employer all your life, you may have earned significant pension benefits. Ask your personnel office for a written statement of any benefits accrued to date. Compare their report with your employee manual to make sure you have been properly credited for your service. If you have any questions, pursue them. By law, your employer must provide you with a full tally of your holdings.

If you are vested with part or all of your benefit, you may be able to cash out that program when you leave. In that case, you can pocket the check now or roll over some or all of those funds into an IRA or a new employer's pension program. If you take the money now, you must pay taxes on it, but you may be able to slash the bill by using the forward averaging formula discussed in Chapter 8. That move makes most sense if you plan to use the money right away, whether to pay basic bills or to start your own business.

By and large, however, no matter how much they think they need such funds now, most women will need them more later. Try to keep this windfall for retirement. If you roll over the funds into an IRA, you put off your tax bill indefinitely and set the entire sum to work; what's more, both principal and earnings accumulate tax-free until withdrawn. While you will pay ordinary income taxes on the money when you retrieve it, tax-free compounding stands to put you substantially ahead. The larger the check, the more likely you are to be better off rolling it over.

In some instances, workers merely are credited for their service. To collect their funds, they will have to notify the company when they reach retirement age. If that is true in your case, get a statement summarizing your future benefits and instructions on how to go about getting them later. Keep it in a safe place. Even if you have not vested in any part of your employer's program, any contributions that you may have made belong to you.

MANAGING A WINDFALL

Money changes everything, but not always in the ways you think. While most women expect stress when money is tight, they are rarely prepared for the mixed feelings that are stirred up by sudden wealth.

Even the best financial changes can spawn anxiety and depression. Just as with losing money, winning a bundle upsets the web of predictability that cushions our lives. Many women are surprised by the responses they feel.

Some of the women who wanted money most badly have the greatest difficulty dealing with its arrival. Becky had often fantasized about the way she would feel when she could one day open her bankbook and see a six-digit balance. But when her father died and left her $80,000, she felt sadness, not elation. Not surprisingly: her richness came at a steep price.

Becky's feelings are shared by a great many women who inherit money. And depending on the quality of their relationship with the person who has died, some women find themselves unable to enjoy their good fortune. Allie, for one, came to resent the money she inherited from her father. A broker, he put in long hours and rarely took time off; never once did the family take a vacation together. "I have this money because my father spent time earning it instead of spending time with me," she says. "It can never make up for the hours we lost."

Other women experience great guilt because they have not earned the money they hold. Especially for women whose work plays a key role in their personal identities, suddenly getting money they did not earn is just as discomfiting as losing their ability to earn it.

The most troublesome feelings, however, tend to flow from our feelings about money in the first place. No matter what we expected money to do for us, in the end we often realize that it does not have that power. Nesters who dreamed of security can find themselves still ill at ease about money matters, only now about whether they will lose their newfound fortune just as suddenly as they got it. Reachers and Drivers are often secretly frustrated by the fact that no amount of financial finagling can buy them self-esteem or control of others in their lives, or free them from situations or relationships they find unsatisfying.

But money can do a great deal, and all heiresses come in to their own when they see that fact. Even small windfalls can play a vital role in helping you meet your financial goals. The lucky few who pocket substantial sums have nothing less than the chance to win financial independence.

The catch is that nothing is won unless you know what you are looking for. Before you take another step with your bonanza, take time to sort out your goals, survey your dreams, and set an agenda for satisfaction.

Savings, Taxes, and Assets

You've got some money? Blow a bit. You deserve it. In fact, celebrating with one big splurge often happens, especially if the money comes from a happy windfall. One woman ordered a brand-new Cadillac Seville the day she won her state lottery. Another booked a trip to Japan.

But proportion counts. **A good rule of thumb: the smaller the windfall, the smaller the splurge. And after the initial spree, settle down a bit.**

No matter what the source, the best rule for the rest of your funds is a simple one: go slow. **Money that has come easy can go the same way.** That was the case for Lisa. She had always believed she had a knack for picking stocks. Her occasional buys had made money. Even better performers were stocks she had thought about buying but hadn't bought. Inevitably, it seemed, they doubled in value in a year's time.

When she inherited $50,000 from her parents, Lisa decided to manage the funds herself. The list of stocks she bought filled a page. Soon she was turning to the stock listings before her morning coffee, and she huddled on the phone with her broker five or six times a day.

At first, the conversations were upbeat. But soon their tenor changed. Her stocks weren't doing well at all. Within two years, Lisa lost $38,000. The only money left was in money market funds and two high-yielding utilities.

Lisa is not alone. By some estimates, as many as 90 percent of those pocketing a windfall blow the money within five years.

For Drivers like Lisa, the real danger is to think you know more than you do. Despite your wealth, your attitudes will change slowly, if at all. In fact, the big mistake is to do something counter to your instincts.

The larger your windfall, the less likely you are to be able to minimize Uncle Sam's initial cut. **While gifts and inheritances come tax-free, you will owe ordinary income taxes on windfalls such as lottery proceeds and hefty bonuses.** An accountant can give specifics. Don't overlook obvious ways to pull down your income. Be sure to pump $2,000 into an IRA and to take advantage of any sheltering packages at work.

Beyond that, you are best advised to devote your energies to cutting the tax on the income your windfall earns. **Parked atop your own salary, it stands to catapult you into the highest tax bracket.** Both stocks and real estate can prove helpful here; they provide the potential for capital growth. Judiciously chosen, a variety of limited partnerships also can offer the chance to shelter income from your investments.

Other ways to whittle your tax bill lie closer to home. You can help to keep a greater share of your wealth in the family if you give money outright. You can shower $10,000 a year to any person you wish without incurring any federal gift taxes.

The precise portfolio mix you adopt will depend on your age.

Just as with any investment decision, you need to determine if your primary aim is to make more or preserve what you've got. In this case, you already have plenty. A prudent course might be to focus on keeping what you have and taking only moderate risks with your funds. Older women might be most comfortable playing it safe, since they have less time to recoup any losses. But young women may prefer to seize the chance to make aggressive investments that hold out the promise of shooting them into the ranks of the very rich.

Your initial moves might look like this:

SHORT-TERM MOVES	
Tax-free money market fund	30%
Second tax-free money fund	30%
Series of short-term Treasury bills	40%

For all your wealth, the first rule of investing remains your watchword as you go to revamp these holdings—diversification. If anything, your list of investments should run into pages. Not just because you have so much money, but so that you divide it up among a range of different areas.

Your hefty capital enables you to lock up assets for a longer time now. As long as interest rates are steady or falling, pump up yields by buying a series of staggered maturities. Put most of your income-oriented holdings into tax-free issues until you drive your tax bracket down to the point where taxable securities offer a better return.

At the same time, of course, investments that seek growth stand to reap the highest rewards. With a solid hoard to back you, you have the priceless ability to wait out sluggish markets. In real estate, as with stocks, those with staying power make the most money.

Depending on whether you want to go for growth or keep what you have, you can tailor a portfolio from these sorts of assets:

LONG-TERM POSITIONS

Growth stocks	30%–50%
Tax-free money fund	5%–20%
Tax-free municipal bonds	10%–30%
Real estate or real estate limited partnerships	0%–30%
Aggressive tax shelters	0%–20%

Insurance: Do You Still Need Any?

A newfound fortune could mean the end of much of the insurance you have carried. Once you hold sufficient assets to protect those who depend upon you, for instance, you have no further need for life insurance. But your burgeoning assets may suggest other coverage. Be sure your homeowner's policy covers any new jewelry or other assets you've acquired. And look into umbrella insurance policies. A wealthy woman is an easy mark for anyone who can claim injury at her hands.

Estate Planning: More Important Than Ever

Before you leave on a round-the-world cruise, rewrite your will. This is important even if you have not yet pocketed the money you expect. It still is yours by right. Your will may not end up substantially different from the one you now hold, but with a great deal more at stake, the exercise is far more important.

The basic principles you should explore with your attorney mirror those discussed in the preceding chapters. In addition, your newfound wealth may make it advisable—as well as easier—for you to cut your tax bills by sharing some of your trove with those you love, enriching all in the process.

III

HOW TO ADD PIZAZZ TO YOUR PLAN

No matter how firm your sense of your own money style, and how well researched your investment choices, you are not ready to implement the plan you've devised until you size up the economy.

In certain markets, your best moves will include borrowing funds to bolster your financial firepower.

In every instance, you can and often should backstop your own insights with a team of money pros.

The last section of this book offers tips on lining up help with all of these tasks.

TEN

HOW TO PLAY THE MARKETS

It's one thing to find an investment that suits your goals. Add to that one that fits your temperament, and you are well on the way toward making a good money move. But even that is no sure index of success. **Bought at the wrong time—when the market is set to tumble or interest rates are poised to rise—no investment will pay off. As much as anything, successful investing is a question of timing.**

When the economy is growing smartly, for instance, certain moves make sense. Boom times signal rising incomes, rousing consumer spending, and often, a surging market for stocks. As interest rates edge upward, wise investors roll over short-term securities at steadily rising rates.

When business slackens, by contrast, interest rates begin to tumble. Bonds and other investments that lock in high yields and stand to gain in value when rates drop would represent wise moves here.

In short, even if your circumstances stay the same, the rest of the world probably won't. Your shrewdest money decisions depend on seizing the opportunities unfolding now and lying in wait as markets shift.

Every day the financial pages are crowded with predictions about the market's moves. Economics, once a topic that you studied (or carefully avoided) in college, is now virtually an industry, with an army of theoreticians, technicians, model-builders and seers bent on calling business turns. Each expert claims a cloudless crystal ball. None exists, of course. And of late, the record of the nation's forecasters has been mixed at best. Most predictions of economic growth and interest rate trends have been painfully wide of the mark.

The din can be confusing. But what's confusing to some can mean opportunities to others.

Women who would rather watch movies than the stock pages, including many Nesters and Reachers, may shy away from this. But every investor must pay attention to overall economic conditions. Changes in the financial markets influence such short-term considerations as whether to take out a loan now or later as well as long-term decisions like whether to invest in CDs or stocks.

Rest assured. Economics has always been an inexact science, and your aim is not to change that now. For your purpose, it matters little whether GNP is jumping ahead by 7 percent or 8 percent. **You need not catch the exact peak or bottom of any trend. It's the direction that counts.** Shrewd investors can make money in almost any market as long as they are with, not behind, the trends.

To succeed, they also need the courage of their convictions. Short-term interest rates topped 15 percent in the early 1980s. Nearly every investment guru warned those returns would not last, and urged savers to lock in sweet yields. Interest rates changed, but many savers didn't. All too many were forced to scramble to pick up far lower returns when rates inevitably came tumbling down.

MAKING SENSE OF MONEY NEWS

Investors trying to make sense of economic news face a jumble of headlines trumpeting shifts in housing starts, the prime rate, orders for durable goods, wholesale prices, and all manner of arcane reports. Written between the lines is a familiar pattern referred to as the business cycle. **Time after time over the years, economic activity has followed a predictable, if erratic, path. Knowing the general outline can help you put the jangle into a more tranquil perspective.**

When the economy begins to slow down, companies scale back production and postpone expansion plans. At the same time, consumers, sensing tough times ahead, begin to tighten their purse strings. As the demand for money from corporate and individual borrowers declines, the supply of funds from savers rises. The upshot: interest rates tend to fall.

In due course, low interest rates discourage consumer saving and encourage spending again. Many shoppers borrow to make purchases postponed during the economy's darker days. As the pace of orders picks up, businesses hire more workers, retailers fill up stores, and builders put up more homes. Encouraged by burgeoning sales and low interest rates, corporations lay plans to expand.

Once the pace of business quickens, the demand for money tends to outstrip supply. As businesses and consumers compete for funds, interest rates begin to creep up. Prices edge up as well, as many businesses have trouble meeting demand. In time, rising costs will start to choke off business and consumer demand. When rates hit painfully high levels, business activity and consumer borrowing slow. Companies lay off workers, who in turn cut down on spending. The economy skids into recession. Eventually interest rates follow it down, and the cycle is poised to begin again.

Like the priestess at Delphi, a wise investor aims to gauge precisely where the economy stands in that cycle. But unlike

the ancient Greeks, she has a clutch of highly sophisticated tools to aid her quest. Market watchers can monitor a wealth of statistics in search of clues to how the economy is faring. So-called economic indicators measure everything from what is going on at the supermarket checkout counter to the size of the crowds in the unemployment lines.

To make any sense of these reports, you first must know how to discern what is important. The U.S. Government, private economic groups, and even your employer churn out mountains of data. All of this information matters to someone, but only a small fraction matters to you. Here's how to cull the news from the noise:

- **Gross national product**—the broadest measure of the economy's performance. Referred to as GNP for short, it tracks the total dollar value of goods and services produced on a quarterly and annual basis. So-called "real" growth eliminates the effects of inflation.
- **Leading economic indicators**—the government's chief forecaster of swings in the economy. This index is a blending of 12 separate measurements, or components, each of which represents decisions or commitments concerning economic activity in the months ahead. As a result, these components tend to signal change before it shows up in the economy as a whole.

Among the forces measured, for instance, are changes in inventories stockpiled or the number of manufacturing hours worked. A rise in either could foreshadow a boost in business output. When companies foresee brisk business, they build up stocks on hand. And managers expecting higher sales are likely to extend the hours logged by existing employees before hiring new ones. Although overtime costs more, the decision is easily reversed; thus the length of the average workweek tends to lengthen before new hiring shows up in other measurements.

If the index is dropping, economists read that to flag a decline in the economy as a whole. A rising index, by contrast, suggests that business activity stands to boom.

Careful here. **The leading indicators can lead you astray.**

While the index does herald broad turns in the economy, it is far less useful a timing tool. The economy could stall out quickly after a downturn, or continue going strong for a few maddening months. Major slumps in the indicators, for example, have occurred anywhere from 3 to 23 months before the actual recession took hold.

A good statistics watcher views monthly reports skeptically. A good rule of thumb: a change of direction lasting at least three consecutive months constitutes a signal of recession or recovery to come. But even that sign is not infallible.

• **Unemployment**—a politically as well as economically sensitive statistic. The unemployment rate measures the percentage of the work force out of work but actively seeking jobs.

By overlooking those too discouraged to look, it can understate the number of idle workers. A better predictor of business activity is *total employment*—those who do have jobs. If that number is surging, then the economy is poised to rise as well, regardless of what the unemployment figures say. Another less well known but useful gauge is the measure of payroll jobs. This index measures business intention to produce goods. A rising number is a sign that employers expect good times ahead.

• **Consumer prices**—the most widely watched measure of inflation. It tracks prices for a specific shopping cart of goods including food, fuel, transportation, housing, medical care, and entertainment.

The index reports average prices only, and averages for goods that many consumers may not even buy. Thus, it often overstates pressures on prices. Its compilers assume shoppers buy the same items month after month. But if fish is costly and consumers switch to beef, that saving is not reflected.

The publicized figures can also be highly alarmist. Although issued as a monthly figure, most news reports promptly convert that number into an annual rate. In doing so, they assume that each future month will be a clone of the one gone by. That is far from likely and can be downright misleading when a given month's numbers prove unrepresentative of overall trends.

• **Interest rates**—the quintessential measure of both the present and the future health of the economy. The most sensitive of economic indicators, interest rates react almost instantly to changes in economic conditions. Their levels in turn influence the conditions themselves. High credit costs put a damper on business, raising the cost of corporate borrowing, slowing down overall economic activity, and cutting corporate profits.

Interest rates also have a direct impact on your own life. Changes in interest rate levels influence whether you can afford to buy a new home or car, whether U.S. business will undertake expansion projects that will produce jobs, whether the stock market will surge or fall, and how much you earn on CDs and other savings.

Gauging the future course of interest rates—which way they are headed and how fast and how far they will travel—is a critical factor in timing your money moves. For years, rate watchers have focused on what is known as the prime rate, traditionally considered the lowest rate available to the bank's most credit-worthy customers. But as banks have rolled out a variety of loans to a broader range of customers, that term has lost its meaning as the best for the best. Many loans now take place at rates below the prime. In fact, the term itself is falling by the wayside in banking circles.

Yet because the figure is so highly publicized, **the prime rate** is a good starting point for understanding how interest rates are determined. Each bank sets its own prime depending on its profit outlook. If a bank's cost of raising money surges, then it will pass some or all of that boost on to its customers.

To predict movements in the prime rate, therefore, you must turn to the marketplace. Dominating the scene is **the Federal Reserve Board,** freely dubbed the Fed. Established in 1913, its charter is to balance the amount of money and credit available with the economy's ability to produce and consume goods and services. To do so, it must steer a careful balance between two extremes—allowing too much money, which can drive up prices and spark inflation, and too little money, which can cramp expansion and cause recession. The decision on what to do, whether to loosen or tighten the money supply or to leave well enough alone, is made by the Fed's Open Market Committee (FOMC).

Clear enough. The problems arise because the Fed rarely discloses its plans or the strategies it will follow to implement them. Even the most far-reaching decisions are couched in the stodgy language of minutes of meetings issued six weeks after the fact. Investors who want to know what is happening now must glean clues from events in the markets.

One of the most closely watched signs of the Fed's intentions is the way it manipulates the rates that banks charge one another for overnight loans. These borrowings occur daily as banks struggle to keep on hand the minimum amount of money reserves they are required to hold by law but lend out any excess to increase their profits. Every evening, after they tally their books, banks with excess funds lend them to those whose reserves come up short. The rate they charge, known as the **federal funds rate,** is determined by the overall supply of funds in the system.

This is where the Fed comes in. By buying and selling securities (usually, but not always, U.S. Government issues) it can cut or increase the supply of such funds and thus edge rates higher or cause them to ease.

When the Fed buys securities, the money it spends to pay for them is pumped into the money supply. The Fed's payment is ultimately deposited in commercial banks, which use it to make loans to individuals and businesses. With a greater supply of money, the cost of money—the rate of interest—falls. The result: more credit at lower rates.

By contrast, if the Fed wants to shrink the money supply, it can sell securities on the open market. The money the buyer uses to purchase these issues is kept by the Fed and simply eliminated from the amount of money used by banks to make loans. Such moves reduce the amount of credit available and drive up its cost. In time, a higher funds rate will be passed along to all of the banks' other borrowers.

In short, the increases or decreases in the federal funds rate give astute investors insight on whether the Fed is intent on keeping the money supply robust, and thus encouraging banks to make more loans and investments. That would imply that interest rates might begin to decline, and it would be an advantageous time to lock in high rates. Money supply shifts can also point up danger ahead. If the money supply balloons, the risk of inflation increases. That might cause the Fed to throttle back the growth of money and possibly the growth of the economy as well.

A second way the Fed influences how much the banks add to the system is by how much it charges them to borrow from its own coffers. That rate, known as **the discount rate,** is a second widely watched indicator. While set independently by each of the Fed's twelve member banks, it varies little from district to district.

When the Fed lifts the discount rate, it becomes more expensive for banks to borrow. They in turn will pass this cost on to their customers. A rise in the discount rate heralds an increase in interest rates overall.

In addition to watching the Fed's movements, several other measures can help you gauge rate trends:

- **Money market tables.** You can get an idea of where professional money managers think interest rates are heading by looking at the money fund tables that run in the financial pages of newspapers each week. These charts usually list the average maturity of each fund's portfolio, that is, the average number of days until its investments become due and must be replaced. When maturities shorten—for example, from 38 to 32 days—fund managers expect rates to climb. They are staying flexible in order to be able to make new investments at higher rates. Lengthening maturity days mean that these experts think rates will drop. Thus they are locking in yields for longer periods of time.
- **Treasury bill rates.** Another easy fix on interest rate trends

TABLE 10.1

The Shape of Things to Come

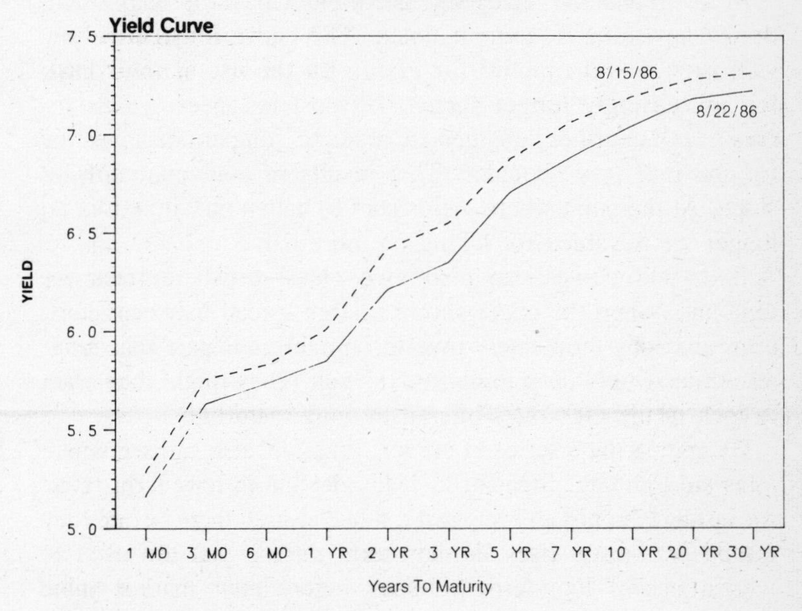

SOURCE: Prudential-Bache Securities

is to watch the yield on six-month Treasury bills. Sold at auction each week, these securities are among the most sensitive barometers of interest rate movements. Any change in interest rates trends usually shows up quickly here.

• **Yield curves.** A more ambitious route is to plot out your own version of what money pros call the "yield curve." Such a graph shows the relationship between short-term and long-term returns on roughly the same type of security. An example appears in Table 10.1.

To plot current levels, take a sheet of paper and draw a graph. Write various rates of return up the left side, with the lowest near the base. Along the bottom, pencil in the dates various securities come due, ranging from one month to 30 years, with the shortest term on the left. Plot each instrument on the appropriate line in the graph. The final step is to connect the dots to create a picture of the price of money over time.

Most frequently, investors use yield curves to help them decide how long to commit funds. **The curve illustrates how well they would be paid for giving up the use of their cash for increasingly longer terms.** In most instances, yields increase as maturities lengthen in order to compensate investors for the risk they shoulder. That results in a gradual upward slope. At the point where yields start to flatten out, investors no longer are rewarded for taking on more risk.

But yield curves can also give clues to where rates are trending. When the curve shows a large spread between short-term and long-term rates, investors might anticipate that long-term rates would drop to narrow the gap. They might then want to lock in the high rates offered by long maturities.

By comparing a series of curves, investors also can see where rates are trending. Sight of a steady decline in long-term rates, for instance, could also suggest a move to grab them before they disappear. Steady rises in short-term rates signal the need to wiggle out of long-term holdings before their market value sinks.

HOW TO USE WHAT YOU READ

Armed with a view on where the economy is heading, an investor must lay a strategy to take advantage of it. Her aim is to profit from changes in two forces—the rise and fall of interest rates and the ups and downs of the business cycle.

To do so, the basic tack is to shift emphasis from income to growth and back. When stocks look favorable, for instance, shuttle more of your capital into equities. When high rates threaten to choke off a market surge yet offer investment values of their own, investors can move to lock in good yields.

Some women perform better in one economic climate than in

another. Many Drivers and other women who prefer to monitor their investments closely enjoy the time devoted to such efforts. But Suzanne is funnelling all her attention now on her quest to make partner at a major law firm. Chances are that she would be happier with a different approach.

In the same vein, a rousing stock market rally can hold perils for some Reachers. When the climate grows buoyant, many an investor adopts an enthusiastic posture. If optimism totally supplants realism, however, she could be stuck with a bum pick bought in good but misplaced faith.

Most vulnerable to interest rate swings are a Nester's core holdings. When rates are rising, her return will soar. But she faces a stiffer challenge to keep yields up when the economy goes into a tailspin.

The table on page 299 outlines many options for women depending on their money styles. While all such decisions are highly individual, the following scenarios can give you ideas.

WHAT TO DO WHEN RATES ARE MOVING UP

Rising rates portend happy times for income-conscious investors. Nesters and all women with an interest in pocketing risk-free returns can profit handsomely by doing very little at all. **The best spot for all income-producing investments in such a climate is short-term issues.** That way, savers can roll over their funds at steadily rising rates as their securities come due. Among the instruments best suited to such an approach are taxable and tax-free money funds, in which the fund managers roll over issues for you, CDs, and Treasury bills.

In some instances, it can make sense to cash in an older CD before it matures to take advantage of rising rates. Many banks have trimmed their penalties for early withdrawal considerably. **If your investment still has a while to go before it matures, and the rate you could get by reinvesting the money is considerably higher than the one you are now collecting, you**

could benefit even after paying a withdrawal penalty. Your bank can help you calculate whether cashing in would prove useful.

Rising rates often throw the stock market into a stall. That is because they increase the cost of borrowing, eating away at corporate profits, and decrease consumer spending, which threatens a company's future earnings. Even so, this can be a good time for some investors to consider stocks.

Growth-conscious investors can reason that the market will turn up eventually as the economy comes out of its trough. To position themselves for that move, daring buyers can begin picking up shares that will benefit from an economic upturn. These include makers of business equipment and farm machinery and providers of the aluminum, steel and other metals used in production. Consider also stocks in industries that prosper in boom times, such as airlines.

It is precisely when things look gloomiest, in fact, that intrepid investors press on. The real money is made in the market by those with the courage to buy stocks at or near their lowest levels, before weeks or months of rising prices have confirmed that a rally is at hand—and driven prices up. One time-honored play is to pick up stock in brokerage firms. Traditionally battered down during the market's nadir, such shares also tend to shoot up when stock prices resurge.

This is also a time Nesters might find opportunities in the stock market. With prices low, many shares offer yields that compare favorably with those on short-term debt securities and hold out the promise of capital gain when the equity markets recover. **The most cautious investors, however, are best advised to swing most of their holdings out of stocks in preparation for the bear market that is likely to come.** With cash on hand, they will be poised to reinvest when prospects are brighter.

As rates forge steadily upward, investments in overseas markets can also prove profitable. High U.S. rates tend to attract foreign funds. That boosts the value of the dollar.

Investors can benefit in two ways. For one thing, their dollar will buy proportionately more shares of Japanese or French or other securities. What's more, overseas companies are likely to profit in such environments. U.S. firms cannot compete as well in foreign markets because the dollar-based prices they must charge are higher.

At the Peak

No one, of course, knows interest rates are poised at their highest level at the exact moment they hit the peak. Not even professional money managers can call the precise turn of any market. Yet **if her reading of the economic smoke signals suggests that rates are peaking and about to begin a long move downward, a wise investor begins to retool her portfolio.**

Nesters and all investors who prize lofty, low-risk yields can begin to lock in returns. If they are right, they now have an opportunity that will shortly slip away. In a gradual fashion, such investors can consider stretching out the maturities on their holdings. Treasury notes can be particularly appealing. They offer relatively high rates along with indisputable safety.

Take it slow. Locking in yields leaves investors vulnerable to a resurgence of inflation. Until the course of rates is clear, shrewd investors should reposition only a portion of their funds. A third to a half of your capital might be a prudent slice. That way, you can reach for yet higher returns from your remaining funds if the softening trend proves short-lived.

Another approach might be to buy shares in a so-called balanced growth mutual fund. These pools aim to conserve capital and generate steady income. To do so, they buy both stocks and bonds and often hold a large chunk of their money in cash.

When rates start to tumble, any investor with the bulk of her assets in short-term holdings begins to reap a gradually diminishing return. Yields that once topped 10 percent in money market funds, for instance, may have slipped a point or more. In such cases, income-conscious investors should step up their efforts to nail down returns.

When rates decline, short-term rates tend to tumble more quickly than those on long-term issues. Companies selling securities with far-off due dates usually offer a higher rate of return to compensate buyers for the risk that rates might shoot up in the meantime. **That gives you a chance to maintain high yields by committing your funds for a somewhat longer term.**

As you begin your search for better rates, seek out banks that offer cash bonuses for new deposits. When interest rates are falling, more aggressive institutions often offer bonuses of $25 to $100 or more for deposits, depending on how much you put up and how long you are willing to park it. The reasoning: the yield they now are paying is lower than prior months and could be less attractive than other investment options.

Investors who are convinced that the economy is shifting into a lower rate environment should position a greater share of their funds. Even so, **they can hedge their bets by staggering maturities. That involves buying CDs, Treasury issues, or bonds that come due in steady succession over the years ahead,** beginning perhaps in three or six months and stretching out for several years. Such a strategy means that some of your capital is always coming due, offering the chance to reinvest funds at whatever rates are available in the market at the time or to take advantage of new opportunities.

Precisely how long your longest-term purchase should be is a thorny question. **Investors buying a fixed-rate issue they intend to hold to maturity in effect are saying they do not expect rates to jump before the instrument comes due.** Do you really believe that? Given the volatile pattern of rates over the past five years, it may not be possible for anyone to know.

Whatever your choice, be sure you are well paid for any long-term commitment. Unless there is a significantly higher yield on a ten-year bond than a six-year note, for instance, it is not worth your while to lock up your funds for the longer period. Even if the promised return is higher, few women should plan to buy securities coming due in the mid-1990s or later unless they are certain they will hold them to maturity and do not care if rates shoot higher before then.

No one, of course, is required to hold any security to maturity. Investors with bonds or Treasury securities paying higher-than-market rates can sell them at a profit now. **If you are tempted to unload, however, be sure to ask yourself what you will do with the proceeds. Only if you have a better alternative for the money should you cash in your fat yields now.** A better move is to wait until rates are poised to rise again and sell just before you stand to lose your gain.

In most instances, high rates eventually will bring the stock market rally to a halt. Because shareholders anticipate economic moves, the market will stall before the economy runs out of steam. Investors who poured money into stocks earlier in the cycle should prepare to cash out. **Take advantage of market rallies to take profits and, if need be, cut losses. In many instances only lower prices lie ahead.** Gutsy speculators can also attempt to make money on bad news by selling stocks short and using other techniques explored in the next chapter.

Drivers and Reachers who are committed to stocks, however, might want to pick up or continue to hold issues that are considered recession-proof. These include issues of companies that tend to do well regardless of the economy as a whole. Even when times are bad, for instance, consumers still eat, smoke, drink beer, and buy soap and over-the-counter drugs.

WHAT TO DO WHEN RATES ARE FALLING

If they did not act quickly enough to lock in favorable yields, Nesters and other investors looking for lucrative income now will have to scramble. The best deals have slipped away. To continue to eke out high rates, they must consider progressively longer maturities and be willing to accept the risks such moves entail. In addition to longer-term CDs, such investors can consider short-term bonds funds holding securities that mature in one to four years. Ginnie Maes, discussed in Chapter 3, also might help out. Because their yields are based on rates on long-term mortgages, they tend to drop more slowly than Treasury securities.

The more rates fall, the more wary investors should be of positioning any money at all for the long term. When rates turn up again, there will be better opportunities. And the market value of any securities posting less attractive returns will drop. The best course at the trough is to keep remaining funds liquid.

Yet better returns may go to investors who swing part of their funds into equities in this climate. **Falling rates can be great news for stockholders.** With the cost of money low, businesses can afford to borrow to expand and consumers can afford to spend. Those trends tend to make stocks do well. This is especially true if rising interest rates are accompanied by spiraling inflation. In that case, the real returns savers are pocketing—the yield less the cost of living—can be slim or nonexistent. What's more, with rates on rival investments such as CDs flagging, stocks gain appeal simply in comparison.

Investors seeking stock market profits, no matter their money styles, do well to buy shares in the early stage of the business cycle. The first companies to benefit will be those whose business is helped by falling rates. These "interest-sensitive" concerns are those whose operating costs are closely tied to the cost of money. As such, they are likely to profit when rates fall. Banks, of course, must pay market rates to attract new deposits. When rates go down their cost of doing business drops. In a similar fashion, utilities tend to borrow heavily to finance their construction projects. Their margins too will blossom when rates tumble.

WHAT TO DO IN ANY MARKET

For many working women, all this can sound like a lot of work. And it is. For those investors with relatively little time to spend monitoring their investments and a commitment to invest for the long haul, it might make sense to follow a single strategy that will see them through thick and thin.

The approach that appeals most is of course highly individual. But some money styles tend to respond better than others to a given philosophy. Outlined below are three different ideas for hands-off investing. Investors should consider each on its merits. Any, or none, might appeal.

Hedging

A Nester might be comfortable hedging her bets no matter what the economic climate. By diversifying broadly among several types of investments, she can reduce the risk of loss of capital regardless of what the economy does. Of course, she also is limiting her potential gains.

The larger your nest egg, the better this strategy works. With $25,000 or more to disperse, you can afford to spread your cash among several different investments. If you now hold $10,000 or less, however, it still makes good sense to diversify your assets among at least four different investments.

Hedgers might apportion cash as follows:

A HEDGED PORTFOLIO

Balanced growth/income fund	15%–20%
Growth stock fund	15%–20%
Second growth stock fund	15%–20%
Bond fund	5%–15%
Second bond fund	5%–15%
REITs	20%–30%
Money fund (tax-free, if appropriate)	15%–20%

All-or-Nothing

Many Reachers might be more attracted to taking an all-or-nothing approach with a large chunk of their funds. Provided that they keep a portion secure in low-risk deals, investors can vastly increase the excitement and their chances of winning big by speeding cash from one market to another as circumstances change.

To use this portfolio well, however, they must be sure to pay attention. Success depends on close-to-precision timing of their moves. When signs of an economic slowdown flicker, they must pull out of stocks fast and rein in any urge to squeeze the last dime of profit out of their holdings.

At each extreme, a portfolio based on this strategy would alternate between heavy emphasis on stocks and heavy emphasis on income-producing assets. Again, the larger your nest egg, the more you can diversify. If you have more than $10,000 to put into a growth stock fund, for instance, spread it among two or more funds.

When the prospects for stocks seem dim, start with:

HUNKERING DOWN

Money funds	70%–80%
Growth stock fund	20%–30%

Then, when the market outlook brightens:

SEEKING HIGH PROFITS

Money funds	20%–30%
Aggressive growth stock fund	30%–40%
Second aggressive growth fund	30%–40%

TABLE 10.2

Using Your Money Style As the Economy Changes

Economic Environment	Nesters	Reachers	Drivers
Economy slowing: inflation down, interest rates falling	Park funds in money market fund. Put the bulk in longer-term CDs and government securities.	Dollar-cost average. Consider bond funds and zero coupon bonds.	Buy interest-sensitive stocks, high-dividend shares, and bond funds.
Economy at bottom	Sit tight.	Buy stocks.	Buy stocks.
Economy surging: inflation rising, interest rates rising	Put money in money market funds and short maturities.	Investigate gold funds.	Sell out fat profits. Consider real estate.
In any market	Hedge.	Switch.	Buy and hold.

Buy and Hold

For the Driver, a buy-and-hold strategy often packs great appeal. This approach builds on her strengths of careful research, patience, and long-term outlook. By choosing two or three good mutual funds and buying shares steadily in good markets and bad, she can increase her odds of pocketing fat profits.

Her portfolio might consist of:

A BUY-AND-HOLD PORTFOLIO

Aggressive growth stocks	25%–30%
Growth stock fund	25%–30%
Second growth stock fund	25%–30%
Growth-and-income stock fund	10%–20%
Money fund	10%–20%

ELEVEN

USING LEVERAGE: WHEN, WHY, AND HOW

"Neither a borrower nor a lender be," Polonius advised his son, "for a loan oft loses both itself and a friend, and borrowing dulls the edge of husbandry."

Not in the stock market. Or in real estate. Or at least not always. In today's economy, investors often find that borrowing gives them an edge in their quest for financial security.

You need money to make money. That advice is so standard it is almost an investment joke. But like all clichés, there is an element of truth, and it speaks precisely to the central problem of many hard-pressed working women today: they do not have enough.

Salaries they have. But even high-earning women often find that savings pile up slowly. Especially in the early years of their careers, women can benefit from borrowing funds to buttress their own. Later on, many are in fact wise to do so.

Borrowing to invest is called leverage. That process buys control of a home, stock, or other asset with just a fraction of its cost. If the value of the purchase appreciates, the investor profits handsomely; she makes money on the cash she borrowed as well as her own funds.

But in the uncompromising financial arena, that move has left her vulnerable as well. **Leverage also magnifies her risk. If the asset drops in value, she will lose money faster—on the funds she borrowed as well as her own—and generally pay interest on the loan to boot.**

The most familiar way for women to leverage their assets is by buying a home. A look at the math behind the purchase can highlight leverage's risks and rewards.

Say you are eyeing a house that is worth $100,000. One way to buy it is for cash. If you put up $100,000, you have no leverage. If the value of the house rises by 5 percent in the next year, your profit comes to $5,000—a 5 percent return on your funds. A plodding passbook savings account will pay you more.

To boost your financial firepower, you can put up only part of the cost. If you make a $10,000 down payment on the same house, and borrow the balance, the $5,000 appreciation represents a 50 percent return on your investment. If real estate values are soaring, and the property value zooms up by 10 percent, that $10,000 paper profit comes to a 100 percent return—or double your money.

Housing values, like those of any assets, fall as well as rise, of course. Another look at these figures illustrates how leverage heightens the risk in any investment. If that property skidded $10,000 or more in value, you would lose your entire investment if you were forced to sell. While many homeowners can sit out swings in property values, those investing in other assets such as stocks may not have the luxury of waiting.

Even generous profits are not all money in the bank. Borrowing money to invest can be costly indeed, depending on the source. Any profit you make is cut by the cost of the loan. The key to making money is to keep your interest costs below the appreciation you are eyeing. Put another way, make sure that any asset you leverage yourself to buy will likely shoot up in value at a higher rate than the interest you are paying.

Buying a Home

Many women regard buying their own home as a prime financial goal. The move symbolizes security and permanence. It also offers great appeal as an investment—it shelters them from the elements and their incomes from the IRS. And many are lured by the prospect of fat profits on the move.

The income tax benefits are predictable. As a homeowner, you are entitled to deduct the interest you pay on any mortgage you hold from your income as long as you itemize. And in the early years of your mortgage, nearly all your payments consist of interest. If you borrowed $75,000 at 10 percent for 30 years, the interest deduction the first year would come to roughly $7,850. Part of the points—a fee of one percent of the sum borrowed—paid when you signed the mortgage also can be written off as long as they are in line with lending practices in your area.

In addition, current law also allows homeowners to deduct any state property taxes they pay. If you live in a condominium, you can write off both the tax on your unit and a share of the tax paid on the property's common grounds. And when you go to sell, any profit you make is not taxed at the time as long as you buy another home that costs at least as much as the old one within two years of the sale.

Together, these breaks make home ownership one of the last, best shelters for most working women. What's more, owning a home can also give you a valuable way to win tax breaks on the money you borrow. As discussed in more detail in Chapter 6, the new tax law makes **home equity loans**—those taken out against the equity in first or second homes—the only consumer loans that qualify for a full interest deduction.

While Congress sharply restricted the tax break on interest paid on most consumer loans beginning in 1987, homeowners still can write off every cent of the money they borrow against their home, as long as the sum does not exceed the original purchase price plus improvements. And those who use the money to pay tuition or medical bills can borrow up to the current value of their homes.

While a woman can quantify the value of such benefits, the overall outlook for any real estate investment is far from clear. Whipped by steady rises in the rate of inflation, property values shot through the roof in the 1970s. Many women saw their own holdings, or those of parents and siblings, double or triple in value.

Inflation's sizzling pace slowed in the early 1980s, and with it the appreciation in property values in many parts of the country. Many experts believe that real estate prices will climb only modestly as long as inflation remains relatively tame.

But so long as they can afford to do so and are not likely to move quickly, most working women are well advised to consider buying a home of their own. Housing promises to offer gains that at least keep pace with the rate of inflation. And it remains one of the easiest ways to leverage.

For most house-hunters, the first question is how much they can borrow. To gauge borrowing power, lenders usually eye a pair of financial yardsticks that compare the prospective homeowner's income with her expenses. Before okaying most conventional home loans, a lender will look for the following:

- **Anticipated monthly housing costs**—including mortgage payments for principal and interest, and in many cases, real-estate taxes, homeowners' insurance and the like—represent no more than 28 percent or so of her pretax income, and
- **All debt outstanding**—housing costs plus payments on obligations such as a car, student loans, credit card bills, or other personal debt—come to no more than 36 percent of gross pay.

A woman's earning power is more than the salary she brings in. Many lenders look for stability as well, and give high marks to applicants who have been working for at least two years and pull down steady paychecks. If a woman's earnings consist largely of commissions, she will need to prove that they are regular.

The size of the down payment she brings can also be a factor.

Most lenders prefer that borrowers ante up at least 20 percent of the purchase price of the property. But there are always exceptions. Some lenders also are reluctant to lend more than the $135,000 or so they can resell to the Federal National Mortgage Association, known as Fannie Mae. This federally chartered company buys mortgages from banks and other lenders who then can use the proceeds to make more mortgages. But many banks are willing to lend far more to well-heeled applicants.

At the same time a bank is scrutinizing her, a borrower should be eyeing the bank's offerings. If part of the profit you make on your investment depends on the rate you pay to borrow, you must shop carefully to get the best deal you can.

Once the best deal was the simplest: find the lowest interest rate and sign up. But the mortgage market has changed dramatically since the days when all loans were made at fixed rates for a fixed term. Stung by the same force of inflation that helped consumers profit so much on soaring real estate values, many lenders made no money at all in those days. The money they were earning on old, low-cost mortgages fell far short of the rates they were paying to attract new funds.

As a result, lenders have tried to inject a measure of self-defense into their portfolios by rolling out a new breed of mortgages (see Table 11.1). With these instruments, known as adjustable-rate loans, consumers take on part of the risk of rising rates that lenders previously shouldered alone. Under these plans, if interest rates tick up, a borrower's mortgage payments will follow in short order.

Among the offerings she will see:

• **Fixed-rate loans,** the time-honored plain vanilla mortgage. Typically, these loans carry the highest interest rate, since the lender alone runs the risk that rates may rocket.

• **Adjustable-rate mortgages (ARMs),** whose interest rate fluctuates with changing economic conditions. How often and how much vary. Lenders generally charge less for these loans, because the borrower shares the risk that rates will climb.

• **Rollover or balloon mortgages,** which pack the bulk of

TABLE 11.1

The Mortgage Market

Type	Description	Considerations
Fixed rate	Fixed interest rate, usually long-term; equal monthly payments of principal and interest until debt is paid in full.	Offers stability and long-term tax advantages; limited availability at times. Interest rates may be higher than other types of financing. New fixed rates are rarely assumable.
Adjustable rate	Interest rate changes are based on a financial index, resulting in possible changes in monthly payments, loan term, and/or principal. Some have rate or payments caps.	Readily available. Starting interest rate is slightly below market, but payments can increase sharply and frequently if index increases. Payment caps prevent wide fluctuations in payments but may cause negative amortization. Rate caps limit amount total debt can expand.

Rollover (renegotiable rate)	Interest rate and monthly payments are constant for several years; changes possible thereafter. Long-term mortgage.	Less frequent changes in interest rate offer some stability.
Balloon	Monthly payments based on fixed interest rate; usually short-term; payments may cover interest only with principal due in full at term end.	Offers low monthly payments but possibly no equity until loan is fully paid. When due, loan must be paid off or refinanced. Refinancing poses high risk if rates climb.
Graduated payment	Lower monthly payments rise gradually (usually over 5–10 years), then level off for duration of term. With adjustable interest rate, additional payment changes possible if index changes.	Easier to qualify for. Buyer's income must be able to keep pace with scheduled payment increases. With an adjustable rate, payment increases beyond the graduated payments can result in negative amortization.
Reverse annuity	Borrower owns mortgage-free property and needs income. Lender makes monthly payments to borrower, using property as collateral.	Can provide homeowners with needed cash. At end of term, borrower must have money available to avoid selling or refinancing.

SOURCE: Federal Trade Commission

the money due into the last payment. Such loans typically run for just five years or so, and borrowers must repay in full or renegotiate at then-current rates so long as the lender is willing to talk.

Ever alert for a bargain, consumers have flocked to ARMs. In recent years, lenders have been dangling rates as much as two to three percentage points below those on fixed-rate deals. But not all ARMs are alike, even if they bear the same price tag. To pick the plan that is best for her pocketbook, a borrower must shop carefully.

To compare deals, get on the phone. What you are aiming for is a thorough understanding of what would happen to each loan under any circumstances, good and bad. Then draw up a strategy based on what you think rates will do.

Among the questions to ask about ARMs:

- **What percentage of the property's price will the lender finance?** If you want to underwrite a greater percentage of your house's cost than the lender commonly will finance, find another bank. Typically, lenders do not make exceptions in this area.
- **What is the initial rate?** The advertised rate will be lower than that on a fixed-rate loan because you are taking on risk. How much lower is the question. Expect a reward of at least two points for your bravery. But watch out for extremely low introductory rates. In many cases, so-called teaser rates can jolt upward in the second year even if the underlying market rates do not.
- **What is the initial monthly payment?** While much about ARMs is shrouded in uncertainty, this is one number that is sure. It is the starting point for all your budget calculations.
- **How often will the interest rate change?** ARMs are recomputed on a preset schedule. Most common: once a year, although some lenders offer adjustments as infrequently as once every three years or five years. The longer the period between adjustments, the less vulnerable you are to rate hikes. But that

also means your payments will stay high even if general rate levels ease.

• **What determines how much the rate will change?** The rate you pay will be based in large part on changes in market rates as measured by a specific yardstick, or index. Indices are worth comparing carefully. Past performance is no guarantee of future rate movements, but as a rule, the shorter the index and the more frequent the changes, the more volatile the rates will be.

• **What is the lender's margin?** In most cases, the lender's profit comes not from the interest rate charged but rather from its margin, an additional percentage point or more that is added to the index rate at the time of the adjustment. Taken together, the interest rate dictated by the index (which fluctuates) and the lender's margin (which remains constant) determine how much you will pay. If the terms of two loans are otherwise equal, a higher margin is likely to result in higher payments.

• **Is there a limit on how much the interest rate can rise at each adjustment period?** Such limits, known as "caps," are valuable safeguards. A two percentage point cap means the rate you are charged could not rise more than two percentage points at any adjustment, regardless of market levels.

• **To what rate does the cap apply?** Careful here. Some lenders do not apply the cap to the low initial rate. Instead, the rate might leap directly to the index level at the first adjustment.

• **What happens to the interest rate if the index declines?** Find out whether the rate you pay will go down by the same amount as the index or whether the lender limits how much it can fall. In many cases, the amount it can drop is equal to the amount by which it can rise at a given adjustment period.

• **What is the highest rate you could ever pay?** A cap on how much the rate can rise over the life of the loan, sometimes called a "ceiling," is the best protection any consumer can write into a loan. The best ARMs have lifetime ceilings of five percentage points, no matter how high the market rates might soar. To pinpoint your risk, ask the lender to quote the maximum monthly payment in dollars as well.

• **Can any unused increases in your monthly payments be saved and added to future periods?** Say interest rates have zoomed. The loan limits rate increases at the time of each adjustment to two percentage points, but you would have been liable to pay three percentage points without the cap. Find out whether the lender can carry the unused percentage point forward to the next adjustment if subsequent rates do not rise to the limit of your cap.

• **Is there a limit to the amount that the payment can increase?** Some loans hold monthly payments to a fixed sum, even if rates rise smartly. While that sounds like a good deal, it can backfire. The amount you owed but did not pay is not forgiven under these plans. Instead, the money is added to the balance on your loan to be repaid at a future date. In times of steady rate increases, the amount of unpaid interest, known as ''negative amortization,'' could mushroom—and with it, the total you owe.

• **What about other fees?** Find out the cost of the application fee as well as how many points the lender charges. Other fees you could pay include title search and insurance, appraisal fees, attorney's fees, recording fees, credit report fees, and mortgage insurance. A prepayment penalty allows the lender to charge a fat fee if you pay off the loan within the first few years.

If you are a shrewd loan shopper, you can outsmart both the economy and the bankers—no mean feat. To do so, you must first assess what you think interest rates might do. The discussion in the last chapter can backstop you here.

If you think rates are set to rise smartly, a fixed-rate loan will pay off. You will lock in what could prove to be extremely attractive rates no matter what happens in the years ahead. By contrast, if you think rates will fall, the right ARM will let you benefit from that trend. If rates stay steady, you probably still are better off with an ARM's relatively lower starting rates.

Another decision to consider is the length of the loan you seek. Shorter loans, running for 15 years instead of the traditional 30, are gaining popularity. These **15-year mortgages** can make a great deal of sense if you can afford to make the slightly higher monthly payments such deals usually entail. For one thing, because you pay back the principal of the loan more quickly, you pay substantially less in interest. That can be a good idea now that marginal tax rates are dropping, since mortgage-interest deductions are not as valuable. What's more, the faster you pay back the principal, the more equity you have to borrow against.

But such loans have drawbacks too. Because you have to pay more each month, they limit your buying power. You probably can afford a more expensive home if you take out a 30-year loan. What's more, larger monthly payments mean you'll have less money left over to save. You might be better off making a lower monthly payment and banking the difference, if you can invest the extra cash at a handsome rate.

Before you make a final choice, give some thought to your life-style. If you have young children or are close to retirement, a 15-year loan might allow you to own your home free and clear before college bills hit or you quit working. By contrast, if you expect to move in two or three years, your best bet is to go for the lowest rate, regardless of the loan term.

Leveraging Other Property

Real estate is not the only property investors can borrow to buy. Stocks, bonds, and other vehicles all can be purchased with borrowed cash, pressing your own funds to work twice as hard.

The most familiar way to leverage with equities is to buy "on margin." The initial down payment, set by the Federal Reserve Board, stands at 50 percent. That means an investor opening a margin account can put up just $5,000 for $10,000 worth of securities. In effect, you buy stock with your own funds, then turn around and use those securities as collateral to take out a loan from your broker and buy more.

Just as with any other leveraged purchase, buying on

margin heightens your rewards as well as your risk. Guess right, and the return on your investment will soar. But a wrong move will magnify your losses. Not only will you lose money on your borrowed funds, you pay higher commissions because you bought twice as much stock.

What's more, aside from the initial down payment requirement, brokers demand that margin borrowers maintain a minimum level of reserves in their account. The amount that is borrowed can represent no more than roughly 30 percent of the stock's value. If a stock you bought skids down past that level, brokers will ask for additional funds that in effect repay part of the loan. **To protect themselves, investors who buy on margin should keep a cushion of cash on hand against such calls.** If you cannot ante up, your broker will sell the stock to repay the debt, and hand over whatever cash remains—at that point, far less than your initial investment.

Brokerage firms charge interest on the funds they lend as well as a loan fee. But such rates tend to be at or close to market levels. In fact, **many women find it advantageous to raise money for other purposes by borrowing on margin against securities they hold.** But like all other borrowing for personal use, if you take out a margin loan for personal use, the amount of interest you can deduct will be phased out gradually by 1991.

In addition, the new tax law sets limits on how much **investment interest** you can write off. In general, the amount of investment interest (interest you pay on funds you borrowed to buy investments) that you can deduct would be limited to the amount of income you collect from all your investments. For tax purposes, **investment income** includes capital gains, interest, dividends, and royalties.

That means if you paid $600 in interest to buy stock, and your only income from investments is $400 from Treasury bills, you can only deduct $400 of your $600 interest bill. The deductibility of any excess interest—in this case, $200—would be phased out over five years under the same terms as consumer interest write-offs outlined in Chapter 4: only 65 percent would be deductible in 1987, 40 percent in 1988, 20 percent in 1989, 10 percent in 1990, and nothing thereafter.

But what you lose is not lost forever. Any disallowed interest could be carried forward indefinitely to offset future income. **Rather than wait to reap your write-off, however, you might consider switching any tax-exempt or low-yielding investments you hold to high-interest savings or high-dividend stocks in order to boost your investment income.**

Buying on margin is most lucrative when investors can pocket a fat profit in a relatively short length of time. That way, they hold interest charges to manageable levels. But no one, of course, can predict whether an investment will turn a profit at all, or if so how quickly. As a result, **buying on margin makes the greatest sense when the market as a whole is roaring ahead and the odds that a given stock will spurt are high.**

If you want to use leverage when the market is tumbling, the better strategy is to do what is known as **selling short.** You borrow stock from your broker, putting up half its value as collateral, and sell the lot in the belief that the share's price will dive. Your plan is to cover your position later, buying the shares at the sharply lower price, and pocket the difference, less commissions and interest.

But just as with any leveraged move, the deal will backfire if the investment goes sour. In fact, selling short involves far more risk than merely buying on margin. The reason is simple: the bottom line. While a stock's price can only fall 100 percent—to zero—it can soar by 200 percent, 300 percent, or more. The higher it rises, the more you lose.

Astute investors can limit their losses on either margin holdings or short sales by entering **a stop-loss order** with their purchase. If a stock sells for $55 a share, the order could be entered for a few dollars more or less than the price you paid. If you bought on margin and you want protection against a falling stock price, you might enter an order for $50. That way, if the shares nose-dive, the loss is held to $5 a share. If you sold the stock short, and do not want to be left stranded if its price surges ahead, you could set the order for $60.

Helpful as stop orders are, they are not surefire solutions. If the stock's value starts to climb or tumble swiftly, due to takeover rumors or a sharp and unexpected loss, a burst of demand to buy or sell could mean that your order would not be filled at the price you set.

Another way to boost financial firepower is to use **options.** An option is not a stock, it is a claim on a stock. Specifically, it is a contract that gives the right—but not the obligation—to buy or sell stock at a specified (called the ''strike'' or ''exercise'') price before a certain date, usually within nine months. At the end of that time, it expires.

Each option represents 100 shares of stock. The right to buy is known as a ''call''; to sell, a ''put.'' The price you pay for this privilege is called a premium. **Because the option sells for a tiny fraction of the total price of the underlying shares, it gives a buyer control over far more stock than outright purchase of securities for the same sum of money.**

Whether a holder exercises that right is up to her. The decision hinges on how well she predicted the change in the price of the stock. Suppose she buys a call for shares in General Motors, expecting their price to jump. If she guessed right, she can use the option to buy the stock at the lower price, sell it at a profit, and keep the difference, less commissions. At the same time, the value of the option itself will have risen as well, usually by an even greater percentage. She may, in fact, make more money by selling the option directly.

While her potential profit is unlimited, an option buyer's losses are not—she can lose everything she invested, but no more. If the price of General Motors shares shuffles sideways, or drops, she does not have to act. But once it expires, an option is worthless, and the investor loses her initial outlay. Though ''limited,'' the loss has been total.

To deal wisely in options, an investor must be familiar with the stock she's trading and fairly certain it is in line for a big move—whether up or down. By buying an option with a relatively far-off expiration date—a few months—at a price somewhat close to the stock's current value, she is likely to pay more, but in return will gain more leeway for the stock to move before the option expires.

Some of today's most popular options are written not on individual stocks but on the whole market as represented by a **stock index.** Best known is the contract based on Standard & Poor's index of 100 stocks, which trades on the Chicago Board Options Exchange. But nearly a dozen crowd the stock index listings.

Essentially, investors in stock index options deal in contracts for an imaginary portfolio of stocks. They are betting on the way stocks in general will perform. They will make or lose money depending on how close the final value of the index comes to the contracted price.

If you figure the market will thunder ahead, the option to buy is a call, or the right to buy the index at a price you suspect will soon look cheap. If you reckon the market is in for tough times, pick up a put, or the right to sell the index at a price you think will be well above the market's eventual landing point.

Just as with conventional options, the appeal is the big win. Small turns in the overall market can lead to sharp swings in the value of the underlying options. If you guess right, you can collect your money either by selling it to an eager buyer or by exercising your option for cash. If your hunch was wrong, sell out or sit around until the option expires.

High leverage also boosts the appeal of investing in **commodities** futures. Trading spans a wealth of goods, from gold and silver to minerals to crops to foreign currencies and, recently, stock indexes like those discussed above. Like options, futures are sold through contracts that give holders the right to buy or sell a specified quantity of the commodity at a preset price by a certain time.

Investors can put down a mere fraction of the cost of the underlying goods, as little as 3 percent to 10 percent of the price. That gives staggering force to any change in price. And unlike options, a contract is an obligation to perform. If the market trades against you, there is no way to shrug your shoulders. You must put up more money or your broker will sell you out. If you do not act quickly enough, you may end up losing more than your initial investment.

As with most speculative investments, holders are wise to limit risks and cut losses. One way to do so is to diversify your bets by buying into a commodities mutual fund. While commissions and fees can eat up much of your initial investment, you can lose no more than the sum you put up. Stop-loss orders also can prove valuable tools with these investments.

Leveraging Your Money Style

Leverage can play a role in every woman's portfolio. When she applies it and how much she takes on depend on her money style.

Many Nesters rule out leveraged investment instinctively. The risk of loss is too much. Most women in most instances who have such feelings should respect them. Fewer than half of all investors, for instance, ever trade options, and their portfolios can prosper nonetheless. Any woman can find all the potential for capital gain she needs in stocks and other less speculative plays.

Buying on margin also could be a mistake for income-seeking investors who buy high-yielding stocks. The interest on the loan will sharply erode the dividends they collect.

But in some cases, leverage can prove useful, even necessary. Few women would own homes if they had to buy them for cash. But even though she embraces a mortgage, a Nester can short-change herself if she is unwilling to stretch a little. So long as she can handle the monthly payments, no one should automatically rule out reaching.

At the same time, Nesters and all women looking to step up

their portfolio's performance can use some of these tools to meet even highly conservative investment goals. **Options are not for speculators only. While buying options on stocks is risky business, selling an option on stock you already hold can be a sensible way to squeeze extra income out of your investments.** In broker parlance, this is known as **writing a covered call.**

As the seller of an option, you give a buyer the right to purchase your shares no later than a specific date at an agreed-upon price, say $42, somewhat higher than their current market value of $38. In return for this privilege, the buyer pays you a premium. In most cases, nothing more happens. The option expires and the seller keeps her shares.

But this strategy does pose risks. The buyer was betting that your stock would soar in price. If it does, she can exercise her option to buy the stock at $42, even if the market price hits $45, $50, or even more. To hold off that move, you can buy back the option, but only at a greater cost than you sold it for.

Whether this approach suits you depends on your underlying investment strategy. If you write calls on stock that already has proven a good investment, the profit you would collect if you sold the stock, plus the premium you earned, may be enough to quell any misgivings about letting it go.

Investors also can use options as a prudent way to hedge their bets. Such women buy a put on a stock that they already own at a price that is close to its current market value. If the share's price plunges, she can sell her holdings before the expiration date for the value set by the put, limiting her losses. If she prefers to hang on to the stock, she has another recourse. The value of the put itself should rise. She can sell the put, and use the profit from that sale to make up for part of the paper loss in her portfolio.

Like any form of insurance, however, hedging with options means that you pay out even if you do not run into trouble. If the value of your shares rises instead of falls, the profit you gain is shaved by the cost of the put.

Because they tend to be watchful of their investments, Nesters and Drivers alike have part of the temperament needed to deal in speculative plays. The riskier the venture, the more closely investors must monitor their holdings. To deal with leverage, however, investors also must be willing to move swiftly to cut their losses, a quality many Nesters tend to lack but an area in which Drivers often shine.

A Driver, in fact, tends to be best suited for highly leveraged plays. She never trades without a reason, and targets her profits in advance. And she must steel herself to take them. The options market is fast-moving. **Investors can double or triple their funds in hours only to find the market suddenly running against them. No one should buy on margin or gamble with leverage unless she is looking for aggressive growth.**

The coolest of calculators can consider the notion of selling something they do not own. Selling short would fit the bill in markets that are tumbling. In addition, it is possible to sell an option, or write a call, without owning the underlying stock. Like selling short, it exposes the seller to unlimited losses. But if successful, this technique allows you to be paid for something you do not have and never want to have to deliver.

Though her spirit may be willing, a Driver's problem may stem from just that eagerness; she may already own so many other investments that her attention could be sidetracked at a critical moment. Or the pace of her job might preclude the kind of daily monitoring such ventures demand. She also should be wary lest she take on more risk than necessary for her own portfolio, even though she may feel personally at ease with the prospect.

Reachers, too, may be more conscious of the excitement of options, high-speed commodities trading and other heady moves than the underlying risks involved. Convinced that fortune is on her side, she can secretly believe she will not lose, and invest far too much in one contract or fail to diversify her bets.

Some of the biggest losses come on the heels of rewarding

plays. Reachers especially must be careful that a spate of easy wins does not lure them into thinking that juggling leverage is child's play.

One way to limit losses is not to invest too much. So-called out-of-the-money options do not look like good bets. If calls, they sport an exercise price above the current market level. If puts, the price is below the market now. The buyer will not make a cent unless the stock moves far and fast. As a result, such options can be bought for next to nothing. Though these deals may stand little chance of turning a profit, they offer investors a chance to learn the markets and satisfy their gambling bent at a relatively low cost.

TWELVE

YOU'RE THE BOSS: HOW TO GET HELP

The financial services industry is in the midst of a revolution that will continue into the 1990s. Spurred by a wave of mergers that rocked the industry earlier in the decade, a growing number of firms are locked in a race to handle our money from our first checking accounts to our Social Security benefits.

The old system had its plusses: shoppers could walk into any bank anywhere or any broker anyplace and walk off with the same product. That era is gone. Now investors face an expanded array of services from a broader group of suppliers.

Traditional money tenders—banks, brokerage firms, mutual funds, insurance companies—are battling one another for customers. And brash new competitors—American Express, retailers such as Sears Roebuck & Co. and K Mart, discount brokerage firms, the whole financial planning industry—also are scrambling for business as well. What's more, the time-honored role of each of these suppliers is changing as bankers sell stocks, brokers sell insurance, and insurers sell mutual funds.

These choices mean that more and increasingly careful shopping now is required to run down the right deal for you. **But**

ultimately, the wealth of choice also stands to mean greater wealth for you—greater satisfaction and a better fit between their products, your needs, and your personality.

At long last, in fact, financial institutions are recognizing the working woman's increasing clout. The life insurance industry has targeted women as a ripe market. A mutual fund has rolled out a portfolio pegged strictly to so-called women's needs. One farsighted California bank even offered a quarter of a percentage point bonus to women opening IRAs before an uproar forced a halt.

How women respond to such lures reflects their money styles. Women whose prime concern is to husband their funds, among them many Nesters, tend to form strong ties with their bankers. That is understandable; much of their assets are stationed in banks. They will serve themselves best, however, by reaching out to other advisors. Accountants and financial planners especially can help them make the most of their funds.

Many Reachers have the opposite weakness: they lean too much on their financial team. Such women take advice without testing it against the standard of their own concerns. Taken to the extreme, they can find themselves falling for any sales pitch that promises instant wealth.

Drivers often fare better with their advisors. By and large, they recognize their need for professionals to implement their plans. But they may be reluctant to defer to wiser heads in devising those plans and can reject sound advice because they want to control the process.

The real problem arises when women are afraid to trust financial advisors enough to let them help. After they have been burned a few times by listening too much to the wrong advisors, even Reachers come to share this view.

If they consider the reasons behind their fear, most often it comes down to two concerns: insufficient knowledge to be able to evaluate suggestions and insufficient knowledge to use to evaluate the advisors themselves. Armed with the information you have read so far, you now stand well equipped to screen a money pro's suggestions. And this chapter will show you how to evaluate the advisors themselves.

The ideal arrangement is a partnership of equals. You are the expert on your needs and your money advisors are the experts who will fill them.

No matter what their financial bent, working women often find their busy schedules leave precious little time to try to find help in the first place. The best managers, however, make time for their finances as well as their jobs.

How to Choose a Money Team

Finding good help takes time. Before settling on any accountant, broker, or lawyer, you should interview at least three candidates for the job. Most professionals are willing to give you up to a half an hour of their time for free to see if you might develop a good working relationship.

To pinpoint candidates worth interviewing, start by gathering recommendations from persons whose judgment you trust. Check with friends and relatives for suggestions. Then broaden your search to include colleagues at work, your boss and other professionals such as bankers.

List in hand, set up meetings with several. You'll want to cover a wide range of questions in your initial meeting. Highlights of the points to raise appear in Table 12.1.

Focus on what you learn from your interview, not what you have heard from others. References are important, of course. But a smart money pro will give out only the names of those she expects to praise her. **In the end, rely on your instincts. Bottom line, you must be *comfortable* with any professional you hire.**

In addition, of course, there are specific questions to ask each candidate, depending on whether you are seeking a lawyer, financial planner, broker, or whatever. Read on for details on topics to cover with each category of professional.

TABLE 12.1

How to Manage Your Financial Team

There are common issues to resolve with any member of your money team—banker, broker, financial planner, insurance agent, lawyer. Here is a checklist of items to consider no matter what money pro and what money question:

TELL YOUR ADVISOR:

——What the problem is and what result you seek.
——Information about your income, assets, or other relevant data.

ASK YOUR ADVISOR:

——What is her educational and professional background?
——How long has she been in business? Where?
——What is her specialty, if any?
——How do the assets or needs of the majority of her clients compare with yours?
——How many clients does she handle personally? Would she handle most or all of your work?
——How often can you expect to hear from her?
——How are fees determined?
——Can she give you a sample of her work or steer you to two or three clients for whom she has worked?

WATCH OUT FOR:

——The kinds of questions she asks. Expect her to draw out information on your needs and expectations.
——Rapport. Do you have good feeling about her?
——Communication. Do you understand her comments and explanations and her answers to your questions? If she says a point is too complicated to explain, for instance, find someone else.
——Courtesy. Did an assistant hold telephone calls, or was the meeting peppered with interruptions?

Financial planner. A financial planner is a personal financial consultant. Her role is to draw upon all your resources to create an integrated plan to win financial security. As the elements of money management increasingly spill across all financial disciplines, and the institutions that will implement them become rapidly more complex, this kind of broad-based approach gains in value.

Provided, that is, that you get good help. Financial planning has become the cult career of the 1980s. Thousands never involved in money management are rushing in to make a buck—for themselves. Other old-line professionals such as insurance agents and brokers also are claiming now to see your finances in a broad, unbiased light.

Don't believe them. **Unlike any other profession dealing with money, planning is virtually unregulated.** There are no federal or state regulations and few if any educational or experience requirements potential planners must meet. Only recently has the industry taken even tentative steps to weed out unqualified and unethical practitioners.

Precisely for this reason, the first question to ask any planner you interview is about her background. Find out where she studied. Perhaps the best-known program is offered by the College for Financial Planning in Denver. Graduates earn a C.F.P. degree. Another well-respected degree, a Chartered Financial Consultant, or Ch.F.C., is offered by the American College in Bryn Mawr, Pennsylvania. In addition, many planners hold other professional licenses such as a stockbroker's or realtor's certificate.

Degrees are just a start, however. These programs provide only the minimum introduction needed to properly manage another person's finances. Another sign that a planner is committed to her work is membership in one of two major professional groups—the International Association for Financial Planning in Atlanta and the Institute of Certified Financial Planners in Denver.

Skills aside, assess the depth of a planner's background. **At a**

minimum, look for at least two or three years' experience in her own or a large planning firm. As financial planning issues grow more complex, give high marks to those affiliated with other professionals who share the burden of keeping up to date with changing markets. Unless she is a tax accountant or lawyer, for instance, she will need help in giving estate planning suggestions. She also should boast access to a computer to make projections or review different tax planning scenarios.

To see if her approach will suit yours, check whether she specializes in a particular type of client. Many planners now are focusing on a specific market, whether corporate executives, doctors, entrepreneurs, or young couples and often tend to specialize in a certain income level, too. You will be best served by someone whose practice is in line with your circumstances. In addition, ask to see a sample plan she has prepared for a client in a situation similar to yours. Be certain that you understand its suggestions and find them neither too simplistic nor too arcane for your needs.

Comes then the question of costs. Financial planners are roughly divided into three camps according to how they are paid. An elite corps bills on an hourly or per-job basis. Another group charges little or nothing for their advice. Instead, they make their money on commissions from the sale of products you buy. A majority do a bit of both.

At the outset, fee-only planners tend to levy the highest fees. But many help to cut down on costs by recommending no-load, or commission-free, products. Even so, many planners who charge commissions are good professionals. Just be sure they are truly well-rounded planners and not salespersons for a single line of goods. **One way to monitor fees: ask the planners how much *they* will earn on any product they suggest you buy.**

In sizing up specific suggestions, ask the planner what alternatives were considered and why they were rejected. Be sure you understand what assumptions the planner made about the rate of inflation in the years ahead, for instance, the rate of return on the recommended investments and the risks involved with your steps.

Banker. Before you can recruit a good banker, you must find a good bank. Even if you have been doing business with the same bank for years, you should take time out periodically to assess the job it is doing.

Start by focusing on the services you use right now. The checklist in Chapter 4 will get you started. In addition, do you write a great many checks or just a few? Do you prefer to keep a fat balance in the account or run it close to the bone? Do you travel widely, and value amenities like automatic teller networks and low-cost travelers' checks, or do you tend to stick closer to home?

With those answers in mind, draw up a checklist of the main areas of importance to you and review how they are handled at each of several banks in your area. **As banks have been forced to pay increasingly higher interest rates to attract and keep deposits, they are slapping steadily higher fees on services to offset those costs.**

Check the minimum balance required for free checking and how much it will cost if your balance drops below that sum. Run down charges to stop payment on a check, wire funds, get a cashier's check, or any other services you routinely use. Then review interest rates offered on deposits and charged on loans. What is the bank paying on six-month CDs or IRA deposits? What is it charging for an auto loan? Watch rates closely for six weeks or so before you decide. From time to time, a bank may in effect run a "sale" on money in order to raise funds. Such rates tend to fall back to normal levels all too soon.

Once you locate a bank that suits your needs, stick with it. It may well be the bank you have been doing business with already. If not, switch your accounts. All your accounts.

The watchword in the banking industry these days is relationship banking. That means that banks are seeking to develop ongoing relationships with customers they value. **If you want a**

bank to do well by you, this means you must do well by it. Consolidate your accounts at one institution. If you are married, bring along your husband's as well. That shows the bank you have assets worth watching and a commitment to serving the bank's interest as well as your own.

Then stay put. Unless the bank's policies change dramatically, don't shop around for an extra sliver of a percentage point return on a CD deposit or discount on your car loan. Not only is it not worth your time, it's not worth the money. A quarter percentage point in additional interest on a $10,000 CD held for six months comes to a piddling $12.50. That's it. More important, by consolidating your funds in one institution, you increase your clout. For other tips on keeping a banker a friend, see Table 12.2.

Your next step is to personalize that clout. That means developing a relationship with a bank officer—or two, if your bank seems to have high turnover among its officers.

How you go about doing so varies with the bank. In smaller institutions, officers are likely to be clearly visible at lobby desks—and just as accessible. Chances are, you can sit down with one without an appointment.

In large cities, the task can be more formidable. Ask a teller whom you know or the receptionist which officer you should see for basic information. **If you need an appointment, feel free to ask for one after bank hours. Contrary to popular belief, bankers don't quit as soon as the doors close.**

When you sit down to talk, your aim is to persuade the banker that you are a good source of business now and are likely to bring in more in the future. Direct the conversation to points that show this. If you are planning to buy a new car or a home soon, ask about loan rates. Or say that you are considering adding to your IRA and would like to see what the bank can do. Even if your plans are tentative, put them on the table. No one will ever know if "soon" means next year.

One area well worth exploring is the matter of fees. Often, consumers pay higher rates than they should because they have not looked into other options. Ask whether there is a way to cut fees by linking your accounts. Often, an individual with a fat CD balance or an IRA, for instance, can get low-cost or free checking. Or you may slice a point or so off the cost of a car loan by emphasizing the five-figure balance in your accounts as a whole.

Before you shake hands, obtain two copies of the banker's card. Keep one for reference, and the other in your wallet. Stranded in a strange city, you may need your banker's quick okay to cash a check at another institution.

Follow up on the meeting from time to time. **As you bring in new business, go back to the same officer. If you've borrowed money, remind the banker pleasantly of that fact.** "We picked up the new car last month and it's running like a dream" keeps your business high in her mind.

That done, watch how well your banker is doing by you. **No bank rules are written in stone, and you should expect an occasional favor if you make this much effort.** Bankers have the power to call you if you are poised to bounce a check, for instance, and let you cover it fast. Or they can press to approve a loan within a day or so if you are truly in a bind. A banker who never gives you a break is one who should be replaced.

Broker. Of all the members of your money team, you have the greatest potential for conflict with your broker. **A broker is a seller, and makes money when you buy or sell. Your best protection is to find someone who at least wants you to make money, too.**

At all costs, avoid dropping into a brokerage office cold to ask for a broker. Chances are, you will be shipped off to the desk of the "broker of the day," usually an inexperienced trainee building a list of clients. While some beginners may be fine, most lack the experience necessary to give you good service. Practice makes perfect, and you don't want a broker practicing on you. What's more, many new brokers leave the business within a year or two, leaving you to start the process all over again.

TABLE 12.2

How to Keep Your Banker Your Friend

When you cultivate a banker, you reap what you sow. Trying too hard can be just as damaging as not trying at all. Here are bankers' thoughts on the five biggest mistakes customers make:

- **Coming on too strong.** While you will never get to know a banker unless you are assertive, customers who *demand* good service rarely get it. That is especially true if you try to pull rank, as in "I have a lot of money here and if you don't help me I will report you to the manager." Never insult, threaten, or dictate terms to your banker.

  Ditto for complaints. You will receive better service if you ask for help in determining why a check was returned than if you angrily accuse a banker of bouncing it.
- **Forgetting good manners.** Consideration counts. If a banker looks harassed, keep any meeting brief. Don't settle in for a chat if she is minding the store alone and managing the phones as well.
- **Being a pest.** Run routine business by a teller, not your banker, or handle it on your own. Many banks offer hotlines that will tell you if a given check has cleared. An ATM can report your current balance at the touch of a button. You are perfectly capable of balancing your checkbook yourself.
- **Procrastinating.** A good banker is usually a busy one. You will win points if you plan ahead. The day you demand immediate action on the loan request that you've carried in your purse for the last several weeks is undoubtedly the day she will be hit with pleas from five other customers with genuine last-minute needs.
- **Taking advantage.** Don't ask for something you know is against the rules. No banker, for instance, can authorize a large loan if you don't pay your bills and your credit is bad. And don't ask her to bend the rules time and again on your behalf. Consistently waiving the fees for bounced checks, for instance, will make a banker look bad with her boss. You'll soon look bad in her eyes, too.

If your request for recommendations left you empty-handed, and you are searching for candidates, go to the most convenient branch of any firm you are considering and ask to see the manager. Outline your present holdings, investment experience, and the types of stocks or other assets you are seeking. The manager then can steer you to the broker or brokers best suited to your needs. Feel free to ask to speak with several before choosing one to work with.

In narrowing down your choices, consider first the broker's questions of you. A good one will aim to determine how much risk you feel comfortable with, the types of investments you prefer, and the financial goals you seek. She should also ask for a rundown of the stocks you hold now and how well—or poorly—they have done. If you don't get a lot of questions about *your* needs, go elsewhere.

In addition, bring up your own list of concerns with any broker you meet. They should include questions about the broker's experience and style of business. How many years has she been in business? How long has she been with this firm? What did she do before? Does she specialize in any investment areas, such as options or undervalued stocks? No broker is completely familiar with the many products now available. If you have special interests, be sure she can work with them.

Next, ask how she finds the stocks she recommends. Does she rely on the firm's research or set off on her own? Will she send you backup information on any stocks you are considering, or brochures on new products? Will she recommend when to sell investments as well as when to buy them?

Find out how she works with her customers. How often should you expect to hear from her? Several times a week? Several times a month? How will you know that she has executed an order you gave? Will she call to confirm or leave that to the mails?

Then, see how you fit into her overall client line-up. **If you are inexperienced, say so up front. Some brokers welcome the chance to educate new customers they think will grow into valued clients. Others would rather not be bothered.** How big is her typical client's portfolio? Find out frankly if the amount you plan to invest is large enough to win much of her time. Are her clients generally long-term investors or traders? Where would you fit in?

Small investors—and many brokers consider any account under $50,000 or so small—have a problem. **A broker will naturally give the bulk of her time to her best clients. To win more attention, you need to either come up with more money or balance your lack of cash with an excess of consideration.** Keep your conversations strictly business. Confine any questions that do not involve an immediate trade to the hours before 9:30 A.M. and after 4:00 P.M. (when the markets are closed.)

Once you have settled on a broker, offer to work with her for six months or so. Then reassess. If you are disappointed with the results, try to figure out why. Perhaps the markets were in an overall downward spiral. That's a tough environment for any broker to make money in. In fact, most professional money managers like to wait at least a year or two before sizing up their recommendations. It often takes that long for a given recommendation to pan out.

Nonetheless, if your personalities have clashed or your broker is making more in commissions than you are in profits, go and find another broker. There's no stigma in that. Many investors have tried four or more brokers before finding one they can work with.

Discount broker. Discount brokers—offering no-frills brokerage services at bargain-basement prices—are the hottest trend in the securities industry. More than 125 independent firms and some 3,000 banks now offer cut-rate plans—and their share of the market is growing.

Discounters offer almost everything that full-service brokers do—except advice. Most discounters have virtually abolished that function. **If you have never traded stocks before, you're probably best off with a full-service broker.** Saving $50 in commissions will not do much good if you lose thousands on the investment itself.

On the other hand, **women who tend to make their own investment decisions or need a broker to handle a onetime trade, such as selling inherited stocks, would do well to consider using a discounter.**

For your bravery, you can do business at rock-bottom rates—as much as 80 percent lower than comparable full-service deals. While you might pay $100 to trade 100 shares of a $50 stock, a discounter might do the same deal for as little as $30.

While all discounters cut fees, the precise way they do so varies. Some base fees on volume, or the number of shares you buy or sell. That gives you a break on large blocks of stock. Others set prices in the traditional brokerage firm manner, that is, on the value of the trade. Such firms are best if most of your trades feature low-priced stocks or small units that will not win volume discounts.

To find the best discounter for your type of trading, ask for a copy of the firm's price list. If you already have a full-service broker, pull out your old statements. Compare the fees you paid your full-service broker with what you would have paid a discounter. If you are just starting out, estimate how much it would cost you to do a given trade at several different firms.

If you trade often, consider lining up two discounters with different fee structures. That way, you can channel a given trade through the organization with the best deal. In any case, check for minimums. **Most discounters impose a minimum on even the smallest trades. If you often buy fewer than 100 shares of stock, or the value of your trades is less than $2,000 or so, you may actually pay less at a full-service house.**

Discounters cut your fees in part by cutting their costs. Many such firms comprise little more than an 800 phone number and a staff. Find out how soon trades are executed and whether and when the firm will let you know your order has been carried out. While full-service firms pay their account executives commissions based on the business they do, discount brokers work strictly on salary. Callers rarely deal with the same person consistently, and it can be hard getting through to anyone at all on the market's busiest days. **Test the level of service before you sign on.**

In addition to screening services, check out products. **Not all discounters offer all products.** Most deal in stocks, bonds, and options. But if you are interested in mutual funds, new issues, or other areas, be sure the discounter can handle your business.

Insurance agent. Or agents. Most tend to specialize in either the broad life insurance area or so-called property/casualty lines, which include homeowners' and other liability policies.

No matter what type of insurance she sells, see that any agent you consider can clearly explain the differences between various policies. That includes differences in cost as well as coverage. A good property/casualty agent, for instance, might recommend one homeowners' policy over another if you own a lot of silver.

Make no mistake, life insurance is a difficult area to shop. A good agent will begin a relationship by quizzing you about your income, assets, and responsibilities as well as any other coverage you might hold. The best make no sales pitch at all the first meeting.

Most life insurance is sold, not bought. Be careful. See that any agent you deal with offers both term and whole life solutions to your needs. **All too often, agents pitch whole life because such policies pay fatter commissions.** In comparing term policies, look first at price. Many companies offer special deals for non-smokers or those in good health. With whole life, compare ratings on the so-called interest adjusted index, which takes into account premiums, dividends, and other variables. Generally, the lower the index number, the better the deal.

Expect good service from any agent you choose. Once you report a claim, for instance, you should be contacted by the company representative within 48 hours. The claims process and final settlement should be fully explained, and any questions you have answered. When a settlement is reached, expect a check to be issued the same day, or within no more than three working days.

Tax specialist. Women with straightforward tax concerns can probably do the job themselves. Straightforward means that you earn most of your income from salary, invest little, and support no one but yourself. Even so, you may lack the time to keep up with the constantly changing tax laws. In that case, you need help.

Start with a national tax preparation chain. Although its staff does not deal with tax matters full-time, they are heavily coached for their seasonal duties. Ask to meet with the person who will prepare your return. If you are uncomfortable with the individual for any reason, you can ask for a new assignment.

As you earn more, or your life grows more complicated, you likely will come to need a tax specialist. Any dramatic shifts in your life-style merit the attention of a tax pro. They include:

- buying a house or condominium
- quitting a job or starting a new one
- piling up substantial medical bills
- getting a big raise or inheritance—or experiencing a large drop in income
- pocketing freelance income
- marrying, divorcing, or having a child
- becoming a widow

Certified public accountants (CPAs) can be your best bet: not only can they prepare your 1040, they can help you keep down future tax bills through judicious planning.

Because tax issues can be downright arcane, the most important talent to look for in a tax pro is the ability to communicate clearly. To see how well you can discuss the topic with a given accountant, bring along copies of your previous year's tax return to the interview. See if the CPA can uncover deductions you missed or suggest other ways to trim your bill—and see how well she can explain her suggestions.

In addition, you want to work with someone who keeps up-to-date on tax law changes. Find out if the CPA offers a newsletter to clients, sends out copies of reference materials, or calls you from time to time over the course of the year. Ask if you can call her with requests for more information and whether a fee will be charged if you do.

In some cases, you will need a tax attorney. They tend to charge more than CPAs, but their advice is worth it if the matter is complex. That would include a serious dispute with the IRS over a previous tax return, a nasty divorce, or starting or buying a business.

Lawyer. Most women need a lawyer at some point in their lives—for instance, when buying or selling property, signing any kind of contract, settling an estate, or dealing with a criminal act such as robbery. All too often, of course, an attorney is needed to advise on a divorce. At times, a lawyer also can help by telling you if you need one. If you've been fired from your job, harassed sexually in the workplace, or stiffed on an agreement, it likely is worthwhile to consult an attorney. She can tell you if she thinks you have a case, how much it would cost to pursue, and the odds of winning.

To round out the list of names supplied by your own contacts, check with the local bar association. Often, there is a woman's bar group that gives suggestions. **Remember that such referrals do not necessarily mean that the lawyer is *good,* only that she practices in the area you need.** Consider asking faculty members at a local law school about a person's reputation or to add to your list of recommended lawyers.

At the interview, determine first the lawyer's experience with the kind of problem you face. General practice lawyers handle a wide variety of legal issues. Specialists concentrate in such areas as criminal work, labor law, wills and estates, or divorce. Ask her to cast a critical eye on your affairs. What is her reading of your case? What kinds of results has she won in similar situations? What steps would she take, how long would it take, and what would the likely outcome be?

Find out, too, who will be doing the work. In larger firms, paralegals or other assistants often take on much of the load. Ask as well how closely you will be involved. Look for a lawyer who will give you copies of all letters and documents prepared on your behalf. Find out how and how frequently she will keep you informed on her progress.

Equally important is a thorough discussion of fees. Lawyers generally are paid at an hourly rate, or in some instances, through a flat fee. Preset prices are most common in routine jobs such as simple wills and property title searches. If she prefers to bill hourly, get her best estimate of the total cost. Depending on your part of the country and the nature of her practice, fees can range from $25 an hour to more than $250. In accident or negligence cases, ask whether a contingent fee might be appropriate. Under such an arrangement, you might pay the full fee only if she wins the case.

Legal clinics are gaining popularity. These storefront operations generally offer cut-rate fees to solve cut-and-dried problems. Bills can run as little as a third of those charged by individual practitioners. Because they make money through high volume, however, do not expect much hand-holding from clinics. And stick with a conventional lawyer if your problem is not typical. Any deviations can run up the bill quickly. They will be happy to let you know. In fact, legal clinics generally are more than willing to describe services and quote fees over the telephone.

Check, too, whether you have access to some sort of group legal plan at work. Many programs represent a good value if they offer easy access to a staff of attorneys who can handle a wide variety of cases.

How to Manage Your Team

All of these individuals exist in your life for just one reason—to help you. Expect them to do so. Every member of your team owes you prompt answers to phone calls, regular progress reports, and courtesy when you call.

Be professional yourself. Make sure you have defined your problem and the results you seek and have given the expert all the information she needs to do the job. Even when you are under great stress, aim to keep your discussions objective and your tears after-hours. Consider carefully the advice you are given, even if it conflicts with measures recommended by your friends' advisors. Raise any questions tactfully.

The actions you avoid are as important as the steps you take. Just like you, professionals are busy people. Plan your conversations. If need be, draw up notes on what you want to say. Don't phone several times a day with questions that could have been handled in one conversation. Find out if your advisor prefers to take calls at a certain time. Brokers, for instance, are happy to book orders while the markets are open, but would rather deal with housekeeping or general questions when trading stops.

From time to time, take a moment to reassess your money relationships. **If you find yourself consistently opposed to an expert's advice or frequently disappointed with the results it yields, schedule a meeting to discuss what's going on. If that session leaves you unsatisfied, move on.** No relationship is permanent. You should never hesitate to renew your search for the best money team for you.

AFTERWORD

WINNING FINANCIAL SECURITY

The greatest threat to winning financial security is not failing to set aside enough money to invest. Or making foolish decisions when you do so.

The greatest threat to your financial security is delay. Constantly shoving your money questions onto the bottom of tomorrow's "To Do" list will guarantee nothing except regret.

Many busy career women feel terrorized by time. To be sure, there are never enough hours in the day. Yet, when it comes to financial security, time can also be your sturdiest ally. Women who lay plans now to achieve their goals, whether a vacation, a new home, or retirement comfort, will find it far more likely to happen and far cheaper to accomplish. Relatively modest sums of money set promptly and properly to work can billow into a generous financial cushion.

This book offers an outline for achieving any goals you set. Resolve now to take the time to tackle them. Doing what you want when the day's work is done is the best reward of all. You deserve nothing less.

GLOSSARY

New investors as well as seasoned money pros can be stumped by financial jargon. Here are definitions of many of the terms you will encounter.

Aggressive growth fund. A type of mutual fund that aims for fast profits, with scant thought to income. When fund managers guess right, they can post spectacular gains. When they are wrong, the value sinks like a stone.

Annual percentage rate. The cost to borrow money for a year, expressed as a percentage of the amount borrowed.

Annuity. A long-term investment offered by insurance companies that guarantees a steady income stream to begin immediately or, in the case of a deferred annuity, at a future date. Like IRAs, all earnings in the account compound tax-free. Fixed annuities, under which your funds are invested in conservative assets such as bonds, guarantee the return of your principal plus a minimum interest rate. Variable annuities, under which you can invest in stocks, real estate, or other risky ventures, offer no guarantees. The value of your investment depends on how well those investments perform.

Asset. An item of value owned by a person, company, or institution. Assets can be tangible, such as cash, or intangible, such as the right to collect a pension when you retire.

Basis point. A term used to describe the amount of change in fixed-income rates. One hundred basis points equals 1 percent. An increase from 7 to 9 percent would be a change of 200 basis points.

Bear market. The opposite of a bull market. A time when stock prices are declining.

Beneficiary. The person named to receive the proceeds of a life insurance policy upon the death of the holder.

Big Board. Another name for the New York Stock Exchange.

Block. A large holding or trade of stock, usually considered to be 10,000 shares or more.

Blue chip. The common stock of a large, well-known company with a record for steady earnings and dividend payments.

Bond. An IOU or debt of a corporation or the U.S. Government or a municipality, usually issued in multiples of $1,000 or $5,000. In return for the use of money you lend it, the issuer agrees to pay a specified amount of interest for a preset time and to repay the loan in full on a given date.

Bond fund. A mutual fund that invests mainly in bonds. Its managers seek to pay out income and preserve principal rather than increase the value of shares.

Broker. An agent who handles orders to buy or sell stocks or other securities. Brokers are also known as account executives or registered representatives. Many financial services firms call brokers financial planners, although the individuals may know little or nothing about the field.

Bull market. The opposite of a bear market. A market in which stock prices are climbing.

Call. See option.

Call privilege. The right of a bond issuer to repay the bond early. Commonly done when interest rates fall, to save money by refinancing at lower rates.

Capital gain or capital loss. The profit or loss from the sale of a capital asset. In 1987, the tax you pay will depend on how long you have held the asset. If you sell within six months, you will owe taxes at current rates, which range as high as 38.5 percent, on any profit you log. Hold the property longer, and you will owe no more than 28 percent of your take. Starting in 1988, all profits will be taxed at ordinary rates no matter how long you have owned the property.

If your losses exceed your gains, starting in January 1987 you can deduct them dollar-for-dollar against your income, up to $3,000 a year. Red ink above that amount can be stockpiled and applied to future gains.

Capital growth. An increase in the market value of stocks or other securities.

Certificate of deposit (CD). A bank account of a fixed duration. In return for your deposit, the bank or savings and loan pays interest, usually at a fixed rate. If you want your money back before the time is up, you generally will pay a penalty fee.

Collateral. An asset that is pledged to back a loan. If you default, the lender can seize the asset.

Collectibles. Non-money assets, ranging from fine art and Persian rugs to baseball cards and other items some souls consider junk.

Commercial paper. Unsecured corporate IOUs, to be repaid within 270 days.

Commission. The broker's basic fee for buying or selling stocks or other investments as your agent.

Commodities. Products that are basic to many industries, usually traded in bulk form. Wheat, pork bellies, and copper are all commodities. Investors who trade in commodities usually deal in a contract, called commodity future contract, to buy or sell a specified amount at a future date.

Common stock. Ownership interest in a portion of a corporation that you can buy or sell.

Confirmation. The written description of a stock trade. It shows the number of shares traded, the price, and the date.

Convertible. A bond or preferred share which can be exchanged for common stock, usually of the same company.

Correction. A short-term decline in stock prices that occurs in the midst of a bull market. Stock prices usually rebound following a correction.

Debenture. A bond with no security other than the issuer's promise to repay.

Deduction. For tax purposes, an expense that can be subtracted from your earnings to arrive at the sum on which you owe taxes.

Deep discount bond. A bond selling for less than 80 percent of its face value.

Diversification. Spreading your dollars among many different investments in order to reduce risk. By investing in several different assets, you lower the odds that one bad pick will swallow your profits. Wise investors diversify among different investments—money market funds, stocks, and bonds—as well as within investments.

Dividend. Your payoff for owning shares in a company. It may be in the form of cash, additional shares of the stock in question, or shares of other stock the company owns. Dividends on preferred stock usually are fixed. On common stock, the company's board of directors votes on the amount each quarter. If times are tough, they may cut the dividend or eliminate it entirely.

Earned income. For tax purposes, income from working, whether wages, salary, or self-employment. This does not include income from investments.

Employee Retirement Income Security Act (ERISA). The 1974 law that set strict rules governing pensions.

Estate. A person's property, usually referring to the holdings of someone who has died.

Ex-dividend. Another way of saying "without dividend." Someone who buys a stock ex-dividend does not receive the recently declared dividend. Identified in the stock tables by the symbol X following the company name.

Executor. The person named in a will to carry out the provisions of the will.

Family of funds. A group of mutual funds managed by the same company. Such concerns let investors switch freely from one fund to another, generally at no cost or for a small fee.

Financial assets. Money assets such as cash and stock.

Fixed annuity. See annuity.

Ginnie Mae. Nickname for Government National Mortgage Association (GNMA), a government-owned corporation that buys home mortgages from private lenders, packages them into bonds (also known as Ginnie Maes) and sells them to private investors.

Growth fund. A mutual fund that aims to increase the value of its shares, primarily by buying common stocks that will gain in value. Portfolio managers usually do not try to pay out current income.

Growth-and-income fund. A mutual fund that aims to provide a high total return through a combination of income now and growth in the value of your shares over time.

Growth stock. Stock in a company whose earnings are growing rapidly and have exceeded or are expected to exceed the rate of growth of the economy or corporations on average.

Hard assets. Tangible assets such as metals, gems, and collectibles.

Income fund. A mutual fund that aims to pay out current income rather than seek capital growth. Bond funds are often called income funds.

Individual Retirement Account (IRA). A retirement plan that allows all wage earners to set aside up to $2,000 a year from earned income and defer taxes on earnings until they are withdrawn. What's more, single persons earning less than $25,000 and married couples filing jointly reporting less than $40,000 can also write off the full value of their contributions. Higher wage earners will see their deductible contributions phase out until they lose them entirely at incomes over $35,000 and $50,000, respectively.

Junk bonds. Bonds issued by companies that just might not be able to repay their debt and hence must offer above-market rates to lure investors.

Keogh account. A retirement plan for self-employed invidividuals and their employees. Holders can in effect contribute up to 20 percent of new income a year, up to $30,000.

Krugerrand. A one-ounce gold coin issued by the South African government.

Leverage. Investing with borrowed money. By using debt, you can increase your own profit on a given investment, but you also increase the risk of loss.

Line of credit. An account which allows you to borrow up to a preset sum of money.

Load fund. A mutual fund that charges a commission, or load, to buy or redeem shares.

Low-load fund. A mutual fund that charges a nominal sales fee, usually 3 percent or less.

Money market account. A bank account that pays current rates of interest on your deposit.

Money market fund. A mutual fund that pays current rates of interest on your deposit.

Municipal bond. IOUs of state or local governments. They generally pay below-market rates of interest, the interest is free of federal (and, in some instances, state and local) taxes. For those in high tax brackets, after-tax returns on tax-free investments can be higher than those on taxable investments.

Municipal bond fund. A mutual fund that invests in municipal bonds.

Mutual fund. An investment company that pools the funds of many different savers with similar investment goals to buy a wide variety of securities packaged in products also known as mutual funds.

Net worth. Your financial value—the difference between what you own (your assets, such as cash, investments, and real estate) and what you owe (your liabilities, or debt).

New issue. A stock or bond sold to the public for the first time.

No-load fund. A mutual fund that does not charge commissions to buy or sell.

Odd lot. A transaction of fewer than 100 shares, the common trading unit.

Option. The right to buy or sell securities, usually stock, at a specified price no later than a preset time. The right to buy is known as a "call"; the right to sell, a "put."

Overdraft checking account. A form of a line of credit that lets you write checks for more than the balance in your account, with interest charged on the amount borrowed.

Par value. The face or dollar value of a security.

Penny stocks. Highly speculative stocks, usually selling for a dollar or less.

Point. In stock parlance, one point is one dollar, three-quarters points is 75 cents. In bonds, one point represents a $10 change in price.

Portfolio. The mix of investments owned by an individual or investment company.

Preferred stock. A "preferred," or privileged, class of stock. Companies must pay any promised dividends on preferred stock before paying any on common stock. Should the company go bankrupt, holders of preferred shares generally are entitled to payment before common shareholders.

Prospectus. The document that describes any new offering of securities to the public, whether a new stock issue or a mutual fund.

Put. See options.

Round lot. One hundred shares of stock, the customary unit of trading.

Secured loan. Loan for which collateral is pledged to guarantee repayment.

Short sale. Selling stock you do not own. A risky technique of borrowing shares from a brokerage firm and selling them in the belief that the price will fall and you can repurchase the shares at the lower level, making money on the spread.

Stop-loss order. Instructions to your broker to sell shares when they reach a specific price.

Street name. Securities held in the name of the firm, rather than the name of the customer who bought them. This is the customary way securities are held.

Tax bracket. The percentage you pay in taxes on the last dollars of income you earn.

Treasury bills, notes, and bonds. All IOUs of the U.S. Treasury. Bills come due in three months, six months, or a year. The minimum investment is $10,000. Backed by the full faith and credit of Uncle Sam, T-bills are considered almost as liquid as cash. Treasury notes mature in one to ten years. Treasury bonds are long-term securities, generally running more than ten years.

Trust. A legal arrangement under which one person (the trustee) holds cash or property for the use and benefit of another.

Underwriter. The firm that buys a new issue of stocks or bonds from the issuer and reoffers them for sale to the public.

Unearned income. For tax purposes, money you make other than through working, including interest, dividends, capital gains, and rental income.

Unit investment trust. A portfolio of professionally selected bonds or securities usually held to maturity. The most popular invest in municipal bonds.

Variable annuity. See annuity.

Vesting. The irrevocable right to receive a portion of your employer's contributions to an employee pension fund and all earnings on that sum when you retire.

Yield. The annual percentage return you pocket on an investment in the form of dividends (on stock) or interest (on bonds or CDs).

Zero coupon bond. A bond that pays no annual interest, hence sells at a very low price. The return on the bond is the difference between the price you pay and the amount you collect when the bond is repaid.

INDEX